Fāṭimah عليها السلام the Gracious

Shaykh Odeh A. Muhawesh

AL-BURĀQ

Copyright

ISBN: 978-1-956276-44-2
Printed and published by al-Burāq Publications.

Ordering Information
We offer discounts and promotions for wholesale purchases, non-profit organizations, and other educational institutions. Contact us at the email below for further information.

www.al-Buraq.org
publications@al-Buraq.org

Second Edition | November 2023

Dedication

The publication of this book was made possible through the generous support of our donors.

Please recite *Sūrat al-Fātihah* and ask God for the Divine reward (*thawāb*) to be conferred upon the donors and also the souls of all the deceased in whose memory their loved ones have contributed graciously towards the publication of *Fāṭimah* عليها السلام *the Gracious.*

We begin by giving all praise and thanks to God ﷻ for giving us the *tawfiq* to translate this book. He has guided us, and without Him, we would not have been guided to the straight path embodied by the Prophet Muḥammad ﷺ and the Ahl al-Bayt عليهم السلام.

This book is dedicated to all the scholars, martyrs, and believers who worked tirelessly to promote the pure Muḥammadan path.

We also want to thank and appreciate all believers worldwide and acknowledge the team that helped al-Burāq Publications complete this work, spending countless hours to make its publication possible. Please recite Sūrat al-Fātiḥah on behalf of them, their families, and their marḥūmīn.

This book is dedicated in honor of the following individuals. Please remember them in your prayers, and may God ﷻ have mercy on them and their loved ones.

Duʿāʾ al-Ḥujjah

اللهم كن لوليك الحجة بن الحسن صلواتك
عليه وعلى آبائه في هذه الساعة وفي كل
ساعة وليا وحافظا وقائدا وناصرا ودليلا
وعينا حتى تسكنه أرضك طوعا وتمتعه فيها طويلا

O God, be, for Your representative, the Ḥujjat (proof), son of al-Ḥasan, Your blessings be upon him and his forefathers, in this hour and in every hour: a guardian, a protector, a leader, a helper, a proof, and an eye - until You make him live on the Earth, in obedience (to You), and cause him to live in it for a long time.

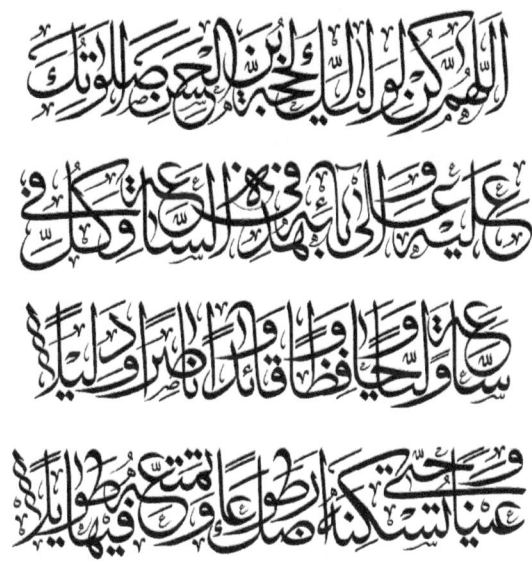

Terms of Respect

The following Arabic phrases have been used throughout this book in their respective places to show the reverence the noble personalities deserve.

عزّ وجلّ

Used for God, meaning:
Exalted and Sublime (Perfect) is He

صلى الله عليه وآله

Used for Prophet Muḥammad, meaning:
Blessings from God be upon him and his family

عليه السلام

Used for a man (singular) of a high status, meaning:
Peace be upon him

عليها السلام

Used for a woman (singular) of a high status, meaning:
Peace be upon her

عليهما السلام

Used for men/women (dual) of high status, meaning:
Peace be upon them both

عليهم السلام

Used for men and women (plural) of high status, meaning:
Peace be upon them all

عجّل الله تعالى فرجه الشريف

Used for Imām Muḥammad al-Mahdī, meaning:
May God hasten his return

قدّس سرّه

Used for a deceased scholar, meaning:
May his resting [burial] place remain pure

Transliteration Table

The method of transliteration of Islamic terminology from Arabic has been carried out according to the standard transliteration table below.

ء	ʾ	ر	r	ف	f
ا	a	ز	z	ق	q
ب	b	س	s	ك	k
ت	t	ش	sh	ل	l
ث	th	ص	ṣ	م	m
ج	j	ض	ḍ	ن	n
ح	ḥ	ط	ṭ	و	w
خ	kh	ظ	ẓ	ه	h
د	d	ع	ʿ	ي	y
ذ	dh	غ	gh		
Long Vowels					
ا	ā	و	ū	ي	ī
Short Vowels					
ـَـ	a	ـُـ	u	ـِـ	i

Table of Contents

Foreword to the Second Edition	1
Preface	5
Introduction	9
The Law of Inheritance	27
The Prophet's ﷺ Marriage	31
On the Way to a Blessed Life	35
Transcendental Events	39
Sayyidah Fāṭimah al-Zahrā’’s ﵇ Birth	51
Naming Sayyidah Fāṭimah ﵇	57
The Event of the Cloak	129
Sayyidah Fāṭimah’s ﵇ Youth	139
Sayyidah Khadījah's ﵇ Death	143
Sayyidah Fāṭimah's ﵇ Immigration	149
Sayyidah Fāṭimah ﵇ at Uḥud	153
Sayyidah Fāṭimah's ﵇ Problems at Home	157
On the Way to Marriage	161
Sayyidah Fāṭimah's ﵇ Dowry	179
Preparations for the Wedding	183
The Year of Her Marriage	193
Sayyidah Fāṭimah's ﵇ House	201
Sayyidah Fāṭimah's ﵇ Marital Life	207
Historical Distortions Regarding Imām ‘Alī's ﵇ Right	211
Imām Ḥasan ﵇ is Born	217
The Birth of Imām Ḥusayn ﵇	221

The Birth of Sayyidah Zaynab عليها السلام 225
Lady Umm Kulthūm 229
Sayyidah Fāṭimah عليها السلام in the Verse of Relationship 231
Sayyidah Fāṭimah عليها السلام in the Verse of Mubāhala 239
Sayyidah Fāṭimah عليها السلام in Sūrat al-Insān 245
Spending in the Path of God ﷻ 253
Sayyidah Fāṭimah's عليها السلام Glorification of God ﷻ 267
The Prophet's ﷺ Love for Sayyidah Fāṭimah عليها السلام 273
Sayyidah Fāṭimah's عليها السلام Knowledge 285
Islamic Dress, a Societal Necessity 293
God's Messenger ﷺ Reveals Sayyidah Fāṭimah's عليها السلام Future 299
The Prophet's ﷺ Death 307
After the Prophet's ﷺ Death 313
Following Imām 'Alī عليه السلام to the Mosque 321
Abū Bakr Versus Sayyidah Fāṭimah عليها السلام 329
Sayyidah Fāṭimah's عليها السلام Protest Against Abū Bakr's Actions 341
Fadak in the Political Arena 359
The House of Grief 363
The Withering Rose 367
Abū Bakr's Family Versus Sayyidah Fāṭimah's عليها السلام Progeny 385
Sayyidah Fāṭimah al-Zahrā''s عليها السلام Will to Imām 'Alī عليه السلام 389
A Quiet Funeral 397
Sayyidah Fāṭimah al-Zahrā' عليها السلام on the Last Day 403
Interceding in the Noble Qur'ān 415
Visitation to Sayyidah Fāṭimah al-Zahrā' عليها السلام 457

Foreword to the Second Edition

بسم الله الرحمن الرحيم

In the Name of God, the Beneficent, the Merciful

This revised edition of "Fāṭimah عليها السلام the Gracious."

With great pleasure, I introduce the latest edition of my book, *Fāṭimah* عليها السلام *the Gracious*. This edition features new scholarly perspectives on the life and legacy of Sayyidah Fāṭimah al-Zahrāʾ عليها السلام, the beloved daughter of the Prophet Muḥammad ﷺ.

This book has always aimed to provide a comprehensive and accessible account of Sayyidah Fāṭimah's عليها السلام life and her contributions to Islamic history. In this new edition, I have worked to include the latest research and scholarship on her life, which provides new insights into her character, her role in Islamic history, and her continued relevance to Muslims today.

Through the blessings of God ﷻ (Alḥamdulilāh), we can share these new perspectives with our readers, which will help to deepen our understanding and appreciation of Sayyidah Fāṭimah's عليها السلام life and legacy. We hope this new edition will be a valuable resource for students, scholars, and anyone interested in learning more about this important figure in Islamic history.

In shāʾAllāh, may this book continue to inspire us to learn more about our beloved Prophet's family عليهم السلام, and may God (Alḥamdulilāh) bless us with the knowledge and understanding to appreciate their contributions to our faith.

Lastly, I wish to remember the late Sayyid Muḥammad Kāẓim Qazwīnī ﵀ for his monumental work, *Sayyidah Fāṭimah from the Cradle to the Grave*, on which I relied heavily to understand much of Sayyidah Fāṭimah's ﷺ life. Although I present opposing scholarly views to his, especially surrounding the life of Sayyidah Khadījah and Sayyidah Fāṭimah's ﷺ family structure, I will forever be grateful for his knowledge and consider him a teacher. May God bless his soul.

Shaykh Odeh A. Muhawesh

Preface

In the name of God, the Beneficent, the Merciful

Praise God ﷻ, who created mankind and made them an example to follow throughout their fierce battle with evil.

Prophet Muḥammad ﷺ was the last apostle sent by God ﷻ to communicate to mankind His Divine code (i.e., Islām). Because this code was comprehensive, it also dealt with the needs of women throughout history. It assigned a perfect example for them to prove beyond doubt that what Islām preaches is practical and, if properly followed, leads to everlasting felicity. It manifested this example set by Islām to women in the person of Sayyidah Fāṭimah al-Zahrā' عليها السلام, daughter of God's Messenger.

Yet, the English library lacks a comprehensive book concerning her life, so I was asked to take upon myself translating the work of a profound Shī'ī speaker – Āyatullāh Sayyid Muḥammad Kāẓim Qazwīnī قدس سره – entitled *Sayyidah Fāṭimah al-Zahrā' Min al-Mahd Ila al-Lahd*, into English. As I translated, I found the book to be a collection of speeches regarding the successive events of Sayyidah Fāṭimah's عليها السلام life; therefore, I mainly relied on the text to record her عليها السلام biography until the Prophet's ﷺ death. However, I disagree with Sayyid Qazwīnī on several facts. For example, he accepts that the Prophet ﷺ had other daughters besides Sayyidah Fāṭimah عليها السلام. He also seems to have a common belief that her عليها السلام mother, Sayyidah Khadījah عليها السلام, was married before she became the Prophet's ﷺ wife. I will prove that Sayyidah Fāṭimah عليها السلام was the only begotten daughter of Prophet Muḥammad ﷺ and that Sayyidah Khadījah عليها السلام was never married before she became his wife.

Because of the susceptible period that followed his death and the everlasting effects those events left upon Islamic ideology and the structure of various Muslim sects and issues, I deemed it necessary to study different historical books, especially those that dealt with Sayyidah Fāṭimah al-Zahrā'’s ﷺ life, to come up with the most accurate information regarding the prime of the post-period of the Prophet's ﷺ death. Various sermons delivered during those events were intentionally included in the book, especially her speeches, to allow researchers to study the historical events independently.

The significant books on which I depended in bringing about the book at hand were:

1. *Sayyidah Fāṭimah al-Zahrā' Min al-Mahd Ila al-Lahd* written in Arabic by Āyatullāh Sayyid Muḥammad Kāẓim Qazwīnī ﷺ, p.680.

2. *Banū-yi Nimūnah-yi Islām Fāṭimah al-Zahrā'* written in Persian by Āyatullāh Ibrāhīm Amīnī ﷺ, p. 246.

3. *Sayyidah Fāṭimah al-Zahrā'* ﷺ *Umm Abīhā* written in Arabic by Sayyid Fāḍil Ḥusaynī Mīlānī, p. 203.

4. *Fadak fī al-Tārīkh* written in Arabic by Āyatullāh Shahīd Sayyid Muḥammad Bāqir al-Ṣadr ﷺ, p. 152.

5. *The Message* in English - written in Persian by Āyatullāh Ja'far Subḥānī, p. 781.

6. *The Early History of Islām*, in English, written by Sayyid Ṣafdar Ḥusayn, p.358.

7. *al-Mīzān fī Tafsīr al-Qur'ān*, English translation, written by 'Allamah Sayyid Muḥammad Ḥusayn Ṭabāṭabā'ī ﷺ, Vol. 1.

8. *Nahj al-Balāgha*, by Imām 'Alī ﷺ.

In conclusion, this book will be handy for information-seeking readers, researchers, and history students.

I extend many thanks to the late Br. Muḥammad Taqī Anṣarīyan for allowing me to serve the cause of this Great Lady of all time.

I beseech God to supply us all with His abundant mercy, which overwhelms every living thing, and to guide all truth seekers to His right path. May His peace, blessings, and grace be upon Muḥammad and his righteous progeny.

Shaykh Odeh A. Muhawesh

Introduction

In the Name of God, the Beneficent, the Merciful.

Sayyidah Fāṭimah is a woman created by God to be a sign of His marvelous and unprecedented might. For, the Lord made Prophet Muḥammad as a sign of His might among prophets; and created from him his daughter Sayyidah Fāṭimah al-Zahrā' to be a sign of His ability to create a woman possessing all moral excellence and talents. God bestowed Sayyidah Fāṭimah with a vast share of greatness and a high level of majesty, which no other woman can ever claim to have reached.

She is one of the prominent people close to God, whose greatness was acknowledged by Heaven before the creation of mankind, and in whose regard verses from the Qur'ān that are and will be read day and night until the Day of Resurrection were revealed.

Humanity will come to appreciate the greatness of Sayyidah Fāṭimah's personality and the deep meanings and characteristics of her actions as they advance in the understanding and realization of facts and secrets.

God praised Sayyidah Fāṭimah al-Zahrā' and showed his satisfaction with her satisfaction and became angered when she was outraged. And the Messenger of God commended her nobility and meritorious personality. At the same time, Imām 'Alī looked to her with respect and admiration, and the holy Imāms of Ahl al-Bayt sanctified and venerated her.

Through Sayyidah Fāṭimah al-Zahrā''s life, one can learn many morals and admonitions and become familiar with the true believers' lifestyles and the viewpoints they held. We can reflect upon a period of Islamic history connected to Sayyidah Fāṭimah's عليها السلام life.

People recognize Sayyidah Fāṭimah's عليها السلام genius as an example of a Muslim woman's adherence to noble traits despite her abuse and lack of attention to her history. Sayyidah Fāṭimah عليها السلام is a perfect example of how a daughter, wife, and mother should act while keeping her decency and pure character; she also shows us the Muslim woman's role in the social field within the guidelines of religion and virtue. Her life confirms that Islām does not deprive women of acquiring scientific, cultural, and literary knowledge, granting that they safeguard themselves from nudity, recklessness, unrestraint, and actions that would bring sorrow upon them and destroy their identities.

Some misguided Muslim and non-Muslim writers have targeted Sayyidah Fāṭimah al-Zahrāʾ عليها السلام with harsh statements despite her greatness, honor, and moral excellence.

Referring to ḥadīth books and studies reveals that agents of past oppressive regimes fabricated and added forged stories to these books. Those agents who spread poisonous speeches and false ḥadīth, revealed to them by their evil masters, have sold their souls to some creatures and achieved nothing save the wrath of God. They used their pens of enmity and daggers of hypocrisy in obedience to those who bought from them their faith and dead consciousnesses, heedless of the Prophet's ﷺ position and indifferent to contradicting the narrations recorded in their books and publications, which praise Sayyidah Fāṭimah al-Zahrāʾ عليها السلام.

It seems as if they are pleased to encroach upon Sayyidah Fāṭimah's عليها السلام honor in response to the call of their evil consciousnesses while they realize she is the Prophet's ﷺ daughter and the most beloved person to him. It is as if they fear announcing their wish to disgrace the great Messenger of God ﷺ directly, so they choose the crooked method of slandering his daughter to fulfill their evil lusts.

Despite that, I do not comprehend the real motives behind these furious and harsh attacks against Sayyidah Fāṭimah al-Zahrāʾ ؑ! Or what the reasons are for this strange and deep enmity against this noble lady!

Is she not the Messenger of God's ﷺ daughter, and "his spirit whom he holds in his heart"?

Was she the Prophet's ﷺ successor, to say that their political motives led them to tarnish her reputation as they did with her great husband ؑ?

What is the reason for this concentrated insistence to put her down? Is it because she is the Prophet's ﷺ daughter? Could it be because she was Imām ʿAlī's ؑ wife? But he married four wives after her; we do not find such agitation and prejudice against them.

The Prophet ﷺ, whose words are no less than revelation from God ﷻ, described Sayyidah Fāṭimah ؑ in many beautiful ways. He ﷺ said:

> "Sayyidah Fāṭimah is a human ḥūrī (a woman from heaven); whenever I long for paradise, I kiss her."[1]

[1] al-Baghdādī, al-Khaṭīb, *Tārīkh al-Baghdādī*, Vol. 5, p.86.

Or:

> "My daughter Sayyidah Fāṭimah is a human ḥūrī."²

Or:

> "Sayyidah Fāṭimah is the true splendor."³

Or as Anas b. Mālik's mother says:

> "Sayyidah Fāṭimah was like a moon on its full night, or the sun covered with no clouds. She was white with a touch of rose color on her face, her hair was black, and she had the beautiful features of the Messenger of God ﷺ."⁴

Sayyidah Fāṭimah's mother, the Mother of the Faithful, Sayyidah Khadījah, may God be pleased with her, said:

> "Sayyidah Fāṭimah used to speak when she was in her mother's womb; when she was born, she fell on the ground in a prostrating position with her finger raised."⁵

---

² al-Haythamī, Ibn Ḥajar, *al-Ṣawāʿiq al-Muḥriqah*, and al-Ṣabān, Muḥammad ʿAlī, *Isʿāf al-Rāghabīn*, p.173.

³ Mūsawī, ʿAbbās ʿAlī, *Nuzhat al-Jalīs wa Munyat al-Adīb al-Anīs*, Vol. 2, p. 222.

⁴ al-Ḥakim al-Nīshābūrī, *al-Mustadrak ʿala al-Ṣaḥīḥayn*, Vol. 3, p.161.

⁵ Majlisī, ʿAllamah Muḥammad Bāqir, *Biḥār al-Anwār*, Vol. 43.

al-Ṭabarī, Muḥib al-Dīn, *Dhakhāʾir al-ʿUqbī*.

Or 'Ā'isha's saying:

> "I have not seen a person more similar to the Prophet's appearance, conduct, guidance, and speech, whether sitting or standing, than Sayyidah Fāṭimah. When she enters, the Messenger of God stands up, kisses and welcomes her, then takes her hand and asks her to sit in his place."[6]

Also, 'Ā'isha said:

> "I have not seen anyone more similar to the Messenger of God's habit of speech and dialogue than Sayyidah Fāṭimah..."[7]

Imām 'Alī, Sayyidah Fāṭimah's husband, who had his share of unfounded attacks by his rivals, had great traits of his own. He had a splendid face as if it was the full moon, his neck appeared like a silver jug[8], and he was cheerful[9]; whenever he smiled, his teeth seemed to be organized pearls.[10]

Abū al-Aswad Du'aliy poetically said that whenever he came face to face with Imām 'Alī, he felt as if he was facing the full moon. Imām 'Alī was well-known for his courage and an invincible knight who participated in many battles and wars.

---

[6] al-Tirmidhī, Muḥammad, *Sunan al-Tirmidhī*.

Ibn 'Abd Rabbih, *al-'Iqd al-Farīd*: Vol. 2, p. 3.

[7] al-Bayhaqī, Aḥmad b. al-Ḥusayn, *Sunan al-Kubra lil Bayhaqī*, vol. 7, p. 101.

[8] Esti'ab: Vol. 2, p.469.

[9] al-Nawawī, Yaḥyā b. Sharaf, *Tahdhīb al-Asmā' wa al-Lughāt*.

[10] al-Isfahānī, Aḥmad, *Ḥilyat al-Awliya' wa-Ṭabaqāt al-Aṣfiya'*, Vol. 1, p. 84.

Imām ʿAlī ؑ was the one who relieved the Messenger of God ﷺ from many inflictions and calamities which had clouded his life since he spoke openly of the righteous religion until he lay down on his death bed, and sacrificed himself for the great Prophet ﷺ until he entered his last dwell.

Has anyone else been granted the verses revealed in their name, like Imām ʿAlī ؑ?

﴿أَجَعَلْتُمْ سِقَايَةَ الْحَاجِّ وَعِمَارَةَ الْمَسْجِدِ الْحَرَامِ كَمَنْ آمَنَ بِاللَّهِ وَالْيَوْمِ الْآخِرِ وَجَاهَدَ فِي سَبِيلِ اللَّهِ ۚ لَا يَسْتَوُونَ عِنْدَ اللَّهِ ۗ وَاللَّهُ لَا يَهْدِي الْقَوْمَ الظَّالِمِينَ﴾

﴿*ʾa-jaʿaltum siqāyata l-ḥājji wa-ʿimārata l-masjidi l-ḥarāmi ka-man ʾāmana bi-llāhi wa-l-yawmi l-ʾākhiri wa-jāhada fī sabīli llāhi lā yastawūna ʿinda llāhi wa-llāhu lā yahdī l-qawma ẓ-ẓālimīna*﴾

﴿*Do you regard the providing of water to* ḥajj *pilgrims and the maintenance of the Holy Mosque as similar [in worth] to someone who has faith in God and [believes in] the Last Day and wages* jihād *in the way of God? They are not equal with God, and God does not guide the wrongdoing lot*﴾[11]

And:

﴿وَمِنَ النَّاسِ مَنْ يَشْرِي نَفْسَهُ ابْتِغَاءَ مَرْضَاتِ اللَّهِ ۗ وَاللَّهُ رَءُوفٌ بِالْعِبَادِ﴾

﴿*wa-mina n-nāsi man yashrī nafsahu btighāʾa marḍāti llāhi wa-llāhu raʾūfun bi-l-ʿibādi*﴾

[11] Sūrat al-Tawbah, Verse 19.

﴾*And among the people is he who sells his soul* seeking the pleasure of God, and God is most kind to [His] servants*﴿[12]

While the Prophet ﷺ declared that Imām ʿAlī ؑ was the best man of his nation, for he was the most patient and best mannered one of them all, and says:

> "ʿAlī is the best of my nation, most knowledgeable and patient from among them."[13]

The Prophet ﷺ said to Sayyidah Fāṭimah ؑ about Imām ʿAlī ؑ,

> "I gave you in marriage to the first one to adhere to Islām from my nation; he is also the most knowledgeable and patient among them."[14]

And:

> "I gave you in marriage to the first Muslim and best-mannered man."[15]

---

12 Sūrat al-Baqarah, Verse 207.

* Or 'his life.'

13 al-Hindī, ʿAlī al-Muttaqī, *Kanz al-ʿUmmāl fī Sunan al-Aqwāl wal-Afʿāl*, Vol. 6, p. 153.

In this volume, the book cites narrations from Ṭabarī, Khaṭīb, and Dūlābī.

14 Ibn Ḥanbal, Aḥmad, *Musnad Aḥmad b. Ḥanbal*, Vol. 5, p. 26 and al-Siʿdī, ʿAbd ur-Raḥman b. Nāṣir, *ar-Riyaḍ an-Naḍirah*, Vol. 2, p.194.

15 al-Siʿdī, ʿAbd ur-Raḥman b. Nāṣir, *ar-Riyaḍ an-Naḍirah*, Vol. 2, p.194.

The Prophet ♣ also said to Sayyidah Fāṭimah ♣:

"Surely God is angered when you are angered and is pleased with your pleasure."[16]

He ♣ also said to Sayyidah Fāṭimah ♣ while holding her hand,

"He who knows this knows her, and he who does not know her; she is part of me, my heart and spirit in my side. Thus, he who harms her harms me."[17]

---

[16] al-Ḥakim al-Nīshābūrī, *al-Mustadrak ʿala al-Ṣaḥīḥayn*, Vol. 3, p.154.

Muḥammad b. Aḥmad al-Dimashqī, *Mīzān al-Iʿtidāl*.

al-Khawārazmī, *Maqtal al-Ḥusayn*: Vol. 1, p.54.

al-Shāfiʿī, Muḥammad b. Yūsuf al-Kanjī, *Kifāyat al-Ṭālib*, p.219.

al-Hindī, ʿAlī al-Muttaqī, *Kanz al-ʿUmmāl fī Sunan al-Aqwāl wal-Afʿāl*, Vol. 7, p.111.

al-Haythamī, Ibn Ḥajar, *al-Ṣawāʿiq al-Muḥriqah*, p.105.

[17] al-Mālikī, Ibn Sabagh, *al-Fuṣūl al-Muhimmah fī Maʿrifat al-Aʾimmah*, p.150.

ash-Shāfiʿī, ʿAbd ur-Rahman, *Nuzhat al-Majālis*, Vol. 2, p.228.

al-Shāfiʿī, Muʾmin b. al-Ḥasan al-Shablanjī, *Nūr al-Abṣār fī Manāqib Āl Bayt an-Nabī al-Mukhtār*, p.45.

He also said:

> "Sayyidah Fāṭimah is part of me; that which annoys her annoys me, and harms me that which harms her."[18]

And:

> "Sayyidah Fāṭimah is part of me, he who angers her angers me."[19]

Did the Prophet ﷺ limit his praise of Imām ʿAlī ؑ to his precedence in adhering to Islām? Did he endeavor to keep this a secret by only informing his daughter to appease her? Indeed not, for he took Imām ʿAlī's ؑ hand and, raised it publicly, and announced:

> "He was the first to believe in me, and he will be the first to shake my hand on the Day of Rising."

---

[18] Bukhārī, Muḥammad b. Ismāʿīl, *Ṣaḥīḥ Bukhārī.*

Muslim b. al-Ḥajjāj, *Ṣaḥīḥ Muslim.*

al-Tirmidhī, Muḥammad, *Sunan al-Tirmidhī.*

Ibn Ḥanbal, Aḥmad, *Musnad Aḥmad b. Ḥanbal*, Vol. 4, p. 328.

al-Nasāʾī, Aḥmad b. Shuʿayb, *Khaṣāʾiṣ Amīr al-Muʾminīn*, p.35.

[19] Bukhārī, Muḥammad b. Ismāʿīl, *Ṣaḥīḥ Bukhārī.*

al-Nasāʾī, Aḥmad b. Shuʿayb, *Khaṣāʾiṣ Amīr al-Muʾminīn*, p.35.

He also informed his companions that:

> "The first among you to appear at my domain (reservoir) is he who was the first among you to follow Islām, ʿAlī b. Abū Ṭālib."

Great companions acknowledged the Prophet's ﷺ praise of Imām ʿAlī ؑ. Men including Salmān the Persian, Anas b. Mālik, Zayd b. Arqam, ʿAbdullāh b. Ḥijl, Hāshim b. ʿUtba, Mālik al-Ashtar, ʿAbdullāh b. Hāshim, Abū Amrah ʿAdī b. Ḥātim, Abū Rāfiʿ, Buraydah, Jundub b. Zuhayr, and Umm al-Khayr b. al-Ḥarash.[20]

Moreover, the Noble Qur'ān declared that Imām ʿAlī ؑ is the same as the Prophet's self (the first verse below) and made the reward for the divine message of the love of Imām ʿAlī ؑ, as it was revealed in the second verse below.

﴿فَمَنْ حَاجَّكَ فِيهِ مِنْ بَعْدِ مَا جَاءَكَ مِنَ الْعِلْمِ فَقُلْ تَعَالَوْا نَدْعُ أَبْنَاءَنَا وَأَبْنَاءَكُمْ
وَنِسَاءَنَا وَنِسَاءَكُمْ وَأَنْفُسَنَا وَأَنْفُسَكُمْ ثُمَّ نَبْتَهِلْ فَنَجْعَلْ لَعْنَتَ اللَّهِ عَلَى الْكَاذِبِينَ﴾

﴿fa-man ḥājjaka fīhi min baʿdi mā jāʾaka mina l-ʿilmi fa-qul taʿālaw nadʿu ʾabnāʾanā wa-ʾabnāʾakum wa-nisāʾanā wa-nisāʾakum wa-ʾanfusanā wa-ʾanfusakum thumma nabtahil fa-najʿal laʿnata llāhi ʿalā l-kādhibīna[a]﴾

﴿*Should anyone argue with* you *concerning him, after the knowledge that has come to* you, say, *'Come! Let us call our sons and your sons,*

[20] Most historical sources mention them.

our women and your women, our souls and your souls, then let us pray earnestly and call down God's curse upon the liars.﴾[21]

﴿إن يَشَأ يُسكِنِ الرِّيحَ فَيَظلَلنَ رَواكِدَ عَلىٰ ظَهرِهِ ۚ إِنَّ في ذٰلِكَ لَآياتٍ لِكُلِّ صَبّارٍ شَكورٍ﴾

﴿*'in yasha' yuskini r-rīḥa fa-yaẓlalna rawākida 'alā ẓahrihī 'inna fī dhālika la-'āyātin li-kulli ṣabbārin shakūr^in*﴾

﴿*If He wishes He stills the wind, whereat they remain standstill on its surface. There are indeed signs in that for every patient and grateful [servant]*﴾[22]

In addition, 'Ā'isha said,

> "Surely 'Alī is the most beloved of all men and precious to me. Therefore, recognize his rights and pay tribute to him."[23]

The Prophet ﷺ also said,

> "The most beloved of all men to me is 'Alī."[24]

---

21 Sūrat Āl 'Imrān, Verse 61.

22 Sūrat al-Shūrā, Verse 33.

23 al-Si'dī, 'Abd ur-Raḥman b. Nāṣir, *ar-Riyaḍ an-Naḍirah*, Vol. 2, p.161.

al-Ṭabarī, Muḥib al-Dīn, *Dhakha'ir al-'Uqbī*, p.62.

24 In another narration: "of my kin."

And:

> "ʿAlī is the best of those I leave behind me (after death)."[25]

And:

> "The best of your men is ʿAlī b. Abū Ṭālib and the best of your women is Sayyidah Fāṭimah, daughter of Muḥammad."[26]

And:

> "ʿAlī is the best of mankind, and he who denies it is an infidel."[27]

And:

> "He who does not say that ʿAlī is the best of mankind is surely an infidel."[28]

---

[25] al-Ījī, al-Qāḍī ʿAḍad al-Dīn, *al-Mawāqif fī ʿIlm al-Kalām*, Vol. 3, p.276.

ʿAlī al-Haythamī, *Majmaʿ al-Zawāʾid*, Vol. 9, p.113.

[26] al-Baghdādī, al-Khaṭīb, *Tārīkh al-Baghdādī*, Vol. 4, p.392.

[27] Ibid.

al-Manāwi, *Kunūz al-Ḥaqāʾiq*.

al-Suyūṭī, ʿAbd al-Raḥmān b. Abī Bakr, *al-Jāmiʿ al-Saghīr*, p.16.

al-Hindī, ʿAlī al-Muttaqī, *Kanz al-ʿUmmāl fī Sunan al-Aqwāl wal-Afʿāl*, p.159.

[28] al-Baghdādī, al-Khaṭīb, *Tārīkh al-Baghdādī*, Vol. 3, p. 192.

al-Hindī, ʿAlī al-Muttaqī, *Kanz al-ʿUmmāl fī Sunan al-Aqwāl wal-Afʿāl*, Vol. 6, p.159.

And in another narration, where it has been unanimously agreed that he ﷺ said:

> "Tomorrow, I will hand over the banner to a man whom God and His Messenger love and who loves God and His Messenger."

And:

> "ʿAlī, to me, is like my head to my body."[29]

And:

> "ʿAlī, to me, is like I am to my Lord."[30]

And:

> "ʿAlī is the most beloved to me and the most beloved to God."[31]

---

[29] al-Baghdādī, al-Khaṭīb, *Tārīkh al-Baghdādī*, Vol. 7, p.12.

al-Haythamī, Ibn Ḥajar, *al-Ṣawāʿiq al-Muḥriqah*, p.75.

al-Suyūṭī, ʿAbd al-Raḥmān b. Abī Bakr, *al-Jāmiʿ al-Saghīr*.

al-Shāfiʿī, Mu'min b. al-Ḥasan al-Shablanjī, *Nūr al-Abṣār fī Manāqib Āl Bayt an-Nabī al-Mukhtār*, p.80.

[30] *al-Sīrah al-Ḥalabiyyah*, Vol. 3, p. 391.

al-Siʿdī, ʿAbd ur-Raḥman b. Nāṣir, *ar-Riyaḍ an-Naḍirah*, Vol. 2, p.163.

[31] al-Baghdādī, al-Khaṭīb, *Tārīkh al-Baghdādī*, Vol. 1, p.160.

He ﷺ also said to Imām ʿAlī ؑ:

"I am from you, and you are from me, or you are from me, and I am from you."³²

And:

"ʿAlī is from me, and I am from him; he is the guardian (wali) of every believer after me."³³

And in the narration regarding sending Imām ʿAlī ؑ to read Sūrat al-Tawbah to the pilgrims on which it has been unanimously agreed, he ﷺ said:

"No one takes it (to the pilgrims) except a man being from me and I from him."³⁴

And:

"Your flesh is my flesh, your blood is my blood, and righteousness is on your side."³⁵

---

³² Ibn Ḥanbal, Aḥmad, *Musnad Aḥmad b. Ḥanbal*, Vol. 5, p.204.

al-Nasāʾī, Aḥmad b. Shuʿayb, *Khaṣāʾiṣ Amīr al-Muʾminīn*, p.36, 51.

³³ Ibn Ḥanbal, Aḥmad, *Musnad Aḥmad b. Ḥanbal*, Vol. 5, p.356.

³⁴ al-Nasāʾī, Aḥmad b. Shuʿayb, *Khaṣāʾiṣ Amīr al-Muʾminīn*, p. 8.

³⁵ al-Bayhaqī, Ibrāhīm b. Muḥammad, *al-Maḥāsin wa al-Masāwī*, Vol. 1, p.31.

And:

> "There is not a prophet who has not had a peer, and 'Alī is my peer."[36]

Also, in a narration that al-Ḥakīm deemed authentic, Ṭabarānī related to Umm Salamah:

> "Whenever the Prophet of God was angered, no one dared to speak to him save 'Alī."[37]

Also, 'Ā'isha said:

> "(I declare) by God that I have not seen anyone more beloved to God 's Messenger than 'Alī, or a woman on earth more beloved to him than his wife ('Alī's wife, Sayyidah Fāṭimah)." [38]

Buraydah and Ubay also said:

> "The most beloved to the Messenger of God from among women is Sayyidah Fāṭimah, and from among men is 'Alī." [39]

---

[36] al-Si'dī, 'Abd ur-Raḥman b. Nāṣir, *ar-Riyaḍ an-Naḍirah*, Vol. 2, p.164.

[37] al-Haythamī, Ibn Ḥajar, *al-Ṣawā'iq al-Muḥriqah*, p.73.

al-Suyūṭī, Jalāl al-Dīn, *Tārīkh al-Khulafā'*, p.116.

[38] al-Ḥakim al-Nīshābūrī, *al-Mustadrak 'ala al-Ṣaḥīḥayn*, Vol. 3, p.154, *Khaṣā'iṣ an-Nisā'ī*: p.29.

[39] al-Nasā'ī, Aḥmad b. Shu'ayb, *Khaṣā'iṣ Amīr al-Mu'minīn*, p.29.

al-Ḥakim al-Nīshābūrī, *al-Mustadrak 'ala al-Ṣaḥīḥayn*, Vol. 3, p.115.

And Jumu'ah b. 'Umayr said:

"I entered 'Alī's house with my aunt when I inquired who was the most beloved of all people to God's Messenger. She said: Sayyidah Fāṭimah. Then she was asked: And from among men? She said her husband has been fasting and praying since I met him."[40]

Imām 'Alī was the first man chosen by God to follow His Messenger from among the dwellers of Earth, as he told Sayyidah Fāṭimah in the following narration:

"Surely God has examined the dwellers of Earth and has chosen your father to be a prophet; he then examined (them) and chose your husband, then He revealed to me that I give (you to him in) marriage and appoint him as my successor."[41]

He also said to Sayyidah Fāṭimah:

"Surely God chose two men from Earth's dwellers, one your father and the other your husband."[42]

---

[40] al-Tirmidhī, Muḥammad, *al-Jāmi' al-Tirmidhī*, Vol. 2, p.227 and other collective books.

[41] al-Hindī, 'Alī al-Muttaqī, *Kanz al-'Ummāl fī Sunan al-Aqwāl wal-Af'āl*, Vol. 6, p.153.

'Alī al-Haythamī, *Majma' al-Zawā'id*, Vol. 9, p.165.

[42] al-Ījī, al-Qāḍī 'Aḍad al-Dīn, *al-Mawāqif fī 'Ilm al-Kalām*.

The Law of Inheritance

It has been proven that children inherit their parent's characteristics. These characteristics are in children's genes before they are transferred into their mothers' wombs. They live with these characteristics as grown unborn children, and after birth, these characteristics become more apparent with the child's growth.

Nursing also has a fantastic effect on nursed children's characteristics, as Imām ʿAlī ﷺ said:

> "Don't have a witless woman nurse your children, for surely nursing is a means for passing on contagious diseases."

Many detailed manuscripts have been published regarding this law. Considering this, it is appropriate to briefly discuss the biographies of the parents of Sayyidah Fāṭimah ﷺ so we may conclude about the magnificence that surrounded her life from the genetic viewpoint. Because this is not the subject of our book, we will briefly cover it.

The chief of prophets and messengers, Muḥammad b. ʿAbdullāh ﷺ is the purest being, the most honorable creature, and the foremost of all the world's people. For his sake, God ﷻ created all beings, and there is not an honor, virtue, or noble deed in the existing universe that the great Prophet ﷺ doesn't enjoy the greatest share of.

This is the least that can be said about the Messenger ﷺ, there is no exaggeration or extravagance in these words; they are like saying: The sun shines, and honey is sweet. For this is the Messenger of God ﷺ from whom Sayyidah Fāṭimah al-Zahrāʾ ﷺ descended.

As for Sayyidah Khadījah ﷺ, she was a beautiful, tall, fair woman, considered noble among her people; she was wise in decision-making and enjoyed great intelligence and sharp discernment. She gave her brilliant insight into economic principles, especially in the export and import field. This was Sayyidah Khadījah ﷺ, the human, the woman, and the wife; she granted thousands of dinars to her husband to use as he saw fit. Thus, her financial support significantly strengthened Islām during its prime days, when it was still in formation and critically needed material aid. Therefore, God ﷻ foreordained her property to help Islām fulfill its goals.

God's Messenger ﷺ said in this regard:

> "No property has ever been so useful to me as Sayyidah Khadījah's."

While in Makkah, the Prophet ﷺ used this property to free slaves, help the needy, support the poor, and rescue his financially inflicted companions. He also paved the way for those who wished to immigrate through Sayyidah Khadījah's ﷺ wealth, from which he spent freely during her life; when she died, he and her children inherited it.[43]

Hence the meaning of the Prophet's ﷺ saying,

> "Religion succeeded and became manifest only through 'Alī's sword and Sayyidah Khadījah's property" becomes clear.

Her conduct throughout her married life with the Messenger ﷺ is worthy of praise and glorification; for this reason, whenever he remembered his wife ﷺ or her name was mentioned to him, he would bless her, and a feeling of sadness overcame him. Perhaps tears would run down his face in her remembrance.

---

[43] Ṣadūq, Shaykh Muḥammad b. 'Alī, *al-Amālī*.

Once the Prophet ﷺ mentioned Sayyidah Khadījah ؑ near ʿĀʾisha, ʿĀʾisha responded,

> "She was not, but a such-and-such of an old lady, and God replaced her with a better one for you."

He ﷺ replied:

> "Indeed, God did not grant me better than her; she accepted me when people rejected me, she believed in me when people doubted me, she shared her wealth with me when people deprived me, and God gave me children only through her."[44]

---

[44] al-Andalusī, Ibn ʿAbd al-Barr, *al-Istīʿāb fī Maʿrifat al-Aṣḥāb.*

The Prophet's ﷺ Marriage

Sunnī Muslims, and some Shīʿī, allege that the Prophet ﷺ married Sayyidah Khadījah ؑ when she was forty years of age and after she had two previous marriages. However, leading researchers like the late ʿAllamah Sayyid Jaʿfar Murtaḍā al-ʿĀmilī ؒ conclude that she was never married before the Prophet ﷺ wedded her. ʿAllamah al-ʿĀmilī ؒ convincingly argues that those who allege Sayyidah Khadījah ؑ married two men before marrying the Prophet ﷺ agree that her alleged former husbands hailed from less-than-noble tribes.

ʿAllamah al-ʿĀmilī ؒ points out that Sayyidah Khadījah ؑ refused all the marriage proposals she received from the noblemen of Quraysh, so why would she agree to marry men of lower-status tribes?[45] ʿAllamah al-ʿĀmilī details the history of the alleged former husbands' of Sayyidah Khadījah ؑ and points out the inconsistencies in those narratives to conclude that the allegation that she was forty years of age and that she had two previous marriages was fabricated by the allies of ʿĀʾisha, who made a great effort to embellish her beauty and status, including the false claim she was the only virgin the Prophet ﷺ married.[46]

The Prophet's ﷺ marriage to Sayyidah Khadījah ؑ was not usual. It was a unique marriage because it was not started because of an emotional relationship, nor were there material or political motives behind it, which were commonplace among the elite classes. There was no correspondence between the Prophet's ﷺ economic position and Sayyidah Khadījah's ؑ. On the one hand, his poor uncle, Abū Ṭālib, sponsored the Messenger ﷺ and Sayyidah

[45] Khūʾī, Āyatullāh Sayyid Abū al-Qāsim Mūsawī, *al-Istighāthah*, Vol. 1, p. 68-69.

[46] al-ʿĀmilī, ʿAllamah Sayyid Jaʿfar Murtaḍā, *Banāt an-Nabī Umm Rabībātuh*, p. 90.

Khadījah عليها السلام was the wealthiest lady in Makkah. Thus, there was a clear gap between them in this peculiarity.

Sayyidah Khadījah عليها السلام heard the Prophet ﷺ had a bright and sacred future ahead of him. Perhaps she heard this from her servant Maysarah, who informed her of what had happened to the Messenger ﷺ during a commercial trip to Sūrīyah (Syria), where he had worked for her. Or perhaps he conveyed to her what the monk in Buṣrā said about the future of the Prophet ﷺ. Upon learning this, Sayyidah Khadījah عليها السلام suggested that the prophet Muḥammad ﷺ marry her and urged him to ask for her hand from her father, Khuwaylid (according to some historians, it was her uncle).

The Prophet, who preferred to marry a poor woman from his economic class, apologized to Sayyidah Khadījah عليها السلام and refused her request. But she, being a wise, reasonable, and honorable woman, informed him she was ready to give him herself in marriage. That property was not difficult to put at his disposal. So, she once again urged him to send his uncles to ask for her hand from her father, Khuwaylid.

The Prophet's uncles and aunts were astonished at this news. Could she have been honest in doing so? Could this news be true? Ṣafīyyah b. 'Abd Muṭṭalib (the Prophet's aunt) rushed to Sayyidah Khadījah's عليها السلام house to validate the information. Sayyidah Khadījah عليها السلام warmly welcomed her and informed her of her earnest desire to do so.

On the Way to a Blessed Life

When Ṣafīyyah returned home and informed her brothers (the Prophet's uncles) of the news's authenticity, happiness and astonishment overtook them.

Sayyidah Khadījah عليها السلام, who refused to marry the princes and lords of the Arabs because she deemed them unworthy to marry, chose to be the wife of a poor man who owned nothing of the ephemeral things of this world or even a square foot of land.

This was the wonder of wonders.

The Prophet's uncles proceeded towards her house and asked for her hand from her father (or uncle), who initially rejected them but later agreed to the proposal.

Inevitably, an appropriate sum of money had to be presented to Sayyidah Khadījah عليها السلام as her dowry; how could it be obtained? And who would donate it?

This was a difficult question until Sayyidah Khadījah عليها السلام once again surprised everyone by giving four thousand dinars as a gift to the Prophet ﷺ and urged him to pay it to her father as her dowry. However, according to another historical finding, Abū Ṭālib paid the dowry with his own money.

Even though Sayyidah Khadījah عليها السلام was a woman of high standards who sacrificed material gains to achieve honor, her father, Khuwaylid, possessed contradicting values. This difference between Sayyidah Khadījah عليها السلام and her father is not rare between parents and their children; we can also find this ideological difference between various classes of people, brothers, spouses, and parents.

Sayyidah Khadījah's ﷺ payment of the dowry was a unique, unforgettable, and unforeseen act, for the Arabs were not accustomed to women giving dowries to their husbands. Thus, it was not unexpected for Abū Jahl to incite an envious commotion and say,

> "O people, we have thus seen men paying dowries for women; we are not used to women giving dowry to men."

In answer to this, Abū Ṭālib angrily replied,

> "What is the matter with you? O, you wicked man! Men like Muḥammad are to be given gifts and grants, but your likes give gifts that people always reject."

He also said:

> "If it was a man like my nephew, then the greatest dowries are to be granted to him, but men like you cannot get married save by paying large sums of money."

The blessed wedding took place in the best possible way. The Messenger moved in with Sayyidah Khadījah ﷺ, who felt she was going through the happiest period because she had reached her best wishes and the sweetest dreams.

Transcendental Events

Sayyidah Fāṭimah al-Zahrā' ﷺ was the daughter of two great people; we briefly spoke about her parents, lives, and virtues and drew a picture through which we can look at her genius and an aspect of genetic inheritance that contributed to this genius.

There are undisputed facts that have been declared by the Sacred Messenger ﷺ and Ahl al-Bayt ﷺ that neither science nor contemporary discoveries have been able to conquer the deep meanings of, despite what science has achieved in these fields. Because these facts are beyond the reach of machines and telescopes, photographers' advanced lenses cannot capture their rays, nor can natural senses realize them.

The truth goes beyond material and logical realization, for the five senses cannot define it. So, if you wish, you may call these facts "transcendental facts."

Before elaborating on these facts, we must make a brief introduction. Thus, we say:

The sperm formed in the womb to become an embryo develops from the blood produced from digesting the food by various body organs. Hence, sperm, a product of eating pork or drinking liquor, differs from lamb meat because of the difference in composition between multiple types of foods. In addition, food has peculiar effects on the human psyche and spirit; some foods bring happiness to the heart and calm nerves, while others do the opposite.

Permissible and pure food benefits man; conversely, impure food such as liquor or impermissible food like stolen or usurped meat harms men. The influence of the food we eat becomes apparent in the sperm. Elaboration on this subject by procuring proof and evidence takes extraordinary effort, which would lead us away from our original topic.

In conclusion, the food the parents eat has an enormous effect on the child's future because it is from this food that the sperm is formed and carried on to the womb to grow and become a human being.

The psychological state of the parents during sexual intercourse has a significant effect on the child's state of mind and psychological behavior in the future. Besides this, persistent want and earnest desire to have sexual intercourse influence the child's appearance and intelligence.

Considering these two points, the nutritional and psychological effects on children, we elaborate on the subject by verifying it through a selection of narrations[47].

Jibrā'īl descended to the Messenger of God and told him:

> "O Muḥammad! The Most Exalted sends His peace upon you and commands you to refrain from (coming close to) Sayyidah Khadījah for forty days."

It was difficult for the Prophet, who loved and adored Sayyidah Khadījah, to do so, but in obedience to God's command, he spent forty days fasting and praying nights. When it was close to the end of the forty days, he summoned 'Ammār b. Yāsir and asked him to go to Sayyidah Khadījah and tell her,

---

[47] Majlisī, 'Allamah Muḥammad Bāqir, *Biḥār al-Anwār*, Vol. 6.

> "O Sayyidah Khadījah! Do not assume that my separation from you means abandoning or forsaking you; instead, my Lord commanded me to do so, so expect nothing save benevolence, for indeed, God ﷻ praises you to His most honorable angels several times a day. Therefore, at nightfall, close the door and sleep; I will stay at Sayyidah Fāṭimah b. Assad's house."

This saddened Sayyidah Khadījah ؑ, who missed having the Prophet ﷺ by her side.

At the end of the forty days, Jibrā'īl once again descended to God's Messenger ﷺ and said:

> "O Muḥammad! The Most Exalted sends His peace upon you and commands you to be prepared for His salutation and gift."

The Prophet ﷺ said:

> "Jibrā'īl! What is the Lord of the world's gift and His salutation?"

Jibrā'īl ؑ said:

> "I do not know."

At that moment, the angel Mīkā'īl ؑ descended with a plate covered with a kerchief made of brocade or sarcenet and presented it to the Prophet ﷺ!

Jibrā'īl ؑ said to him:

> "O Muḥammad, your Lord commands you to break your fasting with this food tonight."

Imām ʿAlī b. Abū Ṭālib ﷺ said:

> "The Prophet ﷺ used to order me to open the door to whoever wanted to join him when he came to break his fast, but that night he called me to guard the door of the house and said to me: `O son of Abū Ṭālib! This food is forbidden to everyone save me."

Then he ﷺ said:

> "I sat at the door, and the Prophet ﷺ uncovered the plate, in privacy, to find a cluster of dates and a bunch of grapes; he ate until satisfied and drank his need of water. He then extended his hands to be washed, so Jibrāʾīl ﷺ poured the water, Mīkāʾīl ﷺ washed his hands, and Isrāfīl ﷺ dried them. After that, the remaining food on the plate ascended to heaven. Then he ﷺ started to prepare himself for prayers when Jibrāʾīl ﷺ said to him:

> "Prayer is forbidden to you until you go to Sayyidah Khadījah's house and perform coition with her, for God ﷻ ordained upon Himself to create noble offspring from you tonight.' So, he rushed to Sayyidah Khadījah's house."

Sayyidah Khadījah ﷺ said:

> "I had gotten used to seclusion by that time, so when night arrived, I covered my head, put down the curtains, locked the doors, performed my prayers, put out the lantern, and retired to my bed. That night, while I was between the states of sleeping and being awake, the Prophet knocked on the door; so, I exclaimed: Who is knocking on the door that only Muḥammad knocks on?"

The Prophet ﷺ gently and politely replied,

"Open the door Sayyidah Khadījah, I am Muḥammad."

Sayyidah Khadījah ؑ said:

"I cheerfully got up and opened the door for the Prophet to come in. He ﷺ usually requested the water jug to perform ablution and two short prayer prostrations before he retired. Rather, that night he ﷺ did not request the jug, nor did he perform prayers... instead, what occurs between a woman and her husband occurred between us. By God, who created the heavens and caused water to come out of springs before the Prophet left me, I felt Sayyidah Fāṭimah's weight in my womb..."

We can conclude from the above narration[48] that:

1. God ﷻ commanded His Messenger to abandon Sayyidah Khadījah ؑ for a period, so his longing for and wanting her increased.

---

[48] The following Sunnī scholars mentioned this narration with minor variations between some of their accounts of it:

al-ʿAsqalānī, Ḥāfiẓ b. Ḥajar, *Lisān al-Mīzān*, Vol. 4, p. 36

adh-Dhahabī, Shams ad-Dīn, *Mīzān al-Iʿtidāl*, Vol. 2, p. 26.

al-Ḥakim al-Nīshābūrī, *al-Mustadrak ʿala al-Ṣaḥīḥayn*, Vol. 3, p. 156.

al-Khawārazmī, *Maqtal al-Ḥusayn*, p. 63, 68.

2. He ﷺ performed more worship to achieve a higher level of spirituality and sacredness because of constant contact with the heavenly world.

3. He ﷺ broke his fast on the pure heavenly gift, which was quickly transformed into sperm because of its delicateness.

4. The sperm was produced from eating delicate heavenly food that differs from material nutrition.

5. The Prophet ﷺ immediately proceeded to Sayyidah Khadījah's ﷺ house to transfer the sperm to her womb after the previously mentioned preparations.

In addition, there are various traditions with minor verbal differences and the same fundamental meaning that Sayyidah Fāṭimah al-Zahrā' ﷺ was created from a sperm produced from heavenly food. We mention some of these narrations and restrict ourselves to the part that is related to our subject for the sake of brevity and omit the rest:

Imām 'Alī al-Riḍā ﷺ said:

> "The Prophet ﷺ said: "On the night of my ascension to Heaven, Jibrā'īl took my hand and led me into Paradise; then he handed me dates from which I ate; those dates were formed into sperm. When I descended to Earth, I came unto Sayyidah Khadījah, who became pregnant with Sayyidah Fāṭimah; thus, Sayyidah Fāṭimah is a human ḥūrī, whom whenever I long for Paradise I smell."[49]

[49] Ṣadūq, Shaykh Muḥammad b. 'Alī, *al-Amālī*.

Imām Muḥammad al-Bāqir ﷺ on the account of Jābir b. ʿAbdullāh said:

"It was said to the Messenger of God: Surely you kiss, embrace, and bring Sayyidah Fāṭimah close to you... and treat her better than your other daughters!"

He ﷺ commented:

"Indeed, for Jibrāʾīl brought me an apple from heaven, which I ate, and it was transformed into sperm that I placed in Sayyidah Khadījah, who later bore Sayyidah Fāṭimah. Hence, I smell paradise's fragrance in her."[50]

Ibn ʿAbbās said:

"ʿĀʾisha entered the house while the Messenger of God was kissing Sayyidah Fāṭimah, so she said: Do you love her, O Messenger of God?'

He replied:

'Indeed, by God, if you knew the extent of my love for her, your love would increase for her. When I was in the fourth heaven... (until he said) that I found these dates softer than butter, more pleasant than musk, and sweeter than honey. So, when I descended to earth, I came unto Sayyidah Khadījah, and she bore Sayyidah Fāṭimah. Thus, Sayyidah Fāṭimah is a human ḥūrī. Whenever I long for paradise, I smell her. '"[51]

---

[50] Ṣadūq, Shaykh Muḥammad b. ʿAlī, *ʿIlal al-Sharāʾiʿ*.

[51] Majlisī, ʿAllamah Muḥammad Bāqir, *Biḥār al-Anwār*, Vol. 6.

This last narration was also mentioned with variations.[52]

> "Some noble narrators said that one day Sayyidah Khadījah ﷺ asked the Master of Creatures (the Prophet ﷺ) to show her fruit from the Dwell of Peace (Paradise). Thus, Jibrā'īl brought him, who was chosen above all two apples from Paradise, and said:
>
> 'O Muḥammad, He who appointed a due proportion for all things says to you: "Eat one apple and give the other to Sayyidah Khadījah, then come unto her, for I will create from you (both) Sayyidah Fāṭimah al-Zahrā'.

"The Chosen One did what the Guardian (Jibrā'īl) told him to do, and... (until he said):

> 'Thus, whenever the Chosen One longed for Paradise and its greatness, he would kiss Sayyidah Fāṭimah and smell her

---

[52] Narrations 1-7 are mentioned on the accounts of 'Ā'isha, Ibn 'Abbās, Saed b. Mālik, and 'Umar b. al-Khaṭṭāb.

al-'Asqalānī, Ḥafīẓ b. Ḥajar, *Lisān al-Mīzān*, Vol. 5, p. 160.

al-Balkhī, Sulaymān b. Ibrāhīm al-Qundūzī, *Yanābī' al-Mawaddah lī-Dhawī l-Qūrbā*.

al-Dimashqī, Muḥammad b. Aḥmad, *Mizān al-I'tidāl*, Vol. 1, p. 38.

al-Ḥanafī, Muḥammad b. Yūsuf al-Zarandī, *Naẓm Durar al-Simṭayn*.

al-Khaṭīb al-Baghdādī in *Tārīkh al-Baghdādī,* Vol. 5, p. 87.

al-Khawārazmī, *Maqtal al-Ḥusayn*, p. 63.

al-Ṭabarī, Muḥib al-Dīn, *Dhakha'ir al-'Uqbī*, p. 43.

beautiful fragrance and say: 'Sayyidah Fāṭimah is a human ḥūrī.'"[53]

There are successive narrations in this regard, but we satisfy ourselves with what we have mentioned.

There remains a point here on which elaboration is somewhat necessary; it is noticeable that the narrations clearly state that Sayyidah Khadījah ؑ bore Sayyidah Fāṭimah ؑ immediately after the Prophet's ﷺ ascension to heaven, which took place in the second or third year after revelation.

There is a collection of narrations from the holy Imāms of Ahl al-Bayt ؑ, which state that Sayyidah Fāṭimah ؑ was born five years after the first revelation to the Prophet. This indicates that she stayed in her mother's womb for over two years, which is incorrect. How can the contradictions between the narrations be explained?

We can give several probabilities as answers to this question.

1. The Messenger of God ﷺ ascended to heaven more than once, as stated in *al-Kāfī*. This is the most accurate account of this matter.

2. Some historians claim that ascension occurred in the third year of revelation and that Sayyidah Fāṭimah ؑ was born in the second or third year after the first revelation.

Among the unique merits of Sayyidah Fāṭimah al-Zahrā' ؑ was that she spoke to her mother while she was still in her mother's womb. Shī'ī scholars are not alone in reporting this merit of

---

[53] al-Miṣrī, Shaykh Shu'ayb, *al-Rawḍ al-Fa'iq*, p. 214

Sayyidah Fāṭimah ﷺ. Several Sunnī scholars and narrators also support this. For instance, ʿAbd ur-Raḥman Shāfiʿī narrated[54] that Sayyidah Khadījah ﷺ said:

> "When I was pregnant with Sayyidah Fāṭimah, which was an easy pregnancy, she would speak to me from inside my womb."

Also, Dahlawī quoted[55] Shaykh al-Shāfiʿī as saying[56]:

> "When Sayyidah Khadījah was pregnant with Sayyidah Fāṭimah, Sayyidah Fāṭimah used to speak to her from her womb, but Sayyidah Khadījah kept this from the Prophet.

One day, the Prophet entered the house and found Sayyidah Khadījah speaking to someone while no one was in the room with her. He inquired as to whom she was saying; she replied:

> 'That which in my womb, surely it speaks to me.'

Then the Prophet said,

> 'Rejoice Sayyidah Khadījah, for this is the girl whom God has made to be the mother of eleven of my successors who will come after me and after their father. "'

---

54 ash-Shāfiʿī, ʿAbd ur-Raḥman, *Nuzhat al-Majālis*.

55 Dahlawī, *Tajhīz al-Jaysh*.

56 al-Shāfiʿī, Shaykh ʿIzz al-Dīn ʿAbd al-Salām, *Madḥ al-Khulafā' ar-Rāshidūn*.

Shuʿayb b. Saʿd al-Miṣrī mentioned the following[57]:

> "At the time when Sayyidah Khadījah's pregnancy had become apparent, the infidels asked the Prophet to show them the splitting of the moon; upon hearing this, Sayyidah Khadījah declared:
>
> "O, what a disappointment it would be! Had Muḥammad lied while he is the best messenger of my Lord?"

It was then that Sayyidah Fāṭimah called Sayyidah Khadījah from her womb and said:

> "O mother, do not be grieved nor sorrowful, for surely God is with my father."

When Sayyidah Fāṭimah عليها السلام was born, the skies became illuminated by the brightness of her face.

Likewise, the narration, which states that Sayyidah Khadījah عليها السلام spoke of Sayyidah Fāṭimah al-Zahrā'’s عليها السلام talking while still in her womb, has already been mentioned at the beginning of this chapter.

57 al-Miṣrī, Shaykh Shuʿayb, *al-Rawḍ al-Fa'iq*, p. 214

Sayyidah Fāṭimah al-Zahrā''s ﷺ Birth

The apparent disagreement on Sayyidah Fāṭimah's ﷺ birth date is surprising. Some scholars say she was born five years after revelation, two or three years before that; others claim she was born five years before Revelation. We should note that while the first statement was narrated by the Imāms of Ahl al-Bayt ﷺ, a group of Sunnī scholars also favor the same viewpoint. Sunnī scholars and narrators alone speak of the second date.

The following are narrations that have been cited concerning the date of Sayyidah Fāṭimah al-Zahrā''s ﷺ birth:

1. "She was born five years after (the beginning of) Prophethood and three years after Ascension to heaven. When the Prophet died, Sayyidah Fāṭimah was eighteen years old...." [58]

2. "Sayyidah Fāṭimah was born five years after (the beginning of) Prophethood and three years after Ascension, namely on the 20th of Jumādā ath-Thāniyah. She lived eight years in Makkah with her father and then immigrated..."[59]

3. Imām Bāqir ﷺ said: "Sayyidah Fāṭimah b. Muḥammad was born five years after the (first) revelation to God's Messenger. She died when she was eighteen years and seventy-five days old."[60]

---

[58] Kulaynī, Shaykh Muḥammad b. Ya'qūb, *al-Kāfī*.

[59] Ibn Shahrāshūb, Muḥammad b. 'Alī, *Manāqib Āl Abī Ṭālib*.

[60] Majlisī, 'Allamah Muḥammad Bāqir, *Biḥār al-Anwār*.

4. "Sayyidah Fāṭimah was born five years after the (first) revelation to the Prophet...."[61]

5. "The 20th of Jumādā ath-Thāniyah was the birthday of Sayyidah Fāṭimah al-Zahrāʾ during the second year after (the first) revelation."[62]

6. "Although some say that she was born five years after (the first) revelation, (Sayyidah Fāṭimah) was born on Friday the 20th of Jumādā ath-Thāniyah, two years after Revelation."[63]

7. "Friday the 20th of Jumādā ath-Thāniyah, two years after Revelation, was the birthday of Sayyidah Fāṭimah, as was cited by some narrations. It has been mentioned in a narration that she was born five years after the revelation. The Sunnis narrate she was born five years before Revelation."[64]

8. Imām Ṣādiq: "Sayyidah Fāṭimah was born on the 20th of Jumādā ath-Thāniyah, forty-five years after the Prophet was born...etc."[65]

---

[61] Nayshābūrī, Muḥammad b. Ḥasan al-Fattāl, *Rawḍat al-Wāʿiẓīn wa Baṣīrat al-Muttaʿiẓīn*.

[62] Sayyid b. Ṭāwūs, *Iqbāl al-Aʿmāl*.

Mufīd, Shaykh Muḥammad, *Ḥadāʾiq ar-Riyāḍ*.

[63] al-Kafʿamī, Ibrāhīm b. ʿAlī, *Miṣbāḥ Kafʿamī*.

[64] *Miṣbāḥayn*.

[65] al-Ṭabarī, Muḥammad b. Jarīr, *Dalāʾil al-ʾImāmat*, as reported in Majlisī, ʿAllāmah Muḥammad Bāqir, *Biḥār al-Anwār*, Vol. 10.

The above statements are a selection of narrations from the Imāms of Ahl al-Bayt ؑ and the old Shīʿī scholars ؒ declaring that Sayyidah Fāṭimah al-Zahrā''s ؑ birth took place after Revelation. Contrary to this, Sunnī scholars have stated[66]:

1. "Sayyidah Fāṭimah was the youngest of God's Messenger's daughters (fostered children of Sayyidah Khadījah). She was born while Quraysh was building the Kaʿbah."[67]

2. "Sayyidah Fāṭimah's birth occurred before revelation while Quraysh was building the Kaʿbah."[68]

More research could reveal that the Sunnis adopted this viewpoint in most books.

After briefly examining the above narrations and because neither Ascension nor Revelation took place before the beginning of Prophethood, Sayyidah Fāṭimah al-Zahrā''s ؑ birth was after Revelation. Therefore, the falsity of the traditions, which claim that she was born five years before the first revelation, becomes apparent.

---

[66] In addition to the following two, other contrary views are reported in:

Ibn al-Athīr, *al-Muhktār min Manāqib al-Akhyār*

al-Ṭabarī, Muḥib al-Dīn, *Dhakhaʾir al-ʿUqbī*

al-Suyūṭī, Jalāl al-Dīn, *al-Thughūr al-Bāsimah*

[67] al-Iṣbahānī, Abū Nuʿaym, *Maʿrifat aṣ-Ṣaḥābah*.

[68] Abu l-Faraj al-Isfahānī, *Maqātil al-Ṭālibiyyīn*.

Two motives can be cited for those who made such false claims:

The first is to refute the prophetic traditions that reveal the story of heavenly food and that Sayyidah Fāṭimah ﷺ was born from sperm produced from an apple that came from paradise.

The second is to prove that Sayyidah Fāṭimah al-Zahrā' ﷺ was unattractive. She was eighteen years old before anyone asked to marry her.

We will shed more light on this subject when we elaborate on Sayyidah Fāṭimah's ﷺ marriage.

It is narrated[69] that Sayyidah Khadījah ﷺ said:

> "... Then, when (Sayyidah Fāṭimah's) delivery came near, I sent for the Qurayshī midwives, who refused to help me because of Muḥammad ﷺ. Four ladies whose beauty and brilliance were indescribable during childbirth entered the house. One said, "I am your Mother Ḥawwā' (Eve)." The second said:
>
> "I am Umm Kulthūm, Mūsā's sister, "

69 al-Ṭabarī, Muḥib al-Dīn, *Dhakha'ir al-'Uqbī*

ash-Shāfi'ī, 'Abd ur-Raḥman, *Nuzhat al-Majālis*

Qundūzī, Sulaymān b. Ibrāhīm, *Yanābī' al-Mawaddah lī-Dhawī l-Qūrbā*

The third said:

> "I am Maryam (the mother of Prophet ʿĪsā ﷺ), and we have come to help you."

Here is the same narration, but differently:

> 'When Sayyidah Khadījah was about to deliver, she sent the Qurayshī women to help her give birth to her child. They refused and said: 'We will not help you, for you became Muḥammad's wife.' In the meantime, four women entered the house; their beauty and brilliance cannot be described. One of them said: 'I am your Mother Ḥawwā'.' The second said: `I am Āsiya b. Muzāḥim.' The third said: 'I am Kulthūm, Mūsā's sister.' The fourth said: "I am Maryam b. ʿImrān, (Prophet ʿĪsā's ﷺ mother). We have come to deliver your child. " Sayyidah Fāṭimah was then born."When Sayyidah Fāṭimah fell on the ground, she prostrated, raising her finger."

The detailed narration was mentioned by Mufaḍḍal b. ʿUmar on the authority of Imām Ṣādiq[70] ﷺ.

Besides what we have already mentioned about Sayyidah Fāṭimah's ﷺ birth, it is narrated that

> "Sayyidah Khadījah gave her children to other women for nursing, but when Sayyidah Fāṭimah was born, Sayyidah Khadījah herself nursed her."[71, 72]

---

70 Majlisī, ʿAllamah Muḥammad Bāqir, *Biḥār al-Anwār*, Vol. 1.

71 Ibn ʿAsākir, *at-Tārīkh al-Kabīr*.

72 Ibn ʿAsākir, *al-Bidāyah wa-l-Nihāyah*.

Naming Sayyidah Fāṭimah

People consider naming newborn children a sacred act. God named Ādam and Ḥawwā' the first day He created them; He also taught Ādam all names. Man, too, has followed this rule and practiced it ever since. Naming is an essential rule for civilized people.

People's names vary according to different times, generations, and languages. There may also be a relationship between the word and its meaning, although this is only sometimes true. We derive some names from entities and others from language.

Adherents of God's religion give names particular importance. This practice has a significant meaning, for a human being is called by his name; hence, a good or bad name leaves its effect on the holder. Indeed, there is particular importance to good terms; it is noteworthy to mention that when Prophet 'Imrān's wife gave birth to a daughter, she said:

> "And I, therefore, call her Maryam."

God chose the name for His prophet Yaḥyā before he was conceived. God says that Zakariyyā, Yaḥyā's father, said:

﴿وَإِنِّي خِفْتُ الْمَوَالِيَ مِن وَرَائِي وَكَانَتِ امْرَأَتِي عَاقِرًا فَهَبْ لِي مِن لَّدُنكَ وَلِيًّا﴾

﴿*wa-'innī khiftu l-mawāliya min warā'ī wa-kānati mra'atī 'āqiran fa-hab lī min ladunka waliyya*^{n}﴾

﴿يَرِثُنِي وَيَرِثُ مِنْ آلِ يَعْقُوبَ ۖ وَاجْعَلْهُ رَبِّ رَضِيًّا﴾

﴿*yarithunī wa-yarithu min 'āli ya'qūba wa-j'alhu rabbi raḍiyya*^{n}﴾

﴿يا زَكَرِيّا إِنّا نُبَشِّرُكَ بِغُلامٍ اسْمُهُ يَحْيى لَمْ نَجْعَل لَهُ مِن قَبلُ سَمِيًّا﴾

﴿yā-zakariyyā ʾinnā nubashshiruka bi-ghulāmin-i smuhū yaḥyā lam najʿal lahū min qablu samiyyaⁿ﴾

﴿Indeed I fear my kinsmen, after me, and my wife is barren. So grant me from Yourself an heir who may inherit from me and inherit from the House of Yaʿqūb, and make him, my Lord, pleasing [to You]!' 'O Zakariyyā! Indeed We give you the good news of a son, whose name is "Yaḥyā." Never before have We made anyone his namesake.﴾[73]

It is also clear from His saying, "On none by that name have we conferred distinction before," that God ﷻ assigns the names of His special worshippers, such as prophets and Imāms, in place of their parents.

We will examine a group of narrations that discuss naming Sayyidah Fāṭimah al-Zahrāʾ ﷺ and the reasons for giving her this name.

Imām Ṣādiq ﷺ said: "Sayyidah Fāṭimah has nine names near God ﷻ, they are Sayyidah Fāṭimah, Ṣiddīqah (the honest), al-Mubārakah (the blessed one), at-Ṭāhirah (virtuous), az-Zakiyyah (the chaste), ar-Raḍīhiyat ul-Marḍiyah (she who is gratified and who shall be satisfied), al-Muḥaddathah (a person, other than a prophet, that the angels speak to), and al-Zahrāʾ (the splendid)."

---

73 Sūrat Maryam, Verses 5-7.

1. Imām Abū Jaʿfar al-Bāqir said: "When Sayyidah Fāṭimah was born, God revealed to an angel to speak the name Sayyidah Fāṭimah with Muḥammad's tongue. God said: "I have given knowledge to you and safeguarded you from menstruation." Then Abū Jaʿfar added: "By God, God bestowed knowledge on her and safeguarded her from menstruation with the covenant."[74]

2. Imām Riḍā and Imām Jawād said: "We heard Maʾmūn narrating from Rashīd, from al-Mahdī, from al-Manṣūr, from his father, from his grandfather, that Ibn ʿAbbās said to Muʿāwiya: 'Do you know why Sayyidah Fāṭimah was given that name?' He said: 'No.' Ibn ʿAbbās said: 'Because she and her followers are protected from Hell, I heard God's Messenger say thus.'

3. Imām Riḍā, quoting his father, said: "The Messenger of God said: 'O Sayyidah Fāṭimah, do you know why you have been given the name Sayyidah Fāṭimah?' ʿAlī said: 'Why was she named (Sayyidah Fāṭimah)?' He replied: 'Because she and her followers (Shīʿī) are protected from hell. "'

4. Imām Ṣādiq said: "Do you know the explanation of (the name) Sayyidah Fāṭimah? I said: 'Inform me, my Master.' He said: 'She is safeguarded from evil.' He then added: 'Had Amīr al-Muʾminīn not married her, no man on Earth from Ādam on would have been suitable for her until the Day of Rising. "'

This narration was also reported by a group of Sunnī scholars, among them being Ibn Shirūyah ad-Daylamī, who said:

---

[74] An explanation of this tradition will soon be made.

"Umm Salamah said: 'The Messenger of God said: 'Had God not created 'Alī, there would not have been an equal to Sayyidah Fāṭimah.'

This tradition was also reported by quoting Umm Salamah and al-'Abbās, the Prophet's uncle.[75]

5. Imām Ṣādiq [76] said:

"The Messenger of God said to 'Alī: 'Do you know the reason Sayyidah Fāṭimah was given that name?'

'Alī said: 'Why was she given that name?'

He said: 'Because she and her followers (Shī'ī) are safeguarded from the fire."

6. Imām Riḍā said that his father quoted Amīr al-Mu'minīn as saying: "I heard God's Messenger say: 'Sayyidah Fāṭimah was given that name because God has safeguarded her and her progeny from the Fire; those who meet God as monotheists and believers in what I preach."[77]

---

[75] al-Khawārazmī, *Kitāb al-Manāqib*

al-Manāwī, *Kunūz al-Ḥaqā'iq*

al-Balkhī, Sulaymān b. Ibrāhīm al-Qundūzī, *Yanābī' al-Mawaddah li-Dhawī l-Qūrbā.*

[76] Kharghūshī, *Sharf an-Nābī*

Ibn Battah, *al-Ibāna*

[77] Majlisī, 'Allamah Muḥammad Bāqir, *Biḥār al-Anwār*, Vol. 10.

Sunnī scholars have also narrated the following:

1. "'Alī b. Abū Ṭālib said: 'The Messenger of God said: 'My daughter was named Sayyidah Fāṭimah because God safeguarded her from the Fire.'" [78]

2. Imām 'Alī b. Abū Ṭālib said[79]:

"The Messenger of God said to Sayyidah Fāṭimah: 'O Sayyidah Fāṭimah, do you know why you have been named Sayyidah Fāṭimah?'

'Alī said: 'O Messenger of God, why was she named Sayyidah Fāṭimah?'

He said: 'Because God will surely safeguard her and her progeny from the Fire on The Day of Resurrection."

Sayyidah Fāṭimah's name was dear to the Ahl al-Bayt; they respected the word and those who held it. For instance, Imām Ṣādiq inquired from one of his companions about the name to be given to his newborn daughter, and the man replied:

"I named her Fāṭimah."

Imām Ṣādiq then said: "Fāṭimah? May the peace of God be upon Fāṭimah. Now that you have given her the name Fāṭimah, refrain from slapping or abusing her; instead, honor her."

---

[78] al-Khawārazmī, *Maqtal al-Ḥusayn*, p. 51.

[79] al-Ṭabarī, Muḥib al-Dīn, *Dhakhā'ir al-'Uqbī*, p. 194.

ash-Shāfi'ī, 'Abd ur-Raḥmān, *Nuzhat al-Majālis*.

Besides this tradition, it was reported on the authority of Sukūnī[80]:

> "O Sukūnī, what grieves you?
>
> I answered: "A girl has been born to me...'"
>
> He said: 'What have you named her?'
>
> I said: 'Fāṭimah.' Then he said: 'Fāṭimah! Oh, Oh, Oh (in admiration). He said, 'Now that you have named her Fāṭimah, refrain from abusing, cursing, or slapping her. "

Imām Abū al-Ḥasan al-Kāẓim عليه السلام said:

> "Poverty shall not enter a house inhabited by people having the names Muḥammad and Sayyidah Fāṭimah from among women."[81]

Imām Bāqir عليه السلام, commenting on the first of these three traditions, stated:

> "By God, He ﷻ bestowed her with knowledge and safeguarded her from menstruation with the covenant."

The covenant mentioned here refers to the Particle (seeds) World said in the Noble Qur'ān in the following verse:

﴿وَإِذْ أَخَذَ رَبُّكَ مِن بَنِي آدَمَ مِن ظُهُورِهِمْ ذُرِّيَّتَهُمْ وَأَشْهَدَهُمْ عَلَىٰ أَنفُسِهِمْ أَلَسْتُ بِرَبِّكُمْ ۖ قَالُوا بَلَىٰ ۛ شَهِدْنَا﴾

---

[80] al-Ḥurr al-ʿĀmilī, Shaykh Muḥammad b. al-Ḥasan, *Wasāʾil al-Shīʿa*, Vol. 7.

[81] Qummī, Shaykh ʿAbbās, *Safīnat al-Biḥār*.

﴿*wa-'idh 'akhadha rabbuka min banī 'ādama min ẓuhūrihim dhurriyyatahum wa-'ashhadahum 'alā 'anfusihim 'a-lastu bi-rabbikum qālū balā shahidnā*﴾

﴿*When your Lord took from the Children of Ādam, from their loins, their descendants and made them bear witness over themselves, [He said to them,] 'Am I not your Lord?' They said, 'Yes indeed! We bear witness.*'﴾[82]

In summary, this means that God ﷻ drew forth from Ādam ﷺ (from his loin), his descendants as seeds (or particles), then presented them to him and said:

> "I will make a covenant with your descendants that they shall worship me, associating nothing with me; I will guarantee their sustenance."

He then said to them:

> "Am I not your Lord?"

They said:

> "Yes, we bear witness that you are our Lord."

He ﷻ said to the angels:

> "Bear witness."

---

[82] Sūrat al-A'rāf, Verse 172.

The angels said:

"We bear witness."

It was mentioned that God ﷻ gave Ādam's ﷺ descendants the ability to realize, understand, and hear His speech. He then placed them back in Ādam's ﷺ loin. Therefore, mankind is held in Ādam ﷺ until God ﷻ brings forth everyone he destined. So, whoever adheres to Islām holds to the covenant, and whoever disbelieves and rejects it violates it.

This account was derived from many traditions and verified narrations. Imām Bāqir ﷺ pointed out that it was decreed that Sayyidah Fāṭimah ﷺ will be safeguarded from menstruation in that world, which is also called the "World of Covenant."

With the many traditions that spoke of the world of Covenant, we mention some of them herein as examples:

1. Imām Ṣādiq ﷺ said[83]: The Prophet was asked: "How do you excel over mankind?" The Prophet answered: "I was the first one to bear witness to my Lord; when God took the oath from the Prophets and made them testify concerning themselves (our Lord said): Am I not your Lord?'They replied: 'Yes. Therefore, I was the first of them to reply."

   Abū Baṣīr: "I asked Abū 'Abdullāh Imām Ṣādiq

   How did they answer Him when they were particles?'

[83] al-Baḥrānī, Hāshim al-Tūbilī, *Tafsīr al-Burhān*.

He said: 'He implemented in them that with which they could answer Him when He asked;

'Ā'isha added: "He means the covenant."

2. Zurārah reported he inquired from Imām Bāqir about what it meant by:

"When thy Lord drew forth from the children of Ādam-from their loins-their descendants. ,"

He said: "(It means that He drew forth) from Ādam's loins his descendants until the Day of Resurrection, so they came forth as particles. He then taught and acquainted them to His creation; had He not done so, no one would have known His Lord."

3. When 'Umar b. al-Khaṭṭāb performed pilgrimage and embraced the (Black) Stone; he said:

"I know by God that you are a stone which neither harms nor benefits, and had I not seen God's Messenger embrace you, I would not have embraced you."

However, Imām 'Alī said:

"Abū al-Ḥafīẓ, do not say this, for God's Messenger did not embrace it (the black stone) save for wisdom he knew, and had you read the Qur'ān and realized its interpretation, as others have, you would have understood that it can harm and bring benefits to you. It has two eyes and two lips and possesses a keen tongue that testifies for those who fulfill their obligations to it."

'Umar said, "Then show me that in God's book, Abū al-Ḥasan."

Imām 'Alī ؑ said: 'God ﷻ said: "When thy Lord drew forth from the children of Ādam (from their loins) their descendants and made them testify concerning themselves (saying): Am I not your Lord? They answered: Yea! We do testify. Thus, when they affirmed their obedience to Him as their Lord and as His slaves, He made a covenant with them that they would make the pilgrimage to His sacred House. He then created parchment finer than water and said to the Pen: Write down My creatures' fulfillment of pilgrimage to my Sacred House. The pen wrote mankind's fulfillment of pilgrimage on the parchment, then it was said to the (Black) Stone: Open your mouth; it opened it, and the parchment was inserted there. He said, 'Safeguard it and testify for My worshippers their fulfillment (of pilgrimage). The Stone then descended in obedience to God.' "O 'Umar, do not you say when you embrace the stone- I have fulfilled my covenant and kept my oath so that you may testify for me?'

'Umar said: "Yes, by God."

Imām 'Alī ؑ said, "It is for this reason that you do so."

Many narrations, which include a study regarding the world of Covenant, were collected by Shaykh al-Kulaynī[84], 'Allamah Majlisī[85], and other collectors of traditions.

---

[84] Kulaynī, Shaykh Muḥammad b. Ya'qūb, *al-Kāfī*.

[85] Majlisī, 'Allamah Muḥammad Bāqir, *Biḥār al-Anwār*.

Some scholars — may God forgive them — misunderstood these narrations, which led them to doubt their authenticity despite the unambiguous meaning of the verse.

In conclusion, it was since or even before the events of the world of seeds (also called the world of Covenant) that the Messenger of God and his Progeny's — including Sayyidah Fāṭimah's — virtue was recognized.

Scholars of both sects (Sunnī and Shīʿī) successively reported many narrations which support this matter. All these narrations support this matter; the traditions that the Shīʿī scholars have mentioned are too many to include here. Examples of those that the Sunnī scholar reported include that Kesay and others said[86]: "When God created Ādam... (until he said) there was a brilliant girl from whom light was illuminating and on her head was a golden crown ornamented with diamonds; the like of whom Ādam had never seen.

Ādam asked:

'My Lord, who is this girl?'

God said:

'Sayyidah Fāṭimah b. Muḥammad.'

Ādam said:

'My Lord, who is her husband?'

---

[86] ash-Shāfiʿī, ʿAbd ur-Raḥman, *Nuzhat al-Majālis*, Vol. 2, p. 223.

God said:

> `O Jibrā'īl, open the gate of the ruby palace;'

When Jibrā'īl did, Ādam saw a dome of camphor, and inside it was a golden bed equipped by a young man as beautiful as Yūsuf.'

He then said:

> "This is her husband, 'Alī b. Abū Ṭālib."

Imām al-Ḥasan b. 'Alī al-Askari ‎ reported that his fathers quoted Jābir b. 'Abdullāh as saying[87]:

> "The Messenger of God ‎ said: 'When God created Ādam and Ḥawwā', they strutted through paradise and said: `Who is better than we?' At that moment, they noticed an image of a girl they had never seen before; from this girl came an illuminating light that almost blinded the eyes.

They said:

> 'O Lord, what is this?'

He answered:

> 'This is the image of Sayyidah Fāṭimah, the mistress of your women descendants.'

---

[87] al-'Asqalānī, Ḥafīẓ b. Ḥajar, *Lisān al-Mīzān*, Vol. 3, p. 346.

Ādam asked:

'What is this crown on her head?'

God said:

'Her husband, 'Alī.'

Ādam then asked:

'What are her two earrings?'

God replied:

'Her (two) sons were ordained in My ever-existent knowledge two thousand years before I created you.'

al-Ṣiddīqah

We have already mentioned that one of Sayyidah Fāṭimah's names was Ṣiddīqah. This word means a woman with scrupulous honesty or sincerity.

Ṣiddīqah differs from Sadooq in that the first is precise in telling facts. Several other meanings have been given to the phrase Ṣiddīqah; among them are:

a. She who is a truth-teller.

b. She never lies.

c. She whose deeds conform to her words.

d. She never lied because she is used to truthfulness.

e. A woman with scrupulous speech and beliefs and whose acts conform to her words.

f. She believes in the commands of God ﷻ and His Prophet's ﷺ, without doubting any of them.

This last opinion is supported by the following Qur'ānic verse:

﴿وَالَّذِينَ آمَنُوا بِاللَّهِ وَرُسُلِهِ أُولَٰئِكَ هُمُ الصِّدِّيقُونَ﴾

﴿wa-lladhīna 'āmanū bi-llāhi wa-rusulihī 'ulā'ika humu ṣ-ṣiddīqūna﴾

﴿Those who have faith in God and His apostles—it is they who are the truthful﴾[88]

Scholars unanimously agree that the various verses and traditions count "Ṣiddīqūn" among the apostles and martyrs who will enjoy special treatment. This becomes apparent when looking at the following Qur'ānic verses:

﴿وَمَن يُطِعِ اللَّهَ وَالرَّسُولَ فَأُولَٰئِكَ مَعَ الَّذِينَ أَنْعَمَ اللَّهُ عَلَيْهِم مِّنَ النَّبِيِّينَ وَالصِّدِّيقِينَ وَالشُّهَدَاءِ وَالصَّالِحِينَ ۚ وَحَسُنَ أُولَٰئِكَ رَفِيقًا﴾

﴿wa-man yuṭi'i llāha wa-r-rasūla fa-'ulā'ika ma'a lladhīna 'an'ama llāhu 'alayhim mina n-nabiyyīna wa-ṣ-ṣiddīqīna wa-sh-shuhadā'i wa-ṣ-ṣāliḥīna wa-ḥasuna 'ulā'ika rafīqan﴾

[88] Sūrat al-Ḥadīd, Verse 19.

﴾*Whoever obeys God and the Apostle —they are with those whom God has blessed, including the prophets and the truthful, the martyrs and the righteous, and excellent companions are they!*﴿[89]

﴿وَاذْكُرْ فِي الْكِتَابِ إِبْرَاهِيمَ ۚ إِنَّهُ كَانَ صِدِّيقًا نَبِيًّا﴾

﴾*wa-dhkur fī l-kitābi 'ibrāhīma 'innahū kāna ṣiddīqan nabiyya*^{n}﴿

﴾*And* mention *in the Book Shu'ayb. Indeed he was a truthful one, a prophet*﴿[90]

﴿وَاذْكُرْ فِي الْكِتَابِ إِدْرِيسَ ۚ إِنَّهُ كَانَ صِدِّيقًا نَبِيًّا﴾

﴾*wa-dhkur fī l-kitābi 'idrīsa 'innahū kāna ṣiddīqan nabiyya*^{n}﴿

﴾*And* mention *in the Book Idrīs. Indeed he was a truthful one, a prophet*﴿[91]

﴿مَا الْمَسِيحُ ابْنُ مَرْيَمَ إِلَّا رَسُولٌ قَدْ خَلَتْ مِنْ قَبْلِهِ الرُّسُلُ وَأُمُّهُ صِدِّيقَةٌ﴾

﴾*mā l-masīḥu bnu maryama 'illā rasūlun qad khalat min qablihi r-rusulu wa-'ummuhū ṣiddīqatun*﴿

﴾*The Messiah, son of Mary, is but an apostle. Certainly [other] apostles have passed before him, and his mother was a truthful one*﴿[92]

---

89 Sūrat al-Nisā', Verse 69.

90 Sūrat Maryam, Verse 41.

91 Sūrat Maryam, Verse 56.

92 Sūrat al-Mā'idah, Verse 75.

When interpreting "His mother was a woman of truth", they said that Maryam ﷺ was called "Ṣiddīqah" because she believed in the signs of the Lord ﷻ, her son's ﷺ position, and that which he preached to her. The verse supported this point:

﴿وَصَدَّقَتْ بِكَلِمَاتِ رَبِّهَا وَكُتُبِهِ﴾

﴾wa-ṣaddaqat bi-kalimāti rabbihā wa-kutubihī﴿

﴾She confirmed the words of her Lord and His Books﴿[93]

Another meaning given to this verse is that Maryam was called "Ṣiddīqah" for her truthfulness and the greatness of her position.

After reviewing the verse, we can easily conclude that some people believe in God, the apostles, the divine books, and religious rules but show contradictory actions. This becomes clear when some people claim they believe God watches them. Yet, they disobey and violate His laws while knowing of God's prohibition of liquor usury and adultery and that He decreed some rules and assigned specific duties to them, which, if they perform, He will grant them paradise. He will subject those who violate them to Hell. These people have yet to reach the level of applying their words and claims to actions.

On the other hand, "Ṣiddīqūn" believe in truth and righteousness and practice what they believe. Their number is small at any given place or time; in fact, a survey might show that in some towns, there is not even one Ṣiddīqah.

---

[93] Sūrat al-Taḥrīm, Verse 75.

Finally, it is easily recognized that Sayyidah Fāṭimah reached this level of "Ṣiddīqūn." God's Apostle[94] gave her the title Ṣiddīqah and then said[95] to Imām ʿAlī:

> "You have been given three things which have been given to no one else, not even me, (they are):
>
> You have been given a father-in-law like me, and my father-in-law was not like me.
>
> You have been given an honest (Ṣiddīqah) wife like my daughter, and I have not been given the like of her as a wife.
>
> And, you have been given Ḥasan and Ḥusayn from your loin, and I was not given two sons like them.
>
> But you are from me, and I am from you."

Also, Mufaḍḍal b. ʿUmar said:

> "I asked Imām Ṣādiq: Who gave major ablution to Sayyidah Fāṭimah (Ghusl al-Mayyit)?

He answered:

> ʾAmīr al--Muʾminīn (Imām ʿAlī) '

I reacted in such a way that made it appear as if I could not believe he would do so. Thus, Imām Ṣādiq said:

---

[94] *al-Riyāḍ al-Nāḍira*, Vol. 2, p.202.

[95] *Sharf an-Nubuwwah*.

It seems you feel uncomfortable about what I told you.

I said:

"May I be your sacrifice; I indeed do."

He then said:

Do not be annoyed by this, for Sayyidah Fāṭimah was a 'Ṣiddīqah', and no one saves a 'Ṣiddīq' can give her ablution. Don't you know no one gave ablution to Maryam save 'Īsā ?"

al-Mubārakah

Barakah means multiplication, felicity, and abundance, as Taj al-'Arus clarifies. Also, Rāghib said: Because divine goodness springs from an ever-continuous source in an unlimited manner, it is said that anything which noticeably multiplies or increases is Mubārak or blessed.

God gifted Sayyidah Fāṭimah abundant blessings and made her the mother of the Prophet's descendants, whom God has bestowed ever-lasting benevolence.

Upon reviewing the history of Sayyidah Fāṭimah's offspring, we find that she left behind two sons and two daughters when she died. They are:

Imām Ḥasan and Imām Ḥusayn, Zaynab and Umm Kulthūm. But when the event of Karbalā' occurred, Imām Ḥusayn and his children achieved martyrdom and 'Alī b. al-Ḥusayn (Imām Zayn al-'Ābidīn) was the only surviving child of Imām Ḥusayn. Also, seven of Imām Ḥasan's children and two of

Zaynab's ﷺ sons achieved martyrdom. Umm Kulthūm had no children.

After the events of Karbalā', inflictions successively befell the Prophet's descendants. Torture and massacres continued against them, starting with the Battle of Ḥarra, Zayd b. 'Alī's and Fakh, and going through the agony they suffered throughout the Umayyad era. But when the Abbasids came to power, they broke the Umayyad record of eradicating and annihilating Sayyidah Fāṭimah's ﷺ offspring.[96]

The struggle continued for two centuries until Imām al-Ḥasan al-'Askarī ﷺ died in Sāmarrā' because of being poisoned, which was placed in his food. Ṣāliḥ ad-Dīn al-Ayyūbī was as savage as the 'Abbāsids in massacring the Prophet's ﷺ descendants and followers. He committed mass murders and brutal crimes, which brought shivers to the spine.

God ﷻ gave benevolence and blessings to Sayyidah Fāṭimah al-Zahrā''s ﷺ descendants. He implemented abundant multiplicity in them.

Interpreting the verse:

﴿إِنَّآ أَعْطَيْنَاكَ الْكَوْثَرَ﴾

﴿*'innā 'a'ṭaynāka l-kawthara*﴾

[96] Details about the sufferings they encountered can be found in Abu l-Faraj al-Isfahānī, *Maqātil al-Ṭālibiyyīn*.

﴾Indeed We have given you abundance﴿[97]

This verse varies according to interpreters. The most popular viewpoint of the meaning of Kawthar is a famous fountain or domain, which will be given to the Apostle on the Day of Resurrection; the literal meaning of Kawthar is abundance or abundant benevolence.

Regarding the meaning of Kawthar, Jalāl al-Dīn al-Suyūṭī writes[98]:

> "Bukhārī, Ibn Jarīr and al-Ḥakīm reported on the authority of Abū Bishr b. Sa'īd b. Jubayr that Ibn 'Abbās said:
>
> `al-Kawthar is abundant goodness which God gave the Apostle.'

Abū Bishr said:

> "I told Ibn Jubayr that some people claim it is a river (fountain) in Paradise.

He said:

> 'The fountain in Paradise is part of the abundant benevolence He (God ﷻ) gave him ﷺ.'

Rāzī's interpretation of the above verse is more appropriate. He held the view that what is meant by Kawthar is Sayyidah Fāṭimah

---

[97] Sūrat al-Kawthar, Verse 1.

[98] al-Suyūṭī, Jalāl al-Dīn, *al-Durr al-Manthūr*.

al-Zahrā' ﷺ. Shaykh Faḍl b. Ḥasan Ṭabrisī writes[99] regarding this subject:

> "It was said that Kawthar means abundant benevolence; it has also been said that it means the multiplicity of a given person; and the descendants of Sayyidah Fāṭimah have enormously multiplied in a way that they will exist until the Day of Resurrection."

Fakhr Rāzī made the following comment in his interpretation of the Qur'ān regarding the last verse:

> "Regarding the third viewpoint, which advocates the meaning of descendants to "Kawthar, " some scholars say:
>
> "Since this chapter was revealed to refute the claim of an infidel who attempted to denounce the Prophet ﷺ for not having sons, the meaning given here is that God gave the Prophet ﷺ offspring, which will be everlasting. We must remember that numerous massacres have been committed against Ahl al-Bayt ﷺ, yet still, the world is full of them, while the Umayyads have vanished, save a few who are worthless. Besides this, prominent scholars have descended from Sayyidah Fāṭimah's ﷺ sons, such as al-Bāqir, al-Ṣādiq, al-Kāẓim, al-Riḍā ﷺ, al-Nafs al-Zakiyyah, and others."

This explanation correlates to an infidel who denounced the Prophet ﷺ when one of his children died and said Muḥammad ﷺ is now without offspring. Therefore, when he dies, his name will die with him. It was because of this incident that God ﷻ revealed this chapter to His Apostle, assuring him; it is as if He ﷻ said:

[99] Ṭabrisī, Shaykh Faḍl b. Ḥasan, *Majma' al-Bayān fī Tafsīr al-Qur'ān.*

> "You have lost your son, but We have given you Sayyidah Fāṭimah; although she is just one, God will make that one many."

A survey of the world's population attests to this conclusion; for Sayyidah Fāṭimah's ﷺ descendants (who are also the Prophet's descendants) are spread around the globe: ʿIrāq: One million, Irān: Three million, Egypt: Five million, al-Maghrib (Morocco): Five million, al-Jazāʾir (Algeria), Tūnis, Lībiyā, al-ʾUrdunn (Jordan), Sūrīyah (Syria), Lubnān (Lebanon), Sūdān, the Persian Gulf countries including Saʿūdīyah (Saudi Arabia), al-Yaman (Yemen), India, Pākistān, Afghānistān, and Indonesia-approximately twenty million descendants of the Prophet of Islām.

An Islamic country in which descendants of Sayyidah Fāṭimah al-Zahrāʾ ﷺ do not live is hard to find. We estimate their number to be thirty-five million; however, if precise and accurate statistics are taken, their number could be much higher.

The Prophet's ﷺ descendants include kings, princes, ministers, scholars, writers, prominent characters, and geniuses. Some are honored by their lineage; others ignore it and give no importance. Some follow Ahl al-Bayt ﷺ, while others violate their doctrine. I have even heard of some descendants of Sayyidah Fāṭimah ﷺ who live in Indonesia and are enemies of Ahl al-Bayt ﷺ!

More impressive is the fact that some Muslims refuse to accept their lineage of Sayyidah Fāṭimah and Imām ʿAlī ﷺ; instead, they claim that such a lineage is forged and unacceptable. These people ferociously fought this idea to the point where they shed innocent blood to implement their ideas.

Ḥajjāj, Manṣūr Dawānīqī, Hārūn al-Rashīd, and others are known advocates for this idea.

ʿAmr al-Shūbe said[100]:

> "One night Ḥajjāj summoned me to his palace; this horrified me, so I performed ablution and wrote my will; then went to meet him. When I entered his room, I saw a sword and a leather mat (usually used for executions). I greeted him, and he replied and said: fear nothing, for I pardon you throughout the night and until tomorrow noon.' He then ordered me to sit next to him; meanwhile, a tied and shackled man was brought to him;

Ḥajjāj said:

> `This old man claims that al-Ḥasan and al-Ḥusayn are the Prophet's children; he shall prove this from the Qur'ān or I will cut his head off.' I said: 'He should be freed from his chains because if he proves his claim, he will surely go free, and if not, then a sword cannot break those chains.' They freed the man of his shackles but kept his hands cuffed. It grieved me when I saw he was Saʿīd b. Jubayr and said: How can he bring proof from the Qur'ān? Ḥajjāj said: `Bring me proof from the Qur'ān or will behead you.' He said: `Wait.' He waited for a while when Ḥajjāj repeated his demand, and Saʿīd asked for more time to think. When Ḥajjāj repeated his demand for the third time, Saʿīd said:
>
> "I seek refuge in God from the cursed devil. In the Name of God the Beneficent, the Merciful.

100 Majlisī, ʿAllamah Muḥammad Bāqir, *Biḥār al-Anwār*, Vol. 10.

﴿وَوَهَبنا لَهُ إِسحاقَ وَيَعقوبَ ۚ كُلًّا هَدَينا ۚ وَنوحًا هَدَينا مِن قَبلُ ۖ وَمِن ذُرِّيَّتِهِ داوودَ وَسُلَيمانَ وَأَيّوبَ وَيوسُفَ وَموسىٰ وَهارونَ ۚ وَكَذٰلِكَ نَجزِي المُحسِنينَ﴾

﴿*wa-wahabnā lahū 'isḥāqa wa-ya'qūba kullan hadaynā wa-nuḥan hadaynā min qablu wa-min dhurriyyatihī dāwūda wa-sulaymāna wa-'ayyūba wa-yūsufa wa-mūsā wa-hārūna wa-ka-dhālika najzī l-muḥsinīn*[a]﴾

﴿وَزَكَرِيّا وَيَحيىٰ وَعيسىٰ وَإِلياسَ ۖ كُلٌّ مِنَ الصّالِحينَ﴾

﴿*wa-zakariyyā wa-yaḥyā wa-'īsā wa-'ilyāsa kullun mina ṣ-ṣāliḥīn*[a]﴾

﴿*And We gave him Isḥāq and Ya'qūb and guided each of them. And Nūḥ We had guided before, and from his offspring, Dāwūd and Sulaymān, Ayyūb, Yūsuf, Mūsā and Hārūn — thus do We reward the virtuous — and Zakariyyā, Yaḥyā, 'Īsā and Ilyās, —each of them among the righteous—*﴾[101]

Then Sa'īd said:

> "How does 'Īsā fit in here?" Ḥajjāj replied: 'He is one of Ibrāhīm's offspring.' Sa'īd said: ''Īsā did not have a father, yet he was Ibrāhīm's descendant because he was his daughter's (Maryam) son; therefore Ḥasan and Ḥusayn are more worthy of being called the Prophet's children, especially because they are closer to him (the Prophet) than 'Īsā was to Maryam.'

When Ḥajjāj heard this, he granted him ten thousand dinars and set him free.

---

[101] Sūrat al-An'ām, Verses 84-85.

Shūbe added:

> "In the morning, I said to myself. 'I must visit that old man and learn the meaning of the Qur'ān, which I thought I knew but do not.' I entered the Mosque and found that old man giving everyone ten dinars; I then heard him say: All this is because of the blessings of al-Ḥasan and al-Ḥusayn ﷺ. We were grieved once but cherished a thousand times. We also pleased God and His Apostle."

Another narration that shows the extent of arrogance and insistence on discrediting Ahl al-Bayt ﷺ and depriving them of the honor of the relationship with the Prophet ﷺ says:

'Allamah Majlisī reported that Abū al-Jārūd said[102]:

> 'Abū Ja'far al-Bāqir ﷺ said to me: 'Abū Jārūd, what do they (followers of other than Ahl al-Bayt) say about al-Ḥasan and al-Ḥusayn ﷺ?'
>
> I said: 'They deny that they are sons of God's Apostle.'
>
> He then said: 'So with what do you debate them?'
>
> I said: 'With God's saying about 'Īsā b. Maryam:

﴿وَمِن ذُرِّيَّتِهِ داوودَ وَسُلَيمانَ وَأَيّوبَ وَيوسُفَ وَموسىٰ وَهارونَ ۚ وَكَذٰلِكَ نَجزِي المُحسِنينَ﴾

102 On the authority of Ṭabrisī, Shaykh Aḥmad b. 'Alī Ṭabrisī, *al-Iḥtijāj*, and al-Qummī, 'Alī b. Ibrāhīm, *Tafsīr al-Qummī*.

⟪*wa-min dhurriyyatihī dāwūda wa-sulaymāna wa-'ayyūba wa-yūsufa wa-mūsā wa-hārūna wa-ka-dhālika najzī l-muḥsinīna*⟫

⟪*and from his offspring, Dāwūd and Sulaymān, Ayyūb, Yūsuf, Mūsā, and Hārūn —thus do We reward the virtuous—*⟫[103]

and that God ﷻ made ʿĪsā a descendant of Ibrāhīm."

He said:

'Then what do they say?'

I said:

'They say: 'A daughter's son can be called a son, but he is not a real descendant.''

He said:

'How do you argue with them?'

I said:

'We quote the following verse for them':

﴿فَمَنْ حَاجَّكَ فِيهِ مِن بَعْدِ مَا جَاءَكَ مِنَ الْعِلْمِ فَقُلْ تَعَالَوْا نَدْعُ أَبْنَاءَنَا وَأَبْنَاءَكُمْ وَنِسَاءَنَا وَنِسَاءَكُمْ وَأَنفُسَنَا وَأَنفُسَكُمْ ثُمَّ نَبْتَهِلْ فَنَجْعَل لَّعْنَتَ اللَّهِ عَلَى الْكَاذِبِينَ﴾

⟪*fa-man ḥājjaka fīhi min baʿdi mā jāʾaka mina l-ʿilmi fa-qul taʿālaw nadʿu ʾabnāʾanā wa-ʾabnāʾakum wa-nisāʾanā wa-*

---

[103] Sūrat al-Anʿām, Verse 84.

nisā'akum wa-'anfusanā wa-'anfusakum thumma nabtahil fa-naj'al la'nata llāhi 'alā l-kādhibīna﴿

﴾*Should anyone argue with you concerning him, after the knowledge that has come to you, say, 'Come! Let us call our sons and your sons, our women and your women, our souls, and your souls, then let us pray earnestly and call down God's curse upon the liars.'*﴿[104]

Then he said:

'Then what do they say?'

I replied:

'They say: "It is common in Arabic for a man to call another man's children Our children while they are in reality others' children."' Imām Bāqir (Abū Ja'far ﷺ) then said: 'By God, Abū al-Jārūd, I shall quote a verse from the Book of God which shows that Ḥasan and Ḥusayn are his ﷺ direct children (form his loins); proof that non-believers can only deny.'

I said:

`May I be your sacrifice? What verse are you speaking of?'

---

[104] Sūrat Āl 'Imrān, Verse 61.

The Prophet ﷺ chose al-Ḥasan and al-Ḥusayn to represent his sons, Sayyidah Fāṭimah for "women, " and himself and 'Alī ﷺ for "ourselves." (Author's note).

He answered:

﴿حُرِّمَت عَلَيكُم أُمَّهاتُكُم وَبَناتُكُم وَأَخَواتُكُم وَعَمّاتُكُم وَخالاتُكُم وَبَناتُ الأَخِ وَبَناتُ الأُختِ وَأُمَّهاتُكُمُ اللّاتي أَرضَعنَكُم وَأَخَواتُكُم مِنَ الرَّضاعَةِ وَأُمَّهاتُ نِسائِكُم وَرَبائِبُكُمُ اللّاتي في حُجورِكُم مِن نِسائِكُمُ اللّاتي دَخَلتُم بِهِنَّ فَإِن لَم تَكونوا دَخَلتُم بِهِنَّ فَلا جُناحَ عَلَيكُم وَحَلائِلُ أَبنائِكُمُ الَّذينَ مِن أَصلابِكُم وَأَن تَجمَعوا بَينَ الأُختَينِ إِلّا ما قَد سَلَفَ ۗ إِنَّ اللَّهَ كانَ غَفورًا رَحيمًا﴾

﴿ḥurrimat ʿalaykum ʾummahātukum wa-banātukum wa-ʾakhawātukum wa-ʿammātukum wa-khālātukum wa-banātu l-ʾakhi wa-banātu l-ʾukhti wa-ʾummahātukumu llātī ʾarḍaʿnakum wa-ʾakhawātukum mina r-raḍāʿati wa-ʾummahātu nisāʾikum wa-rabāʾibukumu llātī fī ḥujūrikum min nisāʾikumu llātī dakhaltum bihinna fa-ʾin lam takūnū dakhaltum bihinna fa-lā junāḥa ʿalaykum wa-ḥalāʾilu ʾabnāʾikumu lladhīna min ʾaṣlābikum wa-ʾan tajmaʿū bayna l-ʾukhtayni ʾillā mā qad salafa ʾinna llāha kāna ghafūran raḥīman﴾

﴿Forbidden to you are your mothers, your daughters and your sisters, your paternal aunts and your maternal aunts, your brother's daughters and your sister's daughters, your [foster-]mothers who have suckled you and your sisters through fosterage, your wives' mothers, and your stepdaughters who are under your care [born] of the wives whom you have gone into —but if you have not gone into them there is no sin upon you— and the wives of your sons who are from your own loins, and that you should marry two sisters at one time — excluding what is already past;*

indeed God is Forgiving, Merciful—﴾[105]

Ask them, Abū al-Jārūd, was it permitted for God's Messenger to marry al-Ḥasan and al-Ḥusayn's wives (had they been divorced)? If their response is affirmative, they have lied and sinned; if their answer is negative, they are his children proceeding from his loins."'

In another debate[106] which took place between Hārūn al-Rashīd and Imām Mūsā b. Ja'far ‎عليه السلام, Hārūn said to the Imām ‎عليه السلام:

"Why did you permit people to trace your ancestry back to God's Messenger ‎ﷺ and call you sons of God's Apostle while you are descendants of 'Alī? Men are traced to their fathers; Sayyidah Fāṭimah was not but a vessel, and her father, the Prophet, your maternal grandfather!"

The Imām ‎عليه السلام replied:

"Had the Prophet been brought back to life and asked you for your daughter's hand in marriage, would you fulfill his wish?"

Rashīd answered:

"Glory be to God! Why wouldn't I fulfill his wish? Indeed, I would be honored among the Arabs, non-Arabs, and Quraysh to do so."

---

[105] Sūrat al-Nisā', Verse 23.

* That is, foster-mothers.

[106] Majlisī, 'Allamah Muḥammad Bāqir, *Biḥār al-Anwār*, on authority of Ṣadūq, Shaykh Muḥammad b. 'Alī, *'Uyūn Akhbār al-Riḍā*.

The Imām said,

> "But he would not ask to marry my daughter, nor could I give her to him in marriage."

Rashīd exclaimed:

> "Why not?"

The Imām said:

> "For he has begotten me and has not begotten you."

Rashīd said,

> "You are right, Mūsā," and added: "But why do you claim to be the Prophet's offspring while he did not beget sons? And since offspring are sons, not daughters, and you are Sayyidah Fāṭimah's children, she did not have offspring."

Upon hearing this, the Imām apologized to Rashīd and asked to be excused; he did not want to answer him in observance of the law of prudence (*taqiyyah*). Nevertheless, Rashīd insisted on hearing his arguments and said:

> "You are obligated to bring me your arguments from the Qur'ān, you children of 'Alī, and since you are their Imām of the time and chief, as I was told, I will not excuse you until you bring me proof from God's Book, from which you know the interpretation of every letter, as has been written in this verse:

﴿ما فَرَّطنا فِي الكِتابِ مِن شَيءٍ﴾

﴿*mā farraṭnā fī l-kitābi min shay'in*﴾

﴿*We have not omitted anything from the Book*﴾[107]

Furthermore, you dispensed with the opinions of other scholars and 'qiyas' (inference)."

The Imām said,

"Am I permitted to give you the answer?"

Rashīd said:

"Indeed you are."

The Imām then said:

"I seek refuge in God from the cursed devil. In the Name of God the Beneficent, the Merciful.

﴿وَوَهَبنا لَهُ إِسحاقَ وَيَعقوبَ ۚ كُلًّا هَدَينا ۚ وَنوحًا هَدَينا مِن قَبلُ ۖ وَمِن ذُرِّيَّتِهِ داوودَ وَسُلَيمانَ وَأَيّوبَ وَيوسُفَ وَموسىٰ وَهارونَ ۚ وَكَذٰلِكَ نَجزِي المُحسِنينَ﴾

﴿*wa-wahabnā lahū 'isḥāqa wa-ya'qūba kullan hadaynā wa-nuḥan hadaynā min qablu wa-min dhurriyyatihī dāwūda wa-sulaymāna wa-'ayyūba wa-yūsufa wa-mūsā wa-hārūna wa-ka-dhālika najzī l-muḥsinīn*[a]﴾

[107] Sūrat al-An'ām, Verse 38.

﴿وَزَكَرِيَّا وَيَحْيَىٰ وَعِيسَىٰ وَإِلْيَاسَ ۖ كُلٌّ مِنَ ٱلصَّالِحِينَ﴾

﴿wa-zakariyyā wa-yaḥyā wa-'īsā wa-'ilyāsa kullun mina ṣ-ṣāliḥīna﴾

﴿And We gave him Isḥāq and Ya'qūb and guided each of them. And Nūḥ We had guided before, and from his offspring, Dāwūd and Sulaymān, Ayyūb, Yūsuf, Mūsā and Hārūn — thus do We reward the virtuous — and Zakariyyā, Yaḥyā, 'Īsā and Ilyās, —each of them among the righteous—﴾[108]

The Imām continued,

"Who is 'Īsā's father?"

The Imām then said:

"Therefore, he is considered among the Prophet's offspring through Maryam; likewise, we are the offspring of the Holy Prophet through our mother, Sayyidah Fāṭimah..."

These were some of the verses that Ahl al-Bayt used as proof of their lineage to God's Apostle through Sayyidah Fāṭimah al-Zahrā'.

There are a significant number of narrations which declare the same thing; among them are:

1. It is reported[109] that Ibn 'Abbās said:

---

[108] Sūrat al-An'ām, Verses 84-85.

[109] al-Baghdādī, al-Khaṭīb, *Tārīkh al-Baghdādī*, Vol. 1, p. 316.

"I was in the company of my father, al-ʿAbbās b. ʿAbd Muṭṭalib, sitting in the presence of God's Messenger ﷺ when ʿAlī b. Abū Ṭālib entered and greeted us. The Prophet ﷺ returned his Salām, stood up, embraced him, and kissed his forehead while smiling. The Prophet then asked him to sit near to him."

al-ʿAbbās asked:

> "Messenger of God, do you love him?"

The Prophet replied:

> "Uncle of God's Messenger! By God, God loves him more than I do. Surely God made every Prophet's progeny proceed from him and made my progeny proceed from this one."

2. Khawārazmī narrates[110]: "God's Apostle declared: "Surely God made every Prophet's progeny proceed from his loins, and made my progeny proceed from 'Alī's loins."

3. On the authority of Muḥammad b. Usama b. Zayd, Nisā'ī mentioned[111] that his (Muḥammad b. Zayd) father said:

   "God's Messenger said:

   > 'As for you 'Alī, you are my son-in-law and the father of my offspring; you are from me, and I am from you.'"

   The same narrator reported that Usama said:

---

[110] al-Khawārazmī, *Kitāb al-Manāqīb*, p. 229.

Also reported in:

al-Ṭabarī, Muḥib al-Dīn, *Dhakha'ir al-'Uqbī*.

al-Juwaynī, Ibrāhīm, *Farā'id al-Simatayn*.

al-Dimashqī, Muḥammad b. Aḥmad, *Mizān al-I'tidāl*.

al-Haythamī, Ibn Ḥajar, *al-Ṣawā'iq al-Muḥriqah*, p. 74.

al-Hindī, 'Alī al-Muttaqī, *Kanz al-'Ummāl fī Sunan al-Aqwāl wal-Af'āl*.

al-Zurqānī, Muḥammad, *Sharh al-Mawāhib al-Ladunniyyah*.

al-Balkhī, Sulaymān b. Ibrāhīm al-Qundūzī, *Yanābī' al-Mawaddah lī-Dhawī l-Qūrbā*, p.138.

[111] al-Nasā'ī, Aḥmad b. Shu'ayb, *Khaṣā'iṣ Amīr al-Mu'minīn*.

"I went to visit the Prophet of God one night; he ﷺ came out carrying something I didn't recognize under his cloak. When I finished my work with him, I said. 'What do you have under your cloak?' When he opened his cloak, I saw al-Ḥasan and al-Ḥusayn on his lap. The Prophet said: 'These are my children and my daughter's sons; O God, you surely know that I love them, therefore love them.'"

Despite the many traditions declaring that al-Ḥasan and al-Ḥusayn ؏ are the Prophet of God's ﷺ children, some ignorant writers try to deny this. These writers quote the following Qurʾānic verse to prove that he ﷺ was not anyone's father:

﴿ما كانَ مُحَمَّدٌ أَبا أَحَدٍ مِن رِجالِكُم﴾

⟨mā kāna muḥammadun ʾabā ʾaḥadin min rijālikum⟩

⟨Muḥammad is not the father of any man among you⟩112

These writers use this verse even though it is an uncontested fact that it was revealed to prove that Zayd, the Prophet's adopted son, is not related to the Prophet ﷺ. The Apostle gave him (Zayd) in marriage to his cousin Zaynab, but when Zayd divorced her, he ﷺ married her in obedience to God's command, and to prove that he ﷺ was not Zayd's father, which would make Zaynab prohibited to him

﴿فَلَمّا قَضىٰ زَيدٌ مِنها وَطَرًا زَوَّجناكَها لِكَي لا يَكونَ عَلَى المُؤمِنينَ حَرَجٌ في أَزواجِ أَدعِيائِهِم إِذا قَضَوا مِنهُنَّ وَطَرًا ۚ وَكانَ أَمرُ اللَّهِ مَفعولًا﴾

---

112 Sūrat al-Aḥzāb, Verse 40.

﴾fa-lammā qaḍā zaydun minhā waṭaran zawwajnākahā li-kay lā yakūna ʿalā l-muʾminīna ḥarajun fī ʾazwāji ʾadʿiyāʾihim ʾidhā qaḍaw minhunna waṭaran wa-kāna ʾamru llāhi mafʿūlaⁿ﴿

﴾so when Zayd had got through with her, We wedded her to you, so that there may be no blame on the faithful in respect of the wives of their adopted sons, when the latter have got through with them, and God's command is bound to be fulfilled﴿[113]

Thus, prohibiting marriage with the previous wives of a son depends on proving their lineage to the father; if such a lineage cannot be established, then marrying the previous wives is not prohibited. It is for this reason that God ﷻ said:

﴿مَا كَانَ مُحَمَّدٌ أَبَا أَحَدٍ مِن رِجَالِكُمْ﴾

﴾mā kāna muḥammadun ʾabā ʾaḥadin min rijālikum﴿

﴾Muḥammad is not the father of any man among you﴿[114]

If this was not the case, what about Ibrāhīm, al-Qāsim, al-Taeeb, and al-Mutahhar, who were all his sons?

It has already been verified that the Prophet ﷺ said to Imām Ḥasan ﷺ:

"This son of mine is a Master."

He also said:

---

[113] Sūrat al-Aḥzāb, Verse 37.

[114] Sūrat al-Aḥzāb, Verse 40.

"al-Ḥasan and al-Ḥusayn, these two sons of mine, are Imāms whether they rise or forebear."

And:

"Every daughter's children are called to their father, save Sayyidah Fāṭimah's children, for I am their Father."

In another interpretation of "of any of your children," some scholars say: "what he meant by "Men", was the mature ones, and none of his children were mature at that time."

In conclusion, whatever has been said about the Apostle's ﷺ sons can be said to include al-Ḥasan and al-Ḥusayn ؑ. They were the sons of the Prophet of God ﷺ.

at-Ṭāhirah

As we already mentioned, one of Sayyidah Fāṭimah al-Zahrā"s ؑ names was "At Ṭāhirah" (the virtuous or pure). This meaning is related to the verse:

﴿إِنَّمَا يُرِيدُ اللَّهُ لِيُذْهِبَ عَنكُمُ الرِّجْسَ أَهْلَ الْبَيْتِ وَيُطَهِّرَكُمْ تَطْهِيرًا﴾

⟨'innamā yurīdu llāhu li-yudhhiba 'ankumu r-rijsa 'ahla l-bayti wa-yuṭahhirakum taṭhīraⁿ⟩

⟨Indeed God desires to repel all impurity from you, O People of the Household, and purify you with a thorough purification⟩[115]

---

[115] Sūrat al-Aḥzāb, Verse 33.

The above verse is important because of its subtle meaning and significance.

We consider this verse the primary source of virtues granted to Ahl al-Bayt عليهم السلام; various debates and many writings took place around it. It might be more appropriate to say that this verse was the field of disputes, contradicting viewpoints, and inconsistent opinions. This is especially true in what "the Family" or Ahl al-Bayt عليهم السلام means.

It is indisputable that this verse, known as "the verse of purification," concerns Sayyidah Fāṭimah at-Ṭāhirah عليها السلام, and both Shīʿī and Sunnī scholars agree on this, except for a few. This fact has been reached considering the traditions, which unanimously state that the said verse includes ʿAlī, Sayyidah Fāṭimah, al-Ḥasan, and al-Ḥusayn عليهم السلام. Yet some hold the view that the verse includes the Prophet's wives because of the word "Family" and the sequence of the surrounding verses that include a speech to them; however, he ﷺ prohibited even his wife, Umm Salamah, from joining them under the cloak before the revelation of this verse.

Although the number of narrators who report that the "verse of purification" was revealed regarding ʿAlī, Sayyidah Fāṭimah, al-Ḥasan, and al-Ḥusayn عليهم السلام reaches several hundred, it will be helpful to include narrations and sources which prominent Sunnī scholars report about this subject. I want to point out that this list should be satisfying for any clear conscience.

1. Baghdādī mentioned[116] that Abū Saʿīd al-Khudrī remarked regarding the verse:

[116] al-Baghdādī, al-Khaṭīb, *Tārīkh al-Baghdādī*, Vol. 10.

﴿إِنَّمَا يُرِيدُ اللَّهُ لِيُذْهِبَ عَنكُمُ الرِّجسَ أَهلَ البَيتِ وَيُطَهِّرَكُم تَطهِيرًا﴾

﴾'innamā yurīdu llāhu li-yudhhiba 'ankumu r-rijsa 'ahla l-bayti wa-yuṭahhirakum taṭhīra^n^﴿

﴾Indeed God desires to repel all impurity from you, O People of the Household, and purify you with a thorough purification﴿[117]

The Messenger of God gathered 'Alī, Sayyidah Fāṭimah, al-Ḥasan, and al-Ḥusayn under a cloak and said: "These are my Ahl al-Bayt (i.e., Family), O God; remove all abominations from them and make them pure and spotless."

Umm Salamah, who was standing near the door, said:

"Am I not one of them, O Messenger of God?"

He said:

"You are (up to a) good ending."

2. Zamakhsharī narrated[118] on account of 'Ā'isha, that God's Messenger ﷺ came out wearing an embroidered, ornamented cloak of woven black hair when al-Ḥasan b. 'Alī came to him and went under it; then al-Ḥusayn followed him, then Sayyidah Fāṭimah, then 'Alī ﷺ.

---

[117] Sūrat al-Aḥzāb, Verse 33.

[118] al-Zamakhsharī, *al-Kashshāf 'an Ḥaqā'iq at-Tanzīl*, Vol. 1, p. 193.

At that moment, the Messenger of God ﷺ quoted the verse:

﴿إِنَّمَا يُرِيدُ اللَّهُ لِيُذْهِبَ عَنكُمُ الرِّجْسَ أَهْلَ الْبَيْتِ وَيُطَهِّرَكُمْ تَطْهِيرًا﴾

﴾*'innamā yurīdu llāhu li-yudhhiba 'ankumu r-rijsa 'ahla l-bayti wa-yuṭahhirakum taṭhīra*^{n}﴿

﴾*Indeed God desires to repel all impurity from you, O People of the Household, and purify you with a thorough purification*﴿[119]

3. Rāzī writes[120]: "When he (the Prophet) came out wearing the black cloak, and al-Ḥasan came under it and al-Ḥusayn, and Sayyidah Fāṭimah and 'Alī the Prophet said [the above-mentioned verse]."

4. Ibn al-Athīr al-Jazarī reported[121] that 'Umar b. Abū Salamah, the Prophet's stepson, said when the above verse[122] was revealed to the Prophet ﷺ, "he had gathered Sayyidah Fāṭimah, Ḥasan, and Ḥusayn under his cloak, while 'Alī was behind him, and said: 'This is my family, therefore, remove all abomination from them, and make them pure and spotless.' Umm Salamah said: Am I one of them, Messenger of God?' He said: 'You will be in good condition."

---

[119] Sūrat al-Aḥzāb, Verse 33.

[120] ar-Rāzī, Fakhr ad-Dīn, *Mafāṭīḥ al-Ghayb* (*al-Tafsīr al-Kabīr*), Vol. 2, p. 700, Istanbul print.

[121] al-Jazarī, Ibn al-Athīr, *Usd al-Ghābah fī Ma'rifat al-Ṣaḥāba*, Vol. 2, p. 12.

[122] Sūrat al-Aḥzāb, Verse 33.

5. Sibṭ b. al-Jawzī reported[123] that Wāthilah b. Asqaʿ said:

"I went to ask Sayyidah Fāṭimah ﷺ about ʿAlī; she told me to go to the Messenger of God ﷺ and ask him, so I went and sat down to wait for him; I then saw the Prophet coming in the company of ʿAlī, al-Ḥasan, and al-Ḥusayn. He held their hands until they entered the room. He then sat al-Ḥasan on his right leg and al-Ḥusayn on his left leg and ordered ʿAlī and Sayyidah Fāṭimah to sit near him. The Prophet ﷺ covered them with his cloak (or garment) and read: And God only wishes... then he ﷺ) supplicated to God and said: "O God, truly these are my Ahl al-Bayt (Family)."

6. Wāhidī reported[124] that Umm Salamah, the Prophet's wife, narrated that God's Messenger ﷺ was present in her house when Sayyidah Fāṭimah brought him an earthenware pot filled with wheat cooked with milk. He ﷺ said: "Call in your husband and two sons for me." Thus, ʿAlī, al-Ḥasan, and al-Ḥusayn came and joined him in eating the food. Meanwhile, he ﷺ sat on a bench, covered with a Khaybariyan cloak.

Umm Salamah added:

"I was in my room performing prayers when the Arch-Angel Jibrāʾīl revealed:

"O God, these are my Family and Kin; therefore, remove all abomination from them and make them pure and spotless."

---

[123] Ibn al-Jawzī, Sibṭ, *Tadhkirat al-Aʾimmah*, p. 244.

[124] al-Wāhidī, ʿAlī b. Aḥmad, *Asbāb al-Nuzūl*.

Hearing that, I looked in the house and said:

"Am I one of them, O Apostle of God?'

Moreover, Tirmidhī reported[125] that God's Messenger ﷺ, since the time this verse was revealed and for six months after that, stood by Sayyidah Fāṭimah's ﷺ house (door) and said: "(Time for) prayers Ahl al-Bayt; God only wished to remove all abomination from you and make you pure and spotless."

7. Ibn Sabagh al-Mālikī narrated[126] a tradition similar to the one already mentioned by Wahidi, but he added:

   Some poets said the following:

Surely Muḥammad and his successor and

Their two sons, and his virtuous and pure daughter;

are the people of the cloak who, in adhering to them, I long for

peace and success on the Last Day.

8. Abū Bakr al-Suyūṭī narrated this tradition on the authority of Umm Salamah, 'Ā'isha, Abū Sa'īd al-Khudrī, Zayd b. Arqam,

[125] al-Tirmidhī, Muḥammad, *al-Jāmi' al-Tirmidhī*.

[126] al-Mālikī, Ibn Sabagh, *al-Fuṣūl al-Muhimmah fī Ma'rifat al-A'immah*, p. 7.

Ibn ʿAbbās, Ḍaḥḥāk b. Muzāḥim, Abū al-Hamra, ʿUmar b. Salamah, and others in his books[127]:

They all reported that the Prophet ﷺ gathered Sayyidah Fāṭimah, ʿAlī, al-Ḥasan, and al-Ḥusayn when the verse[128] was revealed and covered them with a cloak.

He said:

> "By God, these are my Ahl al-Bayt; therefore, remove all abomination from them pure and spotless."

9. Ṭabarī declared[129] that this verse was revealed about the purified five (the Prophet, ʿAlī, Sayyidah Fāṭimah, Ḥasan, Ḥusayn), relying on ʿUmar b. Abū Salamah's narration.

   He also reported that Umm Salamah said:

   > "God's Messenger covered Sayyidah Fāṭimah, ʿAlī, al-Ḥasan, and al-Ḥusayn, including himself with a garment, and read this verse:

﴿إِنَّمَا يُرِيدُ اللَّهُ لِيُذْهِبَ عَنكُمُ الرِّجسَ أَهلَ البَيتِ وَيُطَهِّرَكُم تَطهِيرًا﴾

[127] al-Suyūṭī, Jalāl al-Dīn, *al-Durr al-Manthūr*, Vol. 5, p. 198.

al-Suyūṭī, Jalāl al-Dīn, *al-Khaṣāʾiṣ al-Kubrā*, Vol. 2, p. 264.

al-Suyūṭī, Jalāl al-Dīn, *al-Itqān*, Vol. 2, p. 200.

[128] Sūrat al-Aḥzāb, Verse 33.

[129] al-Ṭabarī, Muḥib al-Dīn, *Dhakhaʾir al-ʿUqbī*, p. 21.

⟨*innamā yurīdu llāhu li-yudhhiba 'ankumu r-rijsa 'ahla l-bayti wa-yuṭahhirakum taṭhīra^n*⟩

⟨*Indeed God desires to repel all impurity from you, O People of the Household, and purify you with a thorough purification*⟩[130]

She added,

"So I came to join them when the Prophet ﷺ said: 'Stay where you are, you will have a pleasant conclusion.'"

In another narration, she was quoted as saying: "God's Messenger said to Sayyidah Fāṭimah:

'Bring your bright cloak, and put his hands on them and said: 'O God, these are the progeny of Muḥammad, thus bless and praise them for surely you are praiseworthy and Exalted.'"

Umm Salamah added:

"I lifted the cloak to join them, but he pulled it away and said: You are all right."

10. Muḥammad b. Aḥmad al-Qurṭubī reported[131] that this verse was revealed regarding Ahl al-Bayt ؑ.

11. Ibn al-'Arabī[132].

---

[130] Sūrat al-Aḥzāb, Verse 33.

[131] al-Qurṭubī, *Tafsīr al-Qurṭubī: al-Jāmiʿ Li Aḥkām al-Qur'ān*, Vol. 14, p. 182.

[132] Ibn 'Arabī, *Aḥkām al-Qur'ān*, Vol. 2, p. 166

12. Ibn ʿAbd al-Barr al-Andalusī[133].

13. al-Bayhaqī[134].

14. al-Ḥakīm al-Nīshābūrī[135].

He narrated a tradition on the authority of Umm Salamah similar to what we have already mentioned and...

He ﷺ said:

"O God, this is my family (Ahl al-Bayt)."

Umm Salamah then said:

"Messenger of God, am I not from Ahl al-Bayt?"

The Prophet answered:

"You are alright, but these are my Ahl al-Bayt..."

15. Aḥmad b. Ḥanbal[136].

---

133 al-Andalusī, Ibn ʿAbd al-Barr, *al-Istīʿāb fī Maʿrifat al-Aṣḥāb*, Vol. 2, p. 460.

134 al-Bayhaqī, Aḥmad b. al-Ḥusayn, *Sunan al-Kubra lil Bayhaqī*, Vol., p. 149.

135 al-Ḥakim al-Nīshābūrī, *al-Mustadrak ʿala al-Ṣaḥīḥayn*, Vol. 2, p. 416.

136 Ibn Ḥanbal, Aḥmad, Musnad Aḥmad b. Ḥanbal, Vol. 1, p. 331.

16. Nasā'ī[137].

17. Muḥammad b. Jarīr at-Ṭabarī[138].

18. al-Khawārazmī[139].

19. 'Alī al-Haythamī[140].

20. Ibn Ḥajar al-Haythamī[141].

It is necessary to further elaborate on this subject since the verse of purification declares, beyond doubt, that Sayyidah Fāṭimah is pure. Explaining the meaning of the word "Rijs" or abomination mentioned in the verse may be beneficial.

"Rijs" means that God purified her from the monthly menstruation and all abominations and depravities. "Rijs" is all that is deemed impure by human nature, conforms to evil doings, deserves punishment, detracts from one's good reputation, brings about sins, and all that is rejected by nature or mard by any of the knightly virtues.

Ibn 'Arabī also said[142] rijs is "anything which detracts from one's character."

---

[137] al-Nasā'ī, Aḥmad b. Shu'ayb, *Khaṣā'iṣ Amīr al-Mu'minīn*, p. 4.

[138] al-Ṭabarī, Muḥammad, *Jāmi' al-Bayān*, Vol. 22, p. 5.

[139] al-Khawārazmī, *Kitāb al-Manāqib*, p. 35.

[140] 'Alī al-Haythamī, *Majma' al-Zawā'id*, Vol. 9, p. 166.

[141] al-Haythamī, Ibn Ḥajar, *al-Ṣawā'iq al-Muḥriqah*, p. 85.

[142] Ibn 'Arabī, *Kitāb al-Futūḥāt al-Makkiyyah*, ch. 29.

The definition that al-ʿArabī gave for the word Rijs is the definition for the word "infallible," which the Shīʿī believe is an inseparable character of all prophets, Imāms, and Sayyidah Fāṭimah al-Zahrāʾ ﷺ. It is indeed an excellent virtue and a great honor that God has bestowed upon some of his servants.

It is worthy of mentioning that infallibility is an inseparable trait of those who propagate divine laws; yet, because infallibility is a prerequisite for prophets and Imāms in their roles of propagating divine rules, it does not mean that others who also propagate are safeguarded from sins.

Imām ʿAlī ﷺ proved Sayyidah Fāṭimah's ﷺ infallibility using the verse of purification in his argument with Abū Bakr.

The Imām ﷺ said:

> "Abū Bakr, do you read God's book?"

He answered:

> "Yes."

Imām ʿAlī ﷺ said:

> "Then tell me about whom was the following verse revealed?

﴿إِنَّمَا يُرِيدُ اللَّهُ لِيُذْهِبَ عَنكُمُ الرِّجْسَ أَهْلَ الْبَيْتِ وَيُطَهِّرَكُمْ تَطْهِيرًا﴾

﴾ʾinnamā yurīdu llāhu li-yudhhiba ʿankumu r-rijsa ʾahla l-bayti wa-yuṭahhirakum taṭhīraⁿ﴿

⟪Indeed God desires to repel all impurity from you, O People of the Household, and purify you with a thorough purification⟫[143]

"Was it not revealed about us, Ahl al-Bayt?"

Abū Bakr said:

"Yes, it was revealed regarding you."

He said:

"If some men testify that Sayyidah Fāṭimah, the Messenger's daughter, committed an abomination, what would you do?"

He answered:

"I would administer the legal punishment to her, just like any other Muslim woman!"

He said,

"If you did so, you would be an infidel in the eyes of God."

Abū Bakr said:

"Why?"

Imām replied:

---

[143] Sūrat al-Aḥzāb, Verse 33.

"Because you would have rejected God's testimony of her purity and virtue (infallibility) and surpassed people's testimony about it..."[144]

A manifestation of this purity is safeguarding the person from impurity upon death, even though any human being, no matter how pious and obedient to God, becomes intensely impure upon passing away, making it obligatory to perform ablution (Ghusl) when touching his body. The dead person, himself, only becomes pure after being washed by others.

Contrarily, the infallible are purified before and after death. al-Ḥasan b. ʿUbayd said[145]

> "I wrote to Imām Ṣādiq and asked him:
>
> "Did the Commander of the Faithful perform ablution (Ghusl) after performing ghusl of the Messenger of God upon his death?"
>
> His answer was:
>
> "The Prophet was pure and safeguarded from all impurities, yet the Commander of the Faithful did so, which became a customary practice (*sunnah*)."

We will elaborate on Sayyidah Fāṭimah's ablution at the end of the book if God wills.

---

[144] Majlisī, ʿAllāmah Muḥammad Bāqir, *Biḥār al-Anwār*, Vol. 10.

[145] al-Ḥasan b. ʿUbayd, *al-Wasāʾil*.

az-Zakiyyah

The word "*tazkiyah*" is mentioned several times and in different forms in the Noble Qur'ān. It means the attestation of someone's honorable record or to purify one's self. For instance, the following verses spoke of "*tazkiyah*":

﴿قَدْ أَفْلَحَ مَن زَكَّاهَا﴾

❨*qad 'aflaḥa man zakkāhā*❩

❨*one who purifies it is felicitous*❩146

﴿قَالَ أَقَتَلْتَ نَفْسًا زَكِيَّةً بِغَيْرِ نَفْسٍ لَقَدْ﴾

❨*qāla 'a-qatalta nafsan zakiyyatan bi-ghayri nafsin la-qad*❩

❨*He said, 'Did you slay an innocent soul, without [his having slain] anyone?*❩147

﴿إِنَّا نُبَشِّرُكَ بِغُلَامٍ﴾

❨*'innā nubashshiruka bi-ghulāmin*❩

❨*Indeed We give you the good news of a son*❩148

---

146 Sūrat al-Shams, Verse 9.

147 Sūrat al-Kahf, Verse 74.

148 Sūrat Maryam, Verse 7.

And

$$\text{﴿ذَٰلِكُمْ أَزْكَىٰ لَكُمْ وَأَطْهَرُ﴾}$$

❮dhālikum 'azkā lakum wa-'aṭharu❯

❮That will be more decent and purer for you❯[149]

The meaning of the first verse is to purify one's self from evil characteristics that develop from corrupt nutrition, excessive speech, anger, envy, greed, self and material worship, conceit, and vanity. This type of purification is performed by abandoning such traits and adhering to the noble characteristics contradicting the ones mentioned above.

The second verse means: Have you killed someone who I attest to his honorable record, for he has not committed a crime or an action, which necessitates punishing?

The third verse speaks of granting a prophet a virtuous son made pure from all sins and whose nations conform to goodness. Sayyidah Fāṭimah al-Zahrā' is Zakiyyah in all the above meanings. This is understood from the verse of purification, which we have already discussed, and concluded that She was pure of all abominations or "Rijs."

As for the fourth verse, you can refer to the study regarding her name, "al-Mubārakah", for here we have explained the purification meant in this verse.

---

[149] Sūrat al-Baqarah, Verse 232.

ar-Raḍiyyah

Accepting what God ordains for oneself is an excellent degree of belief in God ﷻ. Throughout her hard life, Sayyidah Fāṭimah al-Zahrā' ﷺ was delighted with whatever God ﷻ ordained for her. This book discusses the inflictions and disasters that befell Sayyidah Fāṭimah from birth until they martyred her at a young age. During the difficult stages of her life, Sayyidah Fāṭimah was content with the fear, oppression, deprivation, poverty, sorrows, and pains God had predestined for her.

Therefore, Sayyidah Fāṭimah ﷺ is worthy of being included with those mentioned in the verse:

﴿يا أَيَّتُهَا النَّفسُ المُطمَئِنَّةُ﴾

﴿*yā-'ayyatuhā n-nafsu l-muṭma'inna*^tu^﴾

﴿ارجِعي إِلىٰ رَبِّكِ راضِيَةً مَرضِيَّةً﴾

﴿*irji'ī 'ilā rabbiki rāḍiyatan marḍiyya*^tan^﴾

﴿*'O soul at peace! Return to your Lord, pleased, pleasing!*﴾[150]

Because she is satisfied with God's rewards and grants to her and is happy with God's will in this world, He has become well pleased with her.

al-Marḍiyyah

[150] Sūrat al-Fajr, 27-28.

"Marḍiyūn" have an excellent rank and lofty position near God ﷻ.

Just a few of God's worshippers achieve this rank, attained by righteousness and sincerity. Sayyidah Fāṭimah al-Zahrā' ﷺ was one of those who could reach this lofty position. She achieved this rank through her good deeds that pleased God ﷻ and made Him well-satisfied with her.

al-Muḥaddathah

First, we should explain that angels speak, appear, and can be heard by other than prophets.

It is written in the Noble Qur'ān:

﴿وَإِذْ قَالَتِ الْمَلَائِكَةُ يَا مَرْيَمُ إِنَّ اللَّهَ اصْطَفَاكِ وَطَهَّرَكِ وَاصْطَفَاكِ عَلَىٰ نِسَاءِ الْعَالَمِينَ﴾

﴿*wa-'idh qālati l-malā'ikatu yā-maryamu 'inna llāha ṣṭafāki wa-ṭahharaki wa-ṣṭafāki 'alā nisā'i l-'ālamīna*﴾

﴿يَا مَرْيَمُ اقْنُتِي لِرَبِّكِ وَاسْجُدِي وَارْكَعِي مَعَ الرَّاكِعِينَ﴾

﴿*yā-maryamu qnutī li-rabbiki wa-sjudī wa-rka'ī ma'a r-rāki'īna*﴾

﴿*And when the angels said, 'O Mary, God has chosen you and purified you, and He has chosen you above the world's women. O Mary, be obedient to your Lord, and prostrate and bow down with those who bow [in worship].'*﴾[151]

[151] Sūrat Āl 'Imrān, Verses 42-43.

This verse clearly states that angels spoke to Mary by praising her and conveying to her God's commands. It is clear that she heard their speech and realized their intention, for if not, it would be useless to speak to her.[152]

It is even mentioned that the Archangel Jibrā'īl himself spoke to her.

﴿وَاذْكُرْ فِي الْكِتَابِ مَرْيَمَ إِذِ انْتَبَذَتْ مِنْ أَهْلِهَا مَكَانًا شَرْقِيًّا﴾

⟨*wa-dhkur fī l-kitābi maryama 'idhi ntabadhat min 'ahlihā makānan sharqiyyan*⟩

﴿فَاتَّخَذَتْ مِنْ دُونِهِمْ حِجَابًا فَأَرْسَلْنَا إِلَيْهَا رُوحَنَا فَتَمَثَّلَ لَهَا بَشَرًا سَوِيًّا﴾

⟨*fa-ttakhadhat min dūnihim ḥijāban fa-'arsalnā 'ilayhā rūḥanā fa-tamaththala lahā basharan sawiyyan*⟩

﴿قَالَتْ إِنِّي أَعُوذُ بِالرَّحْمَنِ مِنْكَ إِنْ كُنْتَ تَقِيًّا﴾

⟨*qālat 'innī 'a'ūdhu bi-r-raḥmāni minka 'in kunta taqiyyan*⟩

﴿قَالَ إِنَّمَا أَنَا رَسُولُ رَبِّكِ لِأَهَبَ لَكِ غُلَامًا زَكِيًّا﴾

⟨*qāla 'innamā 'ana rasūlu rabbiki li-'ahaba laki ghulāman zakiyyan*⟩

﴿قَالَتْ أَنَّى يَكُونُ لِي غُلَامٌ وَلَمْ يَمْسَسْنِي بَشَرٌ وَلَمْ أَكُ بَغِيًّا﴾

---

[152] Ṭabrisī, Shaykh Faḍl b. Ḥasan, *Majmaʿ al-Bayān fī Tafsīr al-Qurʾān*.

⟪*qālat 'annā yakūnu lī ghulāmun wa-lam yamsasnī basharun wa-lam 'aku baghiyya*ⁿ⟫

﴿قَالَ كَذَلِكِ قَالَ رَبُّكِ هُوَ عَلَيَّ هَيِّنٌ ۖ وَلِنَجْعَلَهُ آيَةً لِلنَّاسِ وَرَحْمَةً مِنَّا ۚ وَكَانَ أَمْرًا مَقْضِيًّا﴾

⟪*qāla ka-dhāliki qāla rabbuki huwa 'alayya hayyinun wa-li-naj'alahū 'āyatan li-n-nāsi wa-raḥmatan minnā wa-kāna 'amran maqḍiyya*ⁿ⟫

⟪And mention in the Book Mary, when she withdrew from her family to an easterly place. Thus did she seclude herself from them, whereupon We sent to her Our Spirit* and he became incarnate for her as a well-proportioned human. She said, 'I seek the protection of the Beneficent from you, should you be Godwary!' He said, 'I am only a messenger of your Lord that I may give you a pure son.' She said, 'How shall I have a child seeing that no human being has ever touched me, nor have I been unchaste?' He said, 'So shall it be. Your Lord says, "It is simple for Me." And so that We may make him a sign for mankind and a mercy from Us, and it is a matter [already] decided.'⟫[153]

The interpreters of the Noble Qur'ān have unanimously agreed that the angel mentioned in the second verse was Jibrā'īl. He "appeared before her as a man in all respects". Then, a dialogue was held between the two of them.

﴿وَامْرَأَتُهُ قَائِمَةٌ فَضَحِكَتْ فَبَشَّرْنَاهَا بِإِسْحَاقَ وَمِن وَرَاءِ إِسْحَاقَ يَعْقُوبَ﴾

---

[153] Sūrat Maryam, Verses 16-21.

* That is, Jibrā'īl.

﴾wa-mra'atuhū qā'imatun fa-ḍaḥikat fa-bashsharnāhā bi-'isḥāqa wa-min warā'i 'isḥāqa ya'qūba﴿

﴿قالَت يا وَيلَتىٰ أَأَلِدُ وَأَنا عَجوزٌ وَهٰذا بَعلي شَيخًا ۖ إِنَّ هٰذا لَشَيءٌ عَجيبٌ﴾

﴾qālat yā-waylatā 'a-'alidu wa-'ana 'ajūzun wa-hādhā ba'lī shaykhan 'inna hādhā la-shay'un 'ajībun﴿

﴿قالوا أَتَعجَبينَ مِن أَمرِ اللَّهِ ۖ رَحمَتُ اللَّهِ وَبَرَكاتُهُ عَلَيكُم أَهلَ البَيتِ ۚ إِنَّهُ حَميدٌ مَجيدٌ﴾

﴾qālū 'a-ta'jabīna min 'amri llāhi raḥmatu llāhi wa-barakātuhū 'alaykum 'ahla l-bayti 'innahū ḥamīdun majīdun﴿

﴾His wife, standing by, laughed as We gave her the good news of [the birth of] Isḥāq, and of Ya'qūb, after Isḥāq. She said, 'Oh, my! Shall I, an old woman, bear [children], and [while] this husband of mine is an old man?! That is indeed an odd thing!' They said, 'Are you amazed at God's dispensation? [That is] God's mercy and His blessings upon you, members of the household. Indeed He is Laudable, Glorious.'﴿[154]

These verses speak of the angels visiting Ibrāhīm ﷺ, bringing him the good news of a son. Ibrāhīm's wife, Sara, who was serving the guests thinking that they were men, spoke to the angels, and they replied to her. This matter is evident from the verses.

---

[154] Sūrat Hūd, Verses 71-73.

﴿وَأَوحَينا إِلىٰ أُمِّ موسىٰ أَن أَرضِعيهِ ۖ فَإِذا خِفتِ عَلَيهِ فَأَلقيهِ فِي اليَمِّ وَلا تَخافي وَلا تَحزَني ۖ إِنّا رادّوهُ إِلَيكِ وَجاعِلوهُ مِنَ المُرسَلينَ﴾

﴿*wa-'awḥaynā 'ilā 'ummi mūsā 'an 'arḍi'īhi fa-'idhā khifti 'alayhi fa-'alqīhi fī l-yammi wa-lā takhāfī wa-lā taḥzanī 'innā rāddūhu 'ilayki wa-jā'ilūhu mina l-mursalīn*[a]﴾

﴿*We revealed to Mūsā' mother, [saying], 'Nurse him; then, when you fear for him, cast him into the river, and do not fear or grieve, for We will restore him to you and make him one of the apostles.*'﴾[155]

Some interpreters claim that Mūsā's ﷺ mother ﷺ was inspired to act in such a manner, while others say that the angels spoke to her to follow the Divine Commands.

al-Manāwi noted[156], on the authority of Qurṭubī: "(Muḥaddathūn) means those who are inspired or whose expectations are accurate and directed by Divine power."

It can also mean those who utter true words, spoken to by angels, or those whose opinions and viewpoints always conform to righteousness as if the Kingdom of Heaven inspired them. Hence, this position is a generous miracle given to a select group of God's pious worshippers and an exalted position granted to God's chosen ones.

Thereupon, it becomes readily easy to distinguish that angels spoke to Sayyidah Fāṭimah al-Zahrā' ﷺ. Because the Mistress of all

---

[155] Sūrat al-Qaṣaṣ, Verse 7.

[156] al-Manāwi, *al-Jāmi' al-Ṣagīr*, Vol. 2, p. 270.

women, and the daughter of the best of all prophets and messengers is not any less significant than Maryam b. 'Imrān, Sarah, Ibrāhīm's wife, or Mūsā's mother ﷺ. Of course, this does not mean that any of these ladies — including Sayyidah Fāṭimah — was a prophet.

Furthermore, Shaykh Ṣadūq narrated[157] that Zayd b. 'Alī said:

> "I heard Abū 'Abdullāh (Imām Ṣādiq ﷺ) say: "Sayyidah Fāṭimah was called "Muḥaddathah" because the angels descended from Heaven and called her as they called Maryam b. 'Imrān and said: "O Sayyidah Fāṭimah! God hath chosen thee above the women of all nations. "

It has been narrated[158] that Imām Ṣādiq ﷺ said to Abū Baṣīr: "... We also possess Sayyidah Fāṭimah's book (*Muṣḥaf Fāṭimah*), and had they known about the book of Sayyidah Fāṭimah. It is three times the size of your Qur'ān; and by God, it has not a letter of your Qur'ān; rather, it was dictated and revealed to her by God ...."[159]

This narration needs elaborate research and explanation, for the Imām ﷺ compared the size of Sayyidah Fāṭimah's ﷺ book to the size of the most familiar book to all Muslims — the Noble Qur'ān. Thus, if the Qur'ān was printed in average-sized letters on standard paper and let us suppose it would fill five hundred such pages, then Sayyidah Fāṭimah's ﷺ book would need fifteen hundred had it

---

[157] Ṣadūq, Shaykh Muḥammad b. 'Alī, *'Ilal al-Sharāi'*.

[158] Majlisī, 'Allamah Muḥammad Bāqir, *Biḥār al-Anwār*, Vol. 10.

[159] Majlisī, 'Allamah Muḥammad Bāqir, *Biḥār al-Anwār*, Vol. 5.

been printed according to the same standards. This is what the Imām ﷺ meant when he said:

> "It is three times the size of your Qur'ān."

This, however, does not mean in any way that the Noble Qur'ān is deficient or that Sayyidah Fāṭimah's ﷺ book completes it, nor does it mean that another divine book was revealed to her. Anyone who makes such a claim is ignorant or a non-Muslim.

The word "Muṣḥaf" does not mean "Qur'ān"; instead, it means volume, book, or a collection of articles in one notebook.

When a group of Imām Ṣādiq's ﷺ companions questioned him about Sayyidah Fāṭimah's ﷺ book, he was quiet for a long time, then explained:

> "Surely you search for what you need and that you need naught".

Sayyidah Fāṭimah ﷺ lived seventy-five days after the Prophet's ﷺ death; when she was intensely depressed, Jibrā'īl ﷺ would visit and condole her on the Prophet's death. He would cheer her up by mentioning the extraordinary situation her father was enjoying and tell her what would come to pass after her death. Imām 'Alī ﷺ wrote what Jibrā'īl ﷺ said, and this is Sayyidah Fāṭimah's ﷺ book.

In addition, Ḥusayn b. Abū al-'Alā' reported that Imām Ṣādiq ﷺ said:

> "...Sayyidah Fāṭimah's book, I don't claim that it is Qur'ān, rather it contains what makes people need us and makes us in need of no one. It even mentions (the legal punishment for) a

lashing, half a lashing, one-fourth of a lashing, and the indemnity for a scratch mark."[160]

We must explain what we mean by "It was revealed to her."

This explanation can be derived from the Qur'ānic verses that revelation is not confined to prophets. Still, God ﷻ reveals to some chosen people, as mentioned in the following verses:

﴿فَخَرَجَ عَلَىٰ قَوْمِهِ مِنَ الْمِحْرَابِ فَأَوْحَىٰ إِلَيْهِمْ أَن سَبِّحُوا بُكْرَةً وَعَشِيًّا﴾

﴿fa-kharaja ʿalā qawmihī mina l-miḥrābi fa-'awḥā 'ilayhim 'an sabbiḥū bukratan wa-ʿashiyyaⁿ﴾

﴿So he emerged before his people from the Temple, and signaled to them that they should glorify [God] morning and evening﴾[161]

﴿فَقَضَاهُنَّ سَبْعَ سَمَاوَاتٍ فِي يَوْمَيْنِ وَأَوْحَىٰ فِي كُلِّ سَمَاءٍ أَمْرَهَا ۚ وَزَيَّنَّا السَّمَاءَ الدُّنْيَا بِمَصَابِيحَ وَحِفْظًا ۚ ذَٰلِكَ تَقْدِيرُ الْعَزِيزِ الْعَلِيمِ﴾

﴿fa-qaḍāhunna sabʿa samāwātin fī yawmayni wa-'awḥā fī kulli samā'in 'amrahā wa-zayyannā s-samā'a d-dunyā bi-maṣābīḥa wa-ḥifẓan dhālika taqdīru l-ʿazīzi l-ʿalīmⁱ﴾

﴿Then He set them up as seven heavens in two days, and revealed in each heaven its ordinance. We have adorned the lowest heaven with*

[160] Ibid., Vol. 6.

[161] Sūrat Maryam, Verse 11.

*lamps, and guarded them**. That is the ordaining of the Mighty, the Knowing*﴿[162]

﴿وَإِذ أَوحَيتُ إِلَى الحَوارِيِّينَ أَن آمِنوا بي وَبِرَسولي﴾

﴾*wa-'idh 'awḥaytu 'ilā l-ḥawāriyyīna 'an 'āminū bī wa-bi-rasūlī*﴿

﴾*And when I inspired the Disciples, [saying], 'Have faith in Me and My apostle,'*﴿[163]

﴿إِذ يوحي رَبُّكَ إِلَى المَلائِكَةِ أَنّي مَعَكُم فَثَبِّتُوا الَّذينَ آمَنوا﴾

﴾*'idh yūḥī rabbuka 'ilā l-malā'ikati 'annī ma'akum fa-thabbitū lladhīna 'āmanū*﴿

﴾*Then your Lord signaled to the angels: 'I am indeed with you; so steady the faithful'*﴿[164]

﴿وَأَوحىٰ رَبُّكَ إِلَى النَّحلِ أَنِ اتَّخِذي مِنَ الجِبالِ بُيوتًا وَمِنَ الشَّجَرِ وَمِمّا يَعرِشونَ﴾

﴾*wa-'awḥā rabbuka 'ilā n-naḥli 'ani ttakhidhī mina l-jibāli buyūtan wa-mina sh-shajari wa-mimmā ya'rishūn*[a]﴿

---

[162] Sūrat Fuṣṣilat, Verse 12.

* Or 'law.'

** Cf. 37:6-7; 67:5.

[163] Sūrat al-Mā'idah, Verse 111.

[164] Sūrat al-Anfāl, Verse 8.

⟪*And* your *Lord inspired the bee [saying]: 'Make your home in the mountains, and on the trees and the trellises that they erect'*⟫165

⟪وَأَوْحَينا إِلىٰ أُمِّ موسىٰ أَن أَرضِعيهِ⟫

⟪*wa-'awḥaynā 'ilā 'ummi mūsā 'an arḍi*⟫

⟪*We revealed to Mūsā' mother, [saying], 'Nurse him'*⟫166

⟪وَلَقَد مَنَنّا عَلَيكَ مَرَّةً أُخرىٰ⟫

⟪*wa-la-qad manannā 'alayka marratan 'ukhrā*⟫

⟪*Certainly, We have done you a favour another time*⟫167

These verses state that revelation is not confined to mankind but includes other creatures such as the Heavens, the Disciples, the angels, the bees, and Mūsā's mother ☙.

Therefore, there can be no doubt that God ﷻ sent revelations to the Mistress of Women and the daughter of the Master of Prophets, as he revealed to Mūsā's mother or Maryam b. 'Imrān ☙.

In conclusion, Sayyidah Fāṭimah's ☙ book is enormous and includes detailed information about the legal punishments and the Islamic penal code, whether major or minor.

---

165 Sūrat al-Naḥl, Verse 68.

166 Sūrat al-Qaṣaṣ, Verse 7.

167 Sūrat Ṭā Ḥā, Verse 37.

It was also declared that her book lists the names of kings who ruled and will rule on Earth until the Day of Resurrection. All this was according to the will of God ﷻ the Knowing, the Omniscient. The book also contains descriptions of all-important events that will take place throughout history.

Sayyidah Fāṭimah's ﷺ book was not a Qur'ān, as is clearly stated in the traditions of Ahl al-Bayt ﷺ, despite the claims of the enemies of the Shī'ī who argue that the Shī'ī believes in another divine book called Sayyidah Fāṭimah's book, intending to undermine their authentic faith.

al-Zahrā'

It was reported[168] that Ibn 'Abbās narrated that God's Messenger ﷺ said:

> "Surely my daughter Sayyidah Fāṭimah is the Mistress of all women from the beginning to the end. She is part of me, and the light of my eyes, She is the flower of my heart, and is my soul, (Sayyidah Fāṭimah) is a human ḥūrī, who whenever she stands in prayers in the presence of Her Lord ﷻ, her light illuminates the skies for the angels like stars shine to people on Earth."

This narration clarifies the reason why Sayyidah Fāṭimah ﷺ was given the name Zahrā'. Other narrations mention that she had a bright and splendid face.

Sayyidah Fāṭimah ﷺ had other titles, and everyone reflected a virtue or noble trait she enjoyed. Among those titles were: al-Batūl,

[168] Majlisī, 'Allamah Muḥammad Bāqir, *Biḥār al-Anwār*, Vol. 10.

al-ʿAdhrā (The Virgin), and al-Hania (the Affectionate one to her children).

Sayyidah Fāṭimah's ﷺ favorite title was "Umm Abīhā," meaning her father's mother.

al-Batūl

God ﷻ created His creatures and implemented specific laws and habits in them. He also subjected these creatures to laws and habits. For instance, a law that rules fire is incendiary, while plants require certain periods and specific environments to grow and produce; likewise, animals need conditions that vary according to their sizes, types, and colors to grow.

Humans are assigned universal laws and physiological, psychological, and spiritual peculiarities. However, certain people chosen by God and, because of His absolute wisdom, have been excluded from these laws. God subjected special rules to the chosen ones. Fire, for example, turns everything on its way to ashes, yet God said to it:

﴿قُلنا يا نارُ كوني بَردًا وَسَلامًا عَلىٰ إبراهيمَ﴾

﴿*qulnā yā-nāru kūnī bardan wa-salāman ʿalā ʾibrāhīm[a]*﴾

﴿*We said, 'O fire! Be cool and safe for Shuʿayb!'*﴾[169]

---

[169] Sūrat al-Anbiyā', Verse 60.

﴿فَنَبَذْنَاهُ بِالْعَرَاءِ وَهُوَ سَقِيمٌ﴾

﴿*fa-nabadhnāhu bi-l-ʿarāʾi wa-huwa saqīm*[un]﴾

﴿وَأَنْبَتْنَا عَلَيْهِ شَجَرَةً مِنْ يَقْطِينٍ﴾

﴿*wa-ʾanbatnā ʿalayhi shajaratan min yaqṭīn*[in]﴾

﴿*Then We cast him on a bare shore, and he was sick. So We made a gourd plant grow above him*﴾[170]

When Yūnus was cast on the shore after the whale swallowed him, God caused the "spreading plant" to proliferate and cover Yūnus's sick body.

Procreation cannot occur without the impregnation and implementation of sperm in the woman's womb, wherein the sperm is made into a clot that grows into a fetus covered with bones that becomes an unborn child. This process takes at least six to nine months, but the natural process God ﷻ implemented in mankind was invalidated with Maryam ﷺ, who gave birth to ʿĪsā ﷺ with none of these steps. It has been said that she carried him for six to nine hours in her womb before giving birth under a palm tree in a secluded location.

Likewise, all miracles through other prophets occurred in environments that did not conform to natural laws. The examples of such events are tremendous. The Noble Qurʾān narrated many stories about prophets' and Imāms' challenges to the laws of nature. Among these stories are Ādam's ﷺ descent from Paradise

[170] Sūrat al-Ṣaffāt, Verse 60.

to Earth, the gushing forth of the fountains of the Earth in the story of Nūḥ ﷺ, Sara's ﷺ pregnancy with Isḥāq ﷺ at an old age, the turning of Mūsā's ﷺ stick into a snake, healing the blind and the lepers and raising of the dead by ʿĪsā ﷺ, and Ascension into the Heavens by God's last Apostle ﷺ.

Now that we understand the above, we can conclude that women's monthly menstruation, which starts at maturity and continues until the fifties or sixties, is nothing but the discharge of spoiled blood and tissues that were to hold the fetus had it been conceived.

God ﷻ says:

﴿وَيَسۡـَٔلُونَكَ عَنِ ٱلۡمَحِيضِۖ قُلۡ هُوَ أَذٗى﴾

﴿wa-yas'alūnaka ʿani l-maḥīḍi qul huwa 'adhan﴾

﴿They ask you concerning [intercourse during] menses. Say, 'It is hurtful'.﴾*[171]

This shows that the discharged blood is a harmful substance, which would harm women if it stayed in their bodies.

God ﷻ relieved Sayyidah Fāṭimah al-Zahrā' ﷺ of such harm, as He removed from her all abomination and purified her with a total purification. Various traditions authenticated this:

---

[171] Sūrat al-Baqarah, Verse 222.

* Or 'offensive.'

1. Qundūzī reported[172] that the Prophet ﷺ said: "She was safeguarded from menstruation and childbed (bleeding)."

2. Muḥammad Ṣāliḥ al-Kashfī al-Ḥanafī reported[173] that the Prophet ﷺ said: "Sayyidah Fāṭimah was called al-Batūl because she was safeguarded and relieved from that which women encounter every month (menstruation)."

3. al-ʿAmr Tasrī narrates[174] that the Prophet ﷺ was asked about the meaning of Batūl — someone said to him: "Messenger of God, we have heard you say that Maryam is Batūl and Sayyidah Fāṭimah, too, is Batūl."

   The Prophet replied: "Batūl is she who never sees blood, meaning that she never discharges menstrual blood because menstruation is resented if it occurs in Prophet's daughters."

   Al-Ḥakīm authenticated the above narration.

4. al-Ḥāfiẓ Abū Bakr ash-Shāfiʿī narrates[175] on the account of Ibn Abbās that the Prophet said: "My daughter is a human ḥūrī, she never menstruates, nor does she encounter any menses."

   al-Nisāʾī also narrates this tradition.

---

172 al-Balkhī, Sulaymān b. Ibrāhīm al-Qundūzī, *Yanābīʿ al-Mawaddah lī-Dhawī l-Qūrbā*, p. 260.

173 al-Ḥanafī, Muḥammad Ṣāliḥ al-Kashfī, *al-Manāqib*.

174 Al-ʿAmr Tasrī, *Arjaḥ al-Muṭṭālib*.

175 al-Baghdādī, al-Khaṭīb, *Tārīkh al-Baghdādī*, Vol. 13, p. 331.

5. Ibn Asākir mentioned[176] on the account of Anas b. Mālik that Umm Salīm said: "Sayyidah Fāṭimah has never menstruated nor discharged childbed blood."

6. al-Ḥāfiẓ al-Suyūṭī said:

'Among Sayyidah Fāṭimah's particularities is that she did not menstruate, and when she gave birth to a child, she would immediately become purified from childbed confinement so as not to miss her prayers."

7. Rāfiʿ mentioned[177] that Umm Salamah said:

"Sayyidah Fāṭimah never discharged blood during her childbed confinement, nor does she menstruate."

8. Ṭabarī narrates[178] that Asmāʾ b. ʿUmays said:

"When Sayyidah Fāṭimah gave birth to al-Ḥasan, she did not bleed; she also does not bleed during menstruation periods. (When I informed the Prophet of this) he said: 'Do you not know that my daughter is pure and chaste; she does not discharge blood as a result of childbirth or menstruation.'"

9. Shāfiʿī narrates[179] this tradition as well.

---

[176] Ibn ʿAsākir, *at-Tārīkh al-Kabīr*, Vol. 1, p. 391.

[177] Rāfiʿ, *at-Tadwīn*.

[178] al-Ṭabarī, Muḥib al-Dīn, *Dhakhaʾir al-ʿUqbī*.

[179] ash-Shāfiʿī, ʿAbd ur-Raḥmān, *Nuzhat al-Majālis*, p. 227.

10. It was mentioned[180] that Abū Baṣīr quoted Imām Ṣādiq as saying: 'God forbade 'Alī from marrying women while Sayyidah Fāṭimah was still alive."

Abū Baṣīr exclaimed:

"Why was that?"

The Imām replied:

"Because she was pure and does not menstruate."

'Allamah Majlisī commented on this narration: "This narration means either. First, Because Sayyidah Fāṭimah did not menstruate, 'Alī had no reason to marry another woman. So, God forbade him to marry other women in the observance of her sanctity. Or, Second: Her eminence disallowed him from marrying another woman, whereas this particularity of hers is part of this eminence."

Sayyidah Fāṭimah's exaltation from encountering menstrual or childbed blood conforms to the verse of purification, which has already been discussed.

al-'Adhrā

This is one name given to Sayyidah Fāṭimah. This name declares she was always a virgin, meaning she was chaste.

We have already mentioned many traditions that attest to the fact that she was conceived of heavenly food and that Sayyidah Fāṭimah

---

[180] Majlisī, 'Allamah Muḥammad Bāqir, *Biḥār al-Anwār*, Vol. 10.

was a human ḥūrī. There is no exaggeration in this expression; instead, stating that Sayyidah Fāṭimah was always a virgin is nothing but the absolute truth. Besides the narrations that verify this, the Noble Qurʾān states:

﴿إِنَّا أَنشَأْنَاهُنَّ إِنشَاءً﴾

⟨ʾinnā ʾanshaʾnāhunna ʾinshāʾan⟩

﴿فَجَعَلْنَاهُنَّ أَبْكَارًا﴾

⟨fa-jaʿalnāhunna ʾabkāran⟩

⟨We have created them with a special creation, and made them virgins⟩[181]

This clarifies that ḥūrīs are always virgins. What is meant by virgin purity "is that whenever their husbands come near them (have sexual intercourse with them), they find them virgins."[182]

Imām Ṣādiq was asked: "How can a ḥūrī always be a virgin (no matter how many times her husband comes near her)?"

The Imām answered: "Because (ḥūrīs) are created from pure goodness where no blight can alter them, nor does decrepitude inflict them... menstruation does not pollute them..."

---

[181] Sūrat al-Wāqiʿah, Verses 35-36.

[182] Ṭabrisī, Shaykh Faḍl b. Ḥasan, *Majmaʿ al-Bayān fī Tafsīr al-Qurʾān*.

The Event of the Cloak[183]

A famous event known as the "Event of the Cloak" was reported in the Shīʿī books regarding "the verse of purification." The context of the event is:

Jābir b. ʿAbdullāh Ansārī (God be pleased with him) narrates from the authority of Sayyidah Fāṭimah ﷺ, the beloved daughter of the Holy Prophet ﷺ that she said:

> "One day when my beloved father, the Holy Prophet ﷺ, visited me in my house, he ﷺ said:
>
> > 'O Sayyidah Fāṭimah! Peace be on you.'
>
> I replied:
>
> > 'O father! Peace be on you, too.'
>
> He then said:
>
> > 'I am feeling some weakness within me.'
>
> I said:
>
> > 'God forbid that you may be sick.'
>
> Then he said:
>
> > 'Sayyidah Fāṭimah! Fetch me a Yamanite cloak and wrap it around me.'

[183] We have depended on the excellent translation of our brothers in the Islamic Seminary of Pakistan to include this event in the book.

I brought the Yamanite cloak and covered my dear father with it. I then noticed that his face was glowing like a full moon. A moment later, my beloved son, Ḥasan, came and said:

'O my dear mother! Peace of God is on you.'

I replied:

'O my loving son, the apple of my eyes, the delight of my heart! Peace be on you, too.'

He then said:

'O my dear mother! I am smelling the fragrance of my loving grandfather!'

I said:

'Yes, your beloved grandfather is under the cloak.'

Ḥasan then approached his grandfather and said:

`O my grandfather! Peace be on you. May I enter the cloak?'

My loving father replied:

`O my son, the owner of my fountain (of Kawthar)! Peace be on you, too. Yes, you may enter.'

Thus, Ḥasan entered the cloak. Soon after, my loving son, Ḥusayn, came and said:

`O my dear mother! Peace be on you.'

I replied:

> `O my loving son, the apple of my eyes, the delight of my heart! peace be on you, too.'

He then said:

> `O my dear mother! I am smelling the fragrance of my affectionate grandfather!'

I replied:

> 'Yes, your loving grandfather and elder brother, Ḥasan, are inside the cloak.'

Ḥusayn then went near the cloak and said:

> `O my dear grandfather, the chosen Prophet of God! Peace be on you. May I also come inside the cloak to be with both of you?'

My loving father replied:

> `O my son, the interceder of my Ummah! Peace be on you, too. Yes, you may enter.'

Thus Ḥusayn, too, entered the cloak. Then ʿAlī b. Abū Ṭālib came and said:

> `O beloved daughter of the Holy Prophet! peace be on you.'

I replied:

> `O Abul-Ḥasan, Commander of the Faithful! Peace be on you, too.'

He then said:

> 'Sayyidah Fāṭimah! I smell the fragrance of my brother, my Uncle's son.'

I replied:

> 'Yes! He and your two sons are inside the cloak.'

'Alī then proceeded towards the cloak and said:

> `O Prophet of God! Peace be on you. May I also come to you inside the cloak?'

My beloved father replied:

> 'Peace be on you also, my brother, my vicegerent, my successor, my standard bearer! You may also come inside.'

Thus, 'Alī also went inside the cloak. Then I went near the cloak and said:

> `Peace be on you, O my loving father! O Prophet of God! May I also come to you inside the cloak?'

My loving father replied:

> 'Peace of God is on you also, my beloved daughter! All dear heart! You, too, have my permission.'

Thus, I also went inside the cloak. When we all assembled inside the Cloak, my affectionate father held the two corners of the cloak and raised his right hand towards the sky, saying:

> 'O God! These are my Ahl al-Bayt.
>
> They are my confidants and my supporters.
>
> Their flesh is my flesh, and their blood is my blood.
>
> Whoever hurts them hurts me.
>
> Whoever displeases them displeases me.
>
> Whoever makes peace with them will make peace with me.
>
> Whoever has enmity against them will have enmity against me.
>
> Whoever is a friend to them is a friend of mine. It is because they belong to me, and I belong to them.
>
> O, God! Bestow Your peace, Benevolence, Mercy, forgiveness, and Pleasures on me and them.
>
> And keep them aloof from uncleanliness and pure and thoroughly purified.'

Then the Lord, God ﷻ said:

> `O my Angels! O inmates of the heavens! I created this solid firmament, well-stretched earth, well-lighted moon, shining sun, rotating planets, rippling oceans, floating boats, and all other things for the sake and love of these five persons inside the cloak.'

At this, the Archangel Jibrā'īl asked:

> `O Lord! Who are they inside the cloak?'

The Lord said:

> `They are Ahl al-Bayt of the Prophet and the assets of the Prophethood. They are Sayyidah Fāṭimah, her father, her husband, and her two sons.'

Jibrā'īl said:

> `O Lord! Permit me to descend to earth and join them as the sixth inside the cloak.'

The Lord said:

> 'You are permitted.'

Thus, Jibrā'īl, the Archangel, came down to earth and said:

> `O Prophet of God! Peace be on you. The Gracious Lord ﷻ sends His Greetings to you to bestow on you His Grace and Mercy and says:

> "By My Grace and Grandeur! I have created this solid firmament, well-stretched earth, well-lighted moon, shining sun, rotating planets, rippling oceans, floating boats, and all other things for the sake and love of you and your chosen people." And the Lord, ﷻ has permitted me to join you inside the cloak.

O Prophet of God! May I come in and be with you?

The Holy Prophet replied:

> 'O Bearer of the Divine revelations! Peace be on you also. Yes, you may come in.'

Then Jibrā'īl, too, came inside the cloak. After that, he spoke to my affectionate father:

> 'God sends His revelation to you people and says:

> "Surely, God has decided that He should keep you and your Ahl al-Bayt clean of all pollution and purify you people with a thorough purification."'

Then ʿAlī said to my loving father,

> 'Tell me! What merit the coming under this cloak have before God ?'

The Holy Prophet replied:

> 'By that Being, Who made me His Prophet and Who, for the salvation of mankind, appointed me to prophethood! When any of our Shīʿī and supporters assemble in a

gathering of the inmates of this earth and narrate this ḥadīth, God will bestow on them His Blessings and Mercy; angels will encircle them, and as long as they do not disperse, the angels will pray for the forgiveness of their sins.'

At this, 'Alī said:

'By God! We and our Shī'ī have now become triumphant.'

Then the Holy Prophet ﷺ said:

'O 'Alī! By that Being, Who made me the righteous prophet and appointed me to the prophet-hood for the sake of people's salvation, whenever in the gathering of the inmates of this earth our Shī'ī and friends will assemble and narrate this ḥadīth of ours, and if some-one amongst them will be in agony, God will remove his trouble; and if someone was sorrowful, God will relieve him of his sorrows; will answer his needs.'

Then 'Alī ؑ said:

'By God! At this moment, we have been crowned with success and blessings; and by the Lord of Ka'bah, in the same way, our Shī'ī too have become triumphant and blessed in this world and the Hereafter.'

Sayyidah Fāṭimah's Youth

Sayyidah Fāṭimah al-Zahrā' opened her eyes to the world to enjoy prophetic fatherly love and to suckle Sayyidah Khadījah's milk, which was mixed with excellent morals and perfection.

Growing up in the house of Revelation allowed her to achieve the highest perfection and excellence. The Prophet ﷺ taught her divine knowledge and endowed her with exceptional intelligence so that she realized the true meaning of faith, piety, and the reality of Islām.

The virtuous upbringing of Sayyidah Fāṭimah by God's Messenger ﷺ was accompanied by her capability to perceive divine facts and her spiritual brilliance and preparedness to ascend to the highest levels of perfection.

Parallel to this was God's will that Sayyidah Fāṭimah al-Zahrā' should face many sorrows and live in anguish from the very beginning of her life. She opened her eyes to see her father being fought by his relatives and strangers and treated with hostility by the infidels and polytheists. For instance, Sayyidah Fāṭimah might have entered the Sacred Mosque and seen her father reading Qur'ān in the private chamber of Ismā'īl (around the Ka'bah) while polytheists were harming him and waging a psychological war against him. One day, Sayyidah Fāṭimah saw the infidels pour camel placenta on her father while he was prostrating to God ﷻ, so she cleaned his back and, while bitterly crying, cursed the unbelievers and supplicated to God to punish them. But the infidels were sarcastic, in the same respect as any lowly people and rubble would be.

Ibn 'Abbās reported that the Qurayshī men once held a meeting in the Sacred Mosque and vowed to their Idols that as soon as they saw Muḥammad ﷺ, they would all take part in killing him; upon hearing this, Sayyidah Fāṭimah ﷺ went crying to her father and informed him of their conspiracy.

The crisis became more intense when the Messenger of God ﷺ was forcefully confined to Abū Ṭālib's trail (valley) along with his family and all the members of Abū Ṭālib's family. They lived in an atmosphere overtaken by fear and anxiety of the constantly expected attack by the infidels at night. The situation worsened when the polytheists signed a treaty to besiege Banī Hāshim and impose economic sanctions against them; this treaty allowed no one to sell or buy anything from them, including food supplies.

Therefore, the cries of starving children reached the ears of all Makkan inhabitants. It divided the people of Makkah into two groups: One who was enjoying the misfortunes of the Banī Hāshim, and the other was deeply saddened by their misery.

This situation continued for over three years. Sayyidah Fāṭimah ﷺ suffered from this siege, which awakened her spirit of struggle, honesty, and endurance; it was as if she was spending a period of training and exercise for the near future.

The predicament was made easier when Sayyidah Fāṭimah ﷺ saw the courageous hero, Abū Ṭālib, aided by Hamza, keeping steadfast and helping her father in every way against the infidels' aggression. Abū Ṭālib declared his adherence to Islām through uttering poetry. Once, the heads of Quraysh objected to Abū Ṭālib's support of the Prophet; they said to him:

> "We will give you a handsome, generous, and courageous Qurayshī youth ('Ammārah b. al-Walīd) to become your son, if you give us your nephew — Muḥammad — who disunites us and humiliates our idols, so that we may kill him!"

Abū Ṭālib said:

> "This is an unfair offer! Do you mean to give me your son so I can feed him for you and give you my nephew to kill? (If this is your way of dealing) then each of you should give me his son to kill if you want me to give you Muḥammad to kill."

Abū Ṭālib's honorable stands in protecting the Prophet were many. Had it not been for his faith and firm adherence to Islām, he would not have been steadfast in defending the Messenger and his divine faith. Contrary to Abū Ṭālib, another uncle of the Prophet ﷺ, Abū Lahab fought fiercely and opposed the Prophet. His shameful conduct was recorded in various history books and the Noble Qur'ān.

Sayyidah Khadījah's عليها السلام Death

Sayyidah Fāṭimah's عليها السلام life was passing by with years full of sorrow and infliction. When she reached her seventh or eighth year, another tragedy clouded her life. The death of Sayyidah Fāṭimah's عليها السلام mother, Sayyidah Khadījah عليها السلام, brought sadness and grief to her heart, for Sayyidah Khadījah عليها السلام was an affectionate mother who had predicted the tough life her darling daughter would live.

During Sayyidah Khadījah's last days, she was confined to bed. One day, the Prophet of God ﷺ said to her:

> "What you are encountering is because of us, Sayyidah Khadījah; when you meet your peers, send my Salām to them!"

Sayyidah Khadījah questioned:

> "Who are they? O Prophet of God?"

He answered:

> "Maryam b. ʿImrān, Kulthūm (Mūsā's sister), and Āsiya — Pharaoh's wife."

She said,

> "May you live in harmony and have sons, O Prophet of God."

The Messenger of God ﷺ used to say:

> "I was commanded to give Sayyidah Khadījah the good news of a dwelling in Paradise made of brocade where there is neither clamoring nor strain."[184]

---

184 Ibn Ḥanbal, Aḥmad, *Musnad Aḥmad b. Ḥanbal.*

Ibn al-Athīr said that the brocade mentioned in this tradition is palace-like hollow pearls.

Sayyidah Khadījah was once crying in the presence of Asmā' b. ʿUmays, who said to her:

> "Why are you crying while you are the Mistress of all women and the Prophet's wife, who will enter Paradise as he has said?"

Sayyidah Khadījah replied:

> "I am not crying (for fear of death); rather, I am crying because every woman needs a close friend on her wedding night to tell her secrets to and help her with certain issues. Sayyidah Fāṭimah is still very young, and I am afraid she will be alone on her wedding night!"

Asmā' said:

> "O my mistress, I vow to you, by God, that if I am alive, I will take your place..."

Sayyidah Khadījah died at sixty-three (according to some historians). Her death brought deep sorrow to the Holy Prophet, especially since her death was followed by the death of Abū Ṭālib, the Prophet's uncle, who died several days (or months) after that. Hence, the year in which the deaths of Sayyidah Khadījah and Abū Ṭālib occurred was called "the year of sorrow" by the Prophet.

Sayyidah Khadījah's death was a disaster for the Prophet, not only because she was his wife but also because she was the first one to believe in his message. Sayyidah Khadījah also supported her husband with abundant shares of her property for the sake of

Islām. She held a unique character in Makkah and among all Arab women.

When Sayyidah Khadījah ؑ was buried at al-Ḥajūn, the Messenger of God ﷺ stepped into her grave to bless it. Meanwhile, Sayyidah Fāṭimah ؑ kept close to her father and asked him,

> "Messenger of God, where is my mother?"

The Prophet ﷺ avoided Sayyidah Fāṭimah's ؑ question, so she looked around for someone to ask where her mother ؑ was! At that point, Jibrā'īl ؑ descended and revealed the following to the Prophet ﷺ:

> "Your Lord commands you to inform Sayyidah Fāṭimah that He sends His blessings upon her and says:
>
> > "Your mother is in a house of brocade, its corners are made of gold, and its poles are of rubies. It is between Āsiya's (Pharaoh's wife) and Maryam b. 'Imrān's houses."

Sayyidah Fāṭimah said,

> "Surely God is as-Salām, and peace is from Him and to Him."

Another mournful event that inflicted the Prophet ﷺ was his uncle's death. Abū Ṭālib had adopted Muhammed when he was eight years old upon the death of his grandfather. Abū Ṭālib was the Prophet's guardian until he was fifty-three years old.

Abū Ṭālib's services and support for Islām and the Prophet ﷺ never ceased throughout those years. Had it not been for Abū

Ṭālib, Islām possibly could not have passed the stage of its prime days of propagation.

These two tragic events had a significant effect on the messenger's life; the death of Abū Ṭālib caused the Prophet to immigrate to Madīnah, for he had lost the strongest supporter and advocate of the religion from among his uncles.

Sayyidah Fāṭimah's ﷺ Immigration

Upon being inflicted with the deaths of Sayyidah Khadījah ﷺ and Abū Ṭālib, the Prophet ﷺ decided to immigrate to Madīnah. He ordered ʿAlī ﷺ to lie in his bed during the night that later became known as (the night of stay). That night, about forty or fourteen polytheist men besieged the Prophet's ﷺ house and were determined to attack and kill him. But the Prophet ﷺ had escaped to a nearby cave, and Sayyidah Fāṭimah ﷺ stayed home expecting the enemy's assault at any minute. She listened to their infidel and atheistic slogans against her father. Only God ﷻ knows how scared and disturbed she was that long night, for she knew the infidels' cruelty and mercilessness.

At dawn, the infidels attacked the house while leveling their swords like ferocious beasts or savage dogs. They proceeded to the Prophet's ﷺ bed intending to kill him but were surprised to find ʿAlī ﷺ laying in it wearing the Prophet's ﷺ clothes. They departed from the house feeling defeated and harboring resentment, fury, and fire against the Prophet ﷺ and Imām ʿAlī ﷺ.

Those hours were the most aggravating, frightening, and anguish-filled for Sayyidah Fāṭimah ﷺ. Soon relief entered her life; Imām ʿAlī ﷺ took her and his mother and Sayyidah Fāṭimah b. Zubayr b. ʿAbd al-Muṭṭalib out toward Madīnah. When the infidels learned this, they intercepted them to prevent their migration out of Makkah. Had it not been for the Mercy and protection of God ﷻ and the heroism and courage of Imām ʿAlī ﷺ, a catastrophe would have occurred. The infidels were driven back by Imām ʿAlī ﷺ, who continued the journey toward Madīnah.

Upon arriving in Madīnah, the Prophet ﷺ met them and took Sayyidah Fāṭimah ﷺ to his home, which was initially Abū Ayyūb Ansārī's. Thus, Sayyidah Fāṭimah ﷺ became the guest of Abū Ayyūb's mother.

Sayyidah Fāṭimah ﻋ lived with the Prophet ﷺ in Madīnah after suffering typhoons of painful incidents, such as the death of her mother ﻋ, her immigration, and the continuous agitations against her. Sayyidah Fāṭimah's miseries did not stop here; her immigration began an era of uninterrupted sorrows.

One year after the Prophet ﷺ immigrated to Madīnah, the infidels mobilized their men and headed towards the Muslim's stronghold, intending to destroy the new faith, but Jibrā'īl ﻋ informed the Prophet of their conspiracy, who ordered the Immigrants and Helpers to leave the city and meet the infidels in a place on the way to Makkah called Badr.

Although the infidels outnumbered the Muslims three to one, the Prophet ﷺ and his followers defeated them and returned to Madīnah triumphant.

Sayyidah Fāṭimah عليها السلام at Uḥud

One year and one month after the battle of Badr, the battle of Uḥud occurred. In this battle, seventy of the Prophet's ﷺ most prominent companions were martyred, including Hamza, the Prophet's uncle and the most notable hero.

Two rocks injured the Prophet on his forehead and mouth in this battle. Because of his injury, the Prophet lost some teeth, and blood clotted on his beard as if it was henna. At that moment, Satan shouted in such a manner that all Muslims heard him; he said:

> "Muḥammad has been killed."

This created disarray among the Muslims, and many men, save the truly faithful, fled the battlefield. Confusion also overtook the Muslim families living in Madīnah.

Ṣafīyya b. 'Abd Muṭṭalib, the Prophet's aunt, accompanied Sayyidah Fāṭimah al-Zahrā' عليها السلام to Uḥud.

When Sayyidah Fāṭimah عليها السلام heard of her father's injuries, she started crying, and the Hāshimīt women rushed to help her.

Sayyidah Fāṭimah's عليها السلام arrival at the battle scene coincided with the Prophet's ﷺ inspection of his soldiers to discover how many had been martyred and wounded. When he reached Hamza, he found him indescribable; the infidels had severely mutilated his body, cut off his fingers, hands, legs, nose, and ears, and ruptured his abdomen to get his liver out. They had also cut off his sexual organs and left him in that horrible state.

The scene of Hamza's defaced body brought sadness and pain to the Prophet's heart. The infidel had abandoned no ugly method of mutilation, which they did not commit against the powerful supporter of God's Apostle ﷺ. While this infliction deeply saddened the Prophet ﷺ, his aunt and Sayyidah Fāṭimah ؑ were rushing towards the scene. When he noticed them, he covered Hamza's body with one of his garments. Ṣafīyya and Sayyidah Fāṭimah ؑ arrived and began crying and condemning the infidels for their crimes. They noticed that the Prophet's ﷺ forehead was severely cut and that blood had become clotted on his face and beard; thus, Sayyidah Fāṭimah al-Zahrā' ؑ started cleaning his face and said,

> "God's punishment will be severe on him who caused the Messenger's face to bleed."

Imām ʿAlī ؑ poured water on the Prophet's ﷺ face, but this did not stop the bleeding, so Sayyidah Fāṭimah ؑ burnt some rope and put its ashes on the cut, which contained the bleeding. Sayyidah Fāṭimah ؑ spent these moments in sadness and tremendous anxiety. She was a faithful and devoted daughter to her father.

When Imām ʿAlī ؑ returned to Madīnah, he gave his sword to Sayyidah Fāṭimah ؑ and said:

> "Take this sword, Sayyidah Fāṭimah; it proved most reliable today."

The Prophet added:

> "Take it, Sayyidah Fāṭimah, for surely your husband has fully performed his duty; God killed the heroes of the Arabs through his hands."

Sayyidah Fāṭimah's help to her father does not mean that she worked as a nurse on the battlefield, despite the claim of some writers who consider this story as proof that Sayyidah Fāṭimah was a battlefield nurse.

Sayyidah Fāṭimah's ﷺ Problems at Home

One problem that disturbed Sayyidah Fāṭimah ﷺ was that some of her father's wives were envious of her. Certain wives of the Prophet ﷺ developed psychological complications against Sayyidah Fāṭimah ﷺ because of the special treatment the Prophet ﷺ gave her and the great love and kindness he favored her with.

Imām Ṣādiq ﷺ said[185]:

> "The Messenger of God entered his house to find 'Ā'isha yelling at Sayyidah Fāṭimah, saying:
>
> > 'By God, O Sayyidah Khadījah's daughter, you feel your mother was better than us, but what favor does she have above us? Is she not saved like us?'
>
> The Prophet ﷺ heard 'Ā'isha's shouting. When Sayyidah Fāṭimah saw him, she cried; the Prophet ﷺ then said:
>
> > 'What makes you cry, O daughter of Muḥammad?'
>
> Sayyidah Fāṭimah said:
>
> > "'Ā'isha degraded my mother, and this has caused me to cry.'
>
> The Messenger of God ﷺ angrily said:
>
> > 'Hush, O Ḥumayrā (reddish woman). Surely God ﷻ blessed this devoted and fertile woman, and Sayyidah Khadījah ﷺ gave birth to my children, al-Ṭāhir ('Abdullāh), who was purified al-Qāsim, Ruqayyah, Umm

---

185 Majlisī, 'Allamah Muḥammad Bāqir, *Biḥār al-Anwār*.

Kulthūm, and Zaynab. Still, God has created you with a sterile womb so you do not give birth to any children."

'Ā'isha made many other unappreciated utterances against Sayyidah Fāṭimah al-Zahrā' ☒, which reflects the profound inborn deviation from which 'Ā'isha suffered, the like of which was not observed in any other of the Prophet's ﷺ wives.

This narration may indicate that Sayyidah Khadījah's ☒ daughters were all the Prophet's ﷺ direct daughters and not fostered daughters. However, we have shown previously that Zaynab, Ruqayyah, and Umm Kulthūm were not the Prophet's nor Sayyidah Khadījah's begotten children.

On the Way to Marriage

When Sayyidah Fāṭimah al-Zahrā' ﷺ reached nine years of age, she was a full-grown woman who enjoyed intellectual maturity and integrity of conduct. God gifted her with a brilliant mentality, cleverness, beauty, grace, and elegance. Her talents were many, and she inherited and gained noble traits that excel those of any female or male.

Sayyidah Fāṭimah's ﷺ religious feelings and literary knowledge were unlimited. You will learn that she was the world's most knowledgeable and honorable woman. History has witnessed no other woman who achieved such a high level of education, knowledge, and social graces that Sayyidah Fāṭimah ﷺ reached, regardless of her not graduating from any educational establishment, save the school of Revelation.

Considering this, it is not strange that prominent companions of the Prophet ﷺ asked to marry her, but he rejected them by saying:

> "Her affair is left to her Lord; whenever He wills, she will marry."

Shuʿayb b. Saʿab al-Miṣrī said[186]:

> "When the sun of her beauty shined in the heavens of the prophetic message and became full on the horizon of the exaltation of the moon of her perfection, the dawns of thoughts reached towards her and the sights of the chosen longed to observe her beauty; so the masters of the Muhājirūn and Ansār asked to marry her, but the one who was bestowed with God's satisfaction (the Prophet ﷺ rejected them and said:

186 al-Miṣrī, Shaykh Shuʿayb, *al-Rawḍ al-Fa'iq*.

`I am waiting for God's ordinance in her regard."'

Abū Bakr and 'Umar were among those who asked to marry Sayyidah Fāṭimah, but the Prophet ﷺ rejected them too and said that she was still too young for marriage. 'Abd ur-Raḥman b. 'Awf also asked for her hand, but the Prophet ﷺ ignored him.

'Alī b. Muttaqī reported[187] that Anas b. Mālik said:

> "Abū Bakr came to see the Prophet ﷺ. After sitting down, he said,
>
> > `O Messenger of God, you surely know of my devotion and long-standing service to Islām...'
>
> The Prophet then said,
>
> > `What is it you want?'
>
> Abū Bakr said,
>
> > 'I want you to give me Sayyidah Fāṭimah in marriage.'
>
> When the Prophet heard this, he said nothing, so Abū Bakr returned to 'Umar and said:
>
> > `I have ruined myself and others.'

---

[187] al-Hindī, 'Alī al-Muttaqī, *Kanz al-'Ummāl fī Sunan al-Aqwāl wal-Af'āl*, Vol. 2, p. 99.

'Umar said:

> 'What happened?'

Abū Bakr replied:

> 'I asked for Sayyidah Fāṭimah's hand from the Prophet, but he ignored me.'

'Umar said:

> 'You stay here, and I will ask the Prophet for the same thing you asked him for.'

'Umar went to the Prophet and, after sitting down, started saying,

> 'O Messenger of God, you surely know of my devotion and long-standing service to Islām...'

The Prophet ﷺ then said:

> 'What is it you want?'

'Umar replied:

> 'I want you to give me Sayyidah Fāṭimah in marriage.'

But the Prophet ﷺ ignored him too. 'Umar returned to Abū Bakr and said:

> 'He is waiting for God's command in her regard."'

al-Haythamī also reported[188] that Abū Bakr and 'Umar sent their daughters to the Prophet ﷺ to ask him to give Sayyidah Fāṭimah in marriage to them; but when the daughters mentioned why they had come, the Prophet said,

"No! Not until God's command in her regard is revealed."

Perhaps the Messenger ﷺ avoided telling Abū Bakr and 'Umar openly that he is keeping Sayyidah Fāṭimah ؑ for the qualified man, 'Alī ؑ, because he did not want to declare to them they were unqualified to marry her, and that his daughter was above their level. The Prophet also wanted everything to occur in its natural order.

Imām 'Alī ؑ was staying in the house of Sa'd b. Mu'ādh (according to one historical finding) since he immigrated to Madīnah. One day, While Imām 'Alī ؑ was in one of the gardens of Madīnah, Sa'd came to him and said:

"What prevents you from asking to marry Sayyidah Fāṭimah from your cousin?"

It has also been mentioned[189] that 'Umar came to 'Alī ؑ and said:

"What prevents you from (marrying) Sayyidah Fāṭimah?"

Imām 'Alī ؑ replied:

---

[188] 'Alī al-Haythamī, *Majma' al-Zawā'id*.

[189] al-Hindī, 'Alī al-Muttaqī, *Kanz al-'Ummāl fī Sunan al-Aqwāl wal-Af'āl*.

> "I fear that he (the Prophet) will not give her to me in marriage!"

'Umar said:

> "If he does not give her to you in marriage, then who will she marry? Besides, you are the nearest of God's creatures to him ...."

'Alī ﵇ had never mentioned his desire to marry Sayyidah Fāṭimah ﵍ for two reasons: first, his shyness to do so in front of the Prophet, and second because of his challenging economic condition. Imām 'Alī ﵇ owned no worldly belongings, not even a house or a piece of land. So how could he get married? And where would he live with his wife? Besides, Sayyidah Fāṭimah ﵍ is not a woman who can be neglected or looked down upon.

The purpose of marriage in Islām is to establish a family. The question of sex is not the primary goal; instead, it is a matter included and taken care of by marriage. In addition, Islām came to break the chains and the blind adoption of concepts that deprived many people of marriage by making it difficult for them to gain partners, thus preventing them from a fundamental and natural necessity needed for the survival of mankind. Therefore, thanks to Islām, marriage became a straightforward affair. The new religion eradicated tribalism and race. The Prophet ﷺ, who was still going through the stage of building Islām, wanted to set an example through his words and deeds in this field, for he is the exemplar and model for the people. So, he fought ignorant and infidel customs through his words and actions.

Imām 'Alī ﵇ finally approached the Prophet ﷺ and asked for Sayyidah Fāṭimah's ﵍ hand in marriage. The Messenger ﷺ, who has absolute guardianship over all Muslim men and women, including his daughter, would not announce his agreement to the wedding without Sayyidah Fāṭimah's ﷺ consent. By this action, he ﷺ clarified that getting the daughter's permission for marriage is inevitable because she is the one to live with the man and share his life. Indeed, giving a girl in marriage to someone without her prior approval or permission violates her honor, degrades her personality, disrupts her soul, and is a practical declaration to her that she is like an animal that is sold or given as a gift to anyone without the right to state her opinion.

The Prophet ﷺ in reply to ʿAlī ﷺ said:

> "Ah, many men have asked before you, and she has rejected them —her resentment to marry them was clear on her face. Yet, wait until I bring you the answer."

The Prophet ﷺ left ʿAlī ﷺ waiting for the answer. The Prophet ﷺ informed his daughter that ʿAlī ﷺ wished to marry her. Sayyidah Fāṭimah ﷺ did not need to ask about ʿAlī's occupation, manners, age, and other traits because she knew all about his talents, excellent characteristics, and long-standing service to Islām. It is for this reason that the Prophet ﷺ only said to her,

> "Sayyidah Fāṭimah, you know ʿAlī b. Abū Ṭālib's relationship to us, his devotion and faithfulness to Islām. I asked God to give you in marriage to the best of His creatures and the most beloved to Him, and he (ʿAlī) has declared his wish to marry you; what do you say?"

Sayyidah Fāṭimah ﷺ did not reply, nor did she show a sign of rejection or resentment, so he ﷺ stood up and said:

> "God is the Greatest! Her silence is her approval."

The Prophet ﷺ considered Sayyidah Fāṭimah's ؏ silence as her consent and approval of the marriage because a shy, virgin girl is not expected to declare her agreement openly. Yes, disagreement and rejection of marriage can be openly expressed by her. However, shyness prevents a girl from declaring her wish to marry a man, but it does not stop her from rejecting it.

The Prophet ﷺ went back to the waiting ʿAlī ؑ and informed him of Sayyidah Fāṭimah's ؏ approval of the marriage. He also inquired about his preparedness to fulfill the requirements for the wedding because, legally and traditionally, there has to be a dowry. Mainly because this marriage would be remembered and be of significant influence to future generations; thus, it was essential to observe every element and event that would play a part in this marriage within the guidelines of simplicity and modesty.

The Prophet ﷺ said to ʿAlī ؑ:

> "Do you possess anything (which you can pay for the dowry) to marry Sayyidah Fāṭimah?'

Imām ʿAlī ؑ answered:

> "May my parents be your sacrifice. By God, there is not a thing of my affairs hidden from you; I own my sword, shield, and the camel, which I use for irrigation."

Indeed, this was everything that ʿAlī ؑ possessed when he was about to get married.

The Messenger ﷺ open-heartedly listened to 'Alī ﷺ and said,

> "'Alī you cannot do without your sword, for you have to struggle with it and defend yourself against the enemies of God. As for your camel, you need it to irrigate palm trees and support your family, and you need it to travel. But I accept the shield as a dowry from you; thus, sell it and bring me the money."

'Alī ﷺ had won this shield from the booty of the battle of Badr. It was given to him by the Messenger ﷺ, who named it al-Hādemah; it destroyed all the swords that stuck it.

The Commander of the Faithful ﷺ sold the shield for 480 or 500 dirhams and brought the money to the Prophet ﷺ. They both agreed that this money would be the dowry of the most honorable girl and the most exalted female of the universe. Yes, Sayyidah Fāṭimah ﷺ was the Mistress of the world's women and the daughter of the Master of Prophets and Messengers ﷺ, the best of God's creatures.

Yet, he gave his daughter in marriage in return for such a modest dowry to teach other Muslim girls not to refrain from marriage because of modest dowries. We can learn many other lessons from Sayyidah Fāṭimah's ﷺ marriage, but this is not the place to mention them.

Despite Sayyidah Fāṭimah's ﷺ modest marriage on Earth, God ﷻ gave her an honorable gift. He ﷻ gave her in marriage to 'Alī b. Abū Ṭālib ﷺ, before the Messenger ﷺ himself did so. This is not abnormal, for God had given women much lower than Sayyidah Fāṭimah ﷺ in marriage to the Prophet ﷺ. For example, He gave

Zaynab b. Jahsh to the Prophet ﷺ in marriage as stated in the Noble Qur'ān.

﴿فَلَمَّا قَضَىٰ زَيْدٌ مِّنْهَا وَطَرًا زَوَّجْنَاكَهَا لِكَيْ لَا يَكُونَ عَلَى الْمُؤْمِنِينَ حَرَجٌ فِي أَزْوَاجِ
أَدْعِيَائِهِمْ إِذَا قَضَوْا مِنْهُنَّ وَطَرًا ۚ وَكَانَ أَمْرُ اللَّهِ مَفْعُولًا﴾

﴿fa-lammā qaḍā zaydun minhā waṭaran zawwajnākahā li-kay lā yakūna ʿalā l-muʾminīna ḥarajun fī ʾazwāji ʾadʿiyāʾihim ʾidhā qaḍaw minhunna waṭaran wa-kāna ʾamru llāhi mafʿūlan﴾

﴿so when Zayd had got through with her, We wedded her to you, so that there may be no blame on the faithful in respect of the wives of their adopted sons, when the latter have got through with them, and God's command is bound to be fulfilled﴾[190]

Therefore, was it impossible for Sayyidah Fāṭimah's ؑ wedding to be celebrated in the exalted heavens and attended by the nearest angels to God ﷻ, as Prophetic traditions state? Indeed, this happened in tribute to Sayyidah Fāṭimah ؑ, her father ﷺ, her husband ؑ, and her future children ؑ, who are the authorities of God on His creatures.

The celebration occurred in the fourth Heaven near al-Bayt al-Maʿmūr (the constantly attended house of God). It was a unique event, the like of which the universe had never encountered before. Angels from all the Heavens gathered in the fourth Heaven and erected the minbar of Honor, made of light. Then God, The ﷻ, revealed to one of His angels, Rāḥīl ؑ, to ascend the minbar and praise and glorify His names as He deserves. Rāḥīl ؑ, who was the

---

[190] Sūrat al-Aḥzāb, Verse 37.

most eloquent of all angels, did what his Lord revealed to him and said:

"Praise be to God, since the creation of the first (creatures); He who is ever-lasting (even) after the cessation of all beings; We praise Him for making us spiritual angels, who are submitting to His Godship, and for making us grateful to Him for His benevolence on us. He safeguarded us from craving for lust and made our only pleasure and enjoyment to glorify and exalt Him. He Who extended His Mercy (upon everything); and gave His benevolence (to everyone). Exalted is His Name from the polytheism of polytheists of the dwellers of Earth, And Elevated by His Creatures from the fabrications of the atheists. God, The Omnipotent King, chose the one who was bestowed with unique Divine Honor and the worshipper of His Greatness, for His worshipper, the Mistress of women and the daughter of the best of prophets, the Master of all messengers and the Imām of the pious; so He brought into relations the Prophet with a man from his kin. One who is his believing companion and was prompt in answering his call — 'Alī the devout, with Sayyidah Fāṭimah the splendid and the daughter of the Messenger."

Then Jibrā'īl added the following words from God:

"Praise is My garment, Greatness is My Magnificence, All the creatures are My slaves, men, and women. I give Sayyidah Fāṭimah, My Worshipper in marriage, to 'Alī, My chosen worshipper. So bear witness, O My angels." [191]

---

[191] Majlisī, 'Allāmah Muḥammad Bāqir, *Biḥār al-Anwār*, Vol. 5.

A group of Sunnī scholars also reported this narration; among them are:

1. ʿAbd ur-Raḥman ash-Shāfiʿī reported[192] that Jābir b. ʿAbdullāh said: "Umm Ayman came to the Prophet crying; the Prophet asked her why she was crying. She replied: "A man from the Ansār just informed me that his daughter has just been married and that he sprinkled sweets and almonds on her. Thus, this reminded me that when Sayyidah Fāṭimah married ʿAlī, you did not sprinkle anything on her." Thereupon the Prophet ﷺ said: "By God Who sent me with honor and gifted me with the Message; when God gave Sayyidah Fāṭimah to ʿAlī in marriage, He ordered the nearest angels to surround the Throne-including Jibrāʾīl, Mīkāʾīl, and Isrāfīl. He also commanded birds to sing and ordered the tree of Tuba to sprinkle them with fresh pearls, white gems, green chrysolites, and red rubies."

According to another tradition, he said,

> "The marriage took place near the Lotus tree in the seventh Heaven, on the night of Ascension. (On that occasion) God revealed to the tree: 'Sprinkle all you bear on them.' So it sprinkled them with gems, jewelry, and corals."

192 ash-Shāfiʿī, ʿAbd ur-Raḥman, *Nuzhat al-Majālis*, Vol. 2, p. 223.

2. al-Ḥafīẓ Abū Nuʿaym reported[193] that ʿAbdullāh b. Masoud said:

   "...then God commanded the Tree of Paradise to bear gems and jewelry; He ordered it to sprinkle them over the angels. So whoever received more than the others on that day will be proud of it until the Day of Resurrection."

3. Khawārazmī, ʿAsqalānī, and Qundūzī mentioned this narration[194].

4. It has been reported[195] that Anas b. Mālik said: "The Prophet ﷺ was in the mosque when he said to ʿAlī: `Here is Jibrā'īl informing me that God gave Sayyidah Fāṭimah to you in marriage, and made forty thousand angels testify to her marriage. He also revealed to the Tree of Tuba to sprinkle them with gems, rubies, jewelry, and embellishments. When it had done this, the Ḥūrī rushed to collect these gems, rubies, jewelry, and embellishments to exchange them for gifts until the Day of Resurrection."

The Messenger ﷺ performed the engagement proceedings in the mosque while he was on the minbar, in the presence of the Muslims, to enact the practice of announcing and assigning witnesses to engagement proceedings and specified the amount of

---

[193] al-Isfahānī, Aḥmad, *Ḥilyat al-Awliya' wa-Ṭabaqāt al-Aṣfiya'*, Vol. 5, p. 59.

[194] al-Balkhī, Sulaymān b. Ibrāhīm al-Qundūzī, *Yanābīʿ al-Mawaddah lī-Dhawī l-Qūrbā*.

[195] ash-Shāfiʿī, ʿAbd ur-Raḥman, *Nuzhat al-Majālis*.

al-Suyūṭī, Jalāl al-Dīn, *Taḥdhīr al-Khawāṣ*.

dowry so that the Muslims could follow his practice in requesting modest dowries for marriages. He ﷺ said:

> "Avoid exaggeration in the (amounts of) dowries because this causes enmity (between you)."

The Prophet ﷺ also assigned the desirable practice of limiting dowry to five hundred dirhams. He and the Holy Imāms of Ahl al-Bayt عليهم السلام never exceeded this amount of dowry in their marriages.

When ʿAlī عليه السلام had sold his sword, he brought the money to the Prophet ﷺ, who divided it into thirds: one-third was for household necessities, one-third was for perfumes and embellishments for the wedding, and the remaining one-third he gave to Umm Salamah, who was to give it back to ʿAlī عليه السلام to assist him in paying for food for the guests attending the ceremony.

Naturally, ʿAlī's عليه السلام marriage to Sayyidah Fāṭimah al-Zahrā' عليها السلام raised envy and enmity in the hearts of some men, especially those rejected by Sayyidah Fāṭimah عليها السلام and her father ﷺ when they had asked for her hand. So it was not strange to see some Qurayshī men come to the Prophet and say,

> "Surely you have taken a lowly dowry for Sayyidah Fāṭimah from ʿAlī."

The Prophet replied:

> "It was not I who gave (Sayyidah Fāṭimah to) ʿAlī in marriage, rather God did so on the night of ascension near the Lotus tree (in the seventh Heaven)..." [196]

---

[196] Ibid., Vol. 6.

He then added:

> "Verily I am a man just like you, I marry (from) your women and give you my (marriageable) women in marriage, save Sayyidah Fāṭimah, for her marriage was revealed in Heaven." [197]

The Prophet ﷺ gave Abū Bakr some money and asked him to accompany Bilāl and Salmān (or 'Ammār b. Yāsir) to buy some household necessities for Sayyidah Fāṭimah's house. The Prophet ﷺ said to Abū Bakr:

> "Buy some appropriate household necessities for my daughter with this money." Abū Bakr said: "He gave sixty-three dirhams, so we went to the market and bought the following:

1. Two mattresses made of Egyptian canvas. (One stuffed with fiber and the other with sheep wool)

2. A leather mat

3. A pillow made of skin, filled with palm tree fiber

4. A Khaybariyan cloak

5. An animal skin for water

6. Some jugs and jars also for water

7. A pitcher painted with tar

8. A thin curtain made of wool

---

[197] Ibn Ḥanbal, Aḥmad, *Musnad Aḥmad b. Ḥanbal*.

9. A shirt costing seven dirhams

10. A veil costing four dirhams

11. A black plush cloak

12. A bed embellished with ribbon

13. Four cushions made of skin imported from aṭ-Ṭā'if, stuffed with a good-smelling plant.

14. A mat from Ḥajar

15. A hand-mill

16. A special copper container used for dyestuff

17. A pestle for grinding coffee

18. A (water) skin

When Abū Bakr and the other companions had bought the above articles, they carried them to Umm Salamah's house. When the Prophet ﷺ saw them, he started kissing every article and supplicated to God, saying:

> "O God, bless them for they are people whose most their belongings are made of natural (simple) materials."

These were all the furnishings they purchased for the daughter of the best of all prophets and messengers. But indeed, marital happiness is not achieved by wealth and overspending, nor can expensive wardrobes, gems, golden ware, luxurious furniture, splendid palaces, or comfortable automobiles provide a person with marital happiness, contrary to most people's beliefs.

How many wealthy women dressed in expensive wardrobes and embellished themselves with gems and jewelry covering their necks, arms, and ears consider life an unbearable misery? On the contrary, how many women live in shacks, cook, bake bread, wash clothes, sweep floors, nurse their children, and struggle hard considering their simple lives, yet think of themselves as happy people and their houses as gardens of Eden?

This fact is also true for men. Yet, unfortunately, many young unmarried women hold the wrong view that marital happiness can only be found through wealth and luxuries. They consider simplicity a sign of misery and deprivation; therefore, these miserable youths remain unmarried, waiting for marital happiness to knock on their doors, accompanied by wealth and luxuries.

Sayyidah Fāṭimah's ﷺ Dowry

Although Sayyidah Fāṭimah's ﷺ dowry was modest, because of the Messenger's wish to set an example for the Muslims and other implicit reasons, Sayyidah Fāṭimah al-Zahrā' ﷺ did not ignore her greatness and exalted identity to get a fantastic gift for her wedding. Sayyidah Fāṭimah's drive for excellence and perfection motivated her to ask for the right of interceding if God willed for the sinners among the Muslims.

Aḥmad b. Yūsuf ad-Dimashqī reported[198]:

> "It was narrated that when she (Sayyidah Fāṭimah) learned about her marriage and that her dowry was a few dirhams, she said:
>
> > 'O Messenger of God, lay girls, take money for dowries; what is the difference between me and them (if my dowry was to be money too)? I kindly ask you to give it back and supplicate to God ﷻ to make my dowry the right to intercede for the sinners among Muslims (on the Day of Rising).'
>
> It was then that Jibrā'īl ﷺ descended with a label on which the following statement was written:
>
> > 'God ordained Sayyidah Fāṭimah al-Zahrā''s dowry to be interceding for the sinners among Muslims.'
>
> When Sayyidah Fāṭimah ﷺ was on her deathbed, she asked that the label be put on her chest under the coffin. Thus, it was done so. Sayyidah Fāṭimah ﷺ said:

---

[198] ad-Dimashqī, Aḥmad b. Yūsuf, *Akhbār al-Duwal wa Āthār al-Awwal.*

> "When I am raised on the Day of Resurrection, I will present this label with my hand to intercede for the sinners from among my father's nation."

The abovementioned narration illustrates the greatness, honor, and excellence Sayyidah Fāṭimah ﷺ enjoyed. The Messenger's ﷺ supplication was answered, so Sayyidah Fāṭimah ﷺ will present the label when it is most needed. Nasafī said: "Sayyidah Fāṭimah ﷺ asked the Prophet ﷺ that her dowry would be interceding for his nation on the day of the Resurrection. So when she passes the path, she will ask for her dowry."

It is worth mentioning that many narrations have been reported on the account of Ahl al-Bayt ﷺ to the effect that interceding is part of Sayyidah Fāṭimah al-Zahrā'"s ﷺ dowry.

Preparations for the Wedding

An unplanned period elapsed between the engagement and the wedding ceremony because Imām ʿAlī ﵇ was too shy to ask the Prophet ﷺ to assign a day for the wedding. At the same time, he wanted to protect Sayyidah Fāṭimah's ﵇ pride by refraining from asking ʿAlī to do so.

A month or more passed before Imām ʿAlī ﵇ said anything about the wedding. ʿAqīl (ʿAlī's brother) asked him about the reason for the delay in holding the wedding ceremony and encouraged him to prepare for the wedding and to ask the Prophet ﷺ to assign a date for it. Despite ʿAlī's ﵇ shyness, he accompanied ʿAqīl to the Prophet's ﷺ house to fulfill his wishes. On their way to the Prophet's ﷺ house, they met Umm Ayman, who, when told the reason for their visit, asked them to leave the matter to her. She then informed Umm Salamah and the Prophet's ﷺ wives who gathered in ʿĀ'isha's house, where the Prophet ﷺ was, and said,

> "May our parents be your sacrifice! We are gathered here regarding that. Had Sayyidah Khadījah been alive, this would have brought happiness to her life."

When hearing Sayyidah Khadījah's ﵇ name, the Prophet ﷺ cried and said,

> "Surely Sayyidah Khadījah believed me when men did not and helped establish God's religion, and granted me her belongings in its path. God ﷻ commanded me to bring the good news to Sayyidah Khadījah that (she has) a house in Paradise made of brocade and emeralds, where there is not roaring nor strain."

Umm Salamah said:

"May our parents be your sacrifice, O Messenger of God! Surely everything you have praised Sayyidah Khadījah for is true, but she departed to her Lord! May He bring happiness to her and gather us with her in the Paradise of His satisfaction and Mercy. Messenger of God! Your brother from among the world's people is also your cousin, 'Alī b. Abū Ṭālib wished that you specify a day for the wedding so that he may be united with his wife, Sayyidah Fāṭimah."

The Prophet answered:

"Why doesn't 'Alī ask me to do so?"

She replied:

"Shyness prevents him!'

He said:

"Umm Ayman, go call 'Alī for me."

When Umm Ayman came out, she found 'Alī waiting for the answer. Upon her request, he entered the house and shyly sat near the Prophet, who said to him:

"Do you wish to be wedded to your wife?"

'Alī replied:

"All right, it is to your honor. If you wish, the wedding can occur tonight or tomorrow night, if God wills."

The Prophet said:

> "So prepare a house for Sayyidah Fāṭimah."

ʿAlī then said:

> "The only house I can acquire is Ḥārithah b. al-Nuʿmān's."

The Prophet said:

> "Surely we are shy for Ḥārithah b. al-Nuʿmān, for we have taken most his houses!"'

When Ḥārithah b. al-Nuʿmān heard about this, he proceeded toward the Prophet ﷺ and said,

> "Messenger of God, I and my property belong to God and His Messenger. By God, there is nothing more beloved to me than that which you take; it surely is more desirable to me (that you take it) than if you leave it (for me)."

Ḥārithah b. al-Nuʿmān, motivated by his strong faith and belief in good deeds, granted ʿAlī ﵇ one of his houses. Imām ʿAlī ﵇ furnished one room by spreading sand on the floor and erecting a pole for hanging the water container. Besides some gifts that were given to him by some companions, he also purchased a jug and jar and laid a piece of wood between two walls for hanging clothes, placed a ram's skin on the floor, and put a pillow made of fiber on it.

The Prophet ﷺ ordered ʿAlī ﵇ to hold a dinner because God ﷻ is pleased with those who do so for the social good it does, such as bringing people together and implementing love and harmony among them.

It is noteworthy that Sayyidah Fāṭimah al-Zahrā' excelled in giving on the path of God; she possessed generosity that no other woman can claim to be equal to:

> "The Prophet had a new dress made for Sayyidah Fāṭimah (as a gift) for her wedding; she had just one old patched dress. On her wedding night, someone knocked on the door and said,
>
> > "I ask the household of Prophethood to give me an old dress."
>
> At first, Sayyidah Fāṭimah was going to give him her old dress, but then remembered the Qurʾānic verse:
>
> ﴿لَن تَنَالُوا الْبِرَّ حَتَّىٰ تُنفِقُوا مِمَّا تُحِبُّونَ ۚ وَمَا تُنفِقُوا مِن شَيْءٍ فَإِنَّ اللَّهَ بِهِ عَلِيمٌ﴾
>
> ⟨lan tanālū l-birra ḥattā tunfiqū mimmā tuḥibbūna wa-mā tunfiqū min shayʾin fa-ʾinna llāha bihi ʿalīm^un⟩
>
> ⟨You will never attain piety until you spend out of what you hold dear, and whatever you may spend of anything, God indeed knows it⟩[199]
>
> She then gave the poor man her new dress. Consequently, Jibrāʾīl descended and said,

---

[199] Sūrat Āl ʿImrān, Verse 92.

> "O Muḥammad! God sends Him peace upon you; He commanded me to greet Sayyidah Fāṭimah and (give her the gift He sent her) which is a dress from Paradise, made of silk brocade, etc."[200]

Returning to the feast, when the food was prepared, the meat cooked, the bread baked, and the dates and butter obtained, the Prophet started splitting the dates and mixing them with the butter to replace sweetmeat for the wedding. When everything was ready, he asked ʿAlī ﷺ to invite the people to the feast.

When ʿAlī ﷺ reached the Mosque, he found it crowded with people all were at the Mosque, from the poor immigrants who lived there to the Ansārs. ʿAlī's ﷺ generosity and noble-heartedness did not allow him to invite some people and exclude others, especially since everyone wanted to be invited to the Prophet's ﷺ daughter's ﷺ wedding feast.

ʿAlī's ﷺ belief in God's ﷻ power and the Prophet's ﷺ blessed heart motivated him to call out loud:

> "O people, answer the call for the feast of Sayyidah Fāṭimah b. Muḥammad."

Men and women from all around Madīnah gathered in the house. They ate, drank, and even took food to their homes. The blessings of the Prophet ﷺ were evident on that day, for not only the food was enough to feed everyone, but it did not decrease. The Prophet ﷺ asked for food containers to be brought and filled and

---

200 ash-Shāfiʿī, ʿAbd ur-Raḥman, *Nuzhat al-Majālis,* Vol. 2, p. 226, on the authority of Ibn al-Ṭāwūs.

sent to his wives and left a special container for Sayyidah Fāṭimah and her husband ﷺ.

By sunset, the wedding night had begun; it was time for Sayyidah Fāṭimah ﷺ to depart to her new home.

Everything went well, for the Prophet ﷺ had made all the preparations for the wedding. Despite the simplicity and modesty of her wedding, Sayyidah Fāṭimah's ﷺ marriage ceremony was surrounded by signs of greatness, excellence, and beauty. al-Haythamī wrote[201] that Jābir said:

> "We were present at Sayyidah Fāṭimah and 'Alī's ﷺ wedding ceremony, and indeed we have seen no ceremony better than that one..."

The Messenger of God ﷺ ordered his wives to embellish Sayyidah Fāṭimah ﷺ before the wedding; they perfumed and dressed her with jewelry. They all helped to ready Sayyidah Fāṭimah ﷺ; some combed her hair while others embellished and dressed her in the dress brought by Jibrā'īl ﷺ from Paradise.

God's Messenger ﷺ paid special attention to Sayyidah Fāṭimah al-Zahrā' ﷺ, which he did not give to his other (fostered) daughters. For while Sayyidah Fāṭimah ﷺ can not be compared to other women, the Prophet ﷺ would not treat his children unequally, proving yet again that Sayyidah Fāṭimah ﷺ was his only begotten daughter.

The night of Sayyidah Fāṭimah's ﷺ wedding arrived. Because every girl needs her mother on her wedding night, Sayyidah Fāṭimah ﷺ

---

201 'Alī al-Haythamī, *Majma' al-Zawā'id*.

missed Sayyidah Khadījah ‎ﷺ and felt like an orphan. With his noble and exceptional attention to Sayyidah Fāṭimah ‎ﷺ, the Prophet ﷺ wished to fill Sayyidah Khadījah's ‎ﷺ space; the Prophet called 'Alī ‎ﷺ and Sayyidah Fāṭimah ‎ﷺ, who proceeded towards him — Sayyidah Fāṭimah ‎ﷺ was in her long heavenly dress overtaken with shyness. He ﷺ brought his gray horse, asked Sayyidah Fāṭimah ‎ﷺ to ride it, and ordered Salmān to lead while he ﷺ followed them.

Yes, indeed, Sayyidah Fāṭimah's ‎ﷺ wedding was attended by heavenly creatures and people, for she is a human ḥūrī.

al-Khaṭīb al-Baghdādī[202] al-Ḥanafī[203], al-Dhahabī[204], Qaramānī[205], and Qundūzī[206] have narrated that Ibn 'Abbās said:

> "When Sayyidah Fāṭimah was taken to 'Alī's house on her wedding night, the Prophet proceeded her, Jibrā'īl was on her right, and Mīkā'īl on her left, and seventy thousand angels followed her. These angels praised and glorified God until dawn. The Hāshimīt men, 'Abd Muṭṭalib's daughters, and Muhājirūn and Ansār's women all accompanied Sayyidah Fāṭimah's caravan that night. The Prophet's wives joyfully led the caravan and were the first to enter the house. Upon

---

[202] al-Baghdādī, al-Khaṭīb, *Tārīkh al-Baghdādī*, Vol. 5, p. 7.

[203] al-Ḥanafī, Muḥammad b. Yūsuf al-Zarandī, *Naẓm Durar al-Simṭayn*.

[204] al-Dimashqī, Muḥammad b. Aḥmad, *Mīzān al-I'tidāl*.

[205] ad-Dimashqī, Aḥmad b. Yūsuf, *Akhbār al-Duwal wa Āthār al-Awwal*.

[206] al-Balkhī, Sulaymān b. Ibrāhīm al-Qundūzī, *Yanābī' al-Mawaddah lī-Dhawī l-Qūrbā*.

arriving, the Prophet placed Sayyidah Fāṭimah's hand in ʿAlī's hand and said:

"May God bless his Messenger's daughter;

ʿAlī, this is Sayyidah Fāṭimah; you are responsible for her (or I entrust her to you)

ʿAlī, what an excellent wife Sayyidah Fāṭimah is.

Sayyidah Fāṭimah, what an excellent husband ʿAlī is.

O God, bless them, bless their lives, and bless their children

O God, indeed they are the most beloved to me from among your creatures, so love them too, and assign for them a guardian

I place them and their progeny under Your protection from the cursed devil."

The Prophet then asked for a jug of water; he sipped a small amount of the water and, after gargling with it, placed it back in the jug. He then called for Sayyidah Fāṭimah, sprayed her head and shoulders with that water, and did the same thing to ʿAlī. After that, he ordered the women to leave the house. They all left except Asmāʾ b. ʿUmays. When he noticed that she had stayed behind, he exclaimed:

'Didn't I ask you to leave?'

She answered:

> 'Indeed, O Messenger of God! May my parents be your sacrifice; I did not intend to disobey you, but I promised Sayyidah Khadījah to take her place this night.'

The Prophet ﷺ was moved by this; he cried and said to Asmā':

> 'By God, is this the reason that made you stay behind?'

She said:

> 'Yes, by God!'

He ﷺ then said:

> 'Asmā', may God fulfill for you the needs of this world and the Hereafter.'

The Year of Her Marriage

Opinions of historians and narrators differ from one to another regarding the year of Sayyidah Fāṭimah al-Zahrā'’s ﷺ marriage.

> "Sayyidah Fāṭimah's marriage took place on the night of the 21st of Muharram, 3 A.H."[207]

al-Miṣbāḥ:

> "Dhū al-Ḥijjah first or sixth."

and al-Āmalī:

> "Her marriage took place sixteen days after the death of Ruqayyah, ʿUthmān's wife, after he returned from Badr. This means that it took place at the beginning of Shawwal."

Ambiguous Findings Asmā' b. Umays and Umm Salamah under the Spotlight

Asmā' was Jaʿfar b. Abū Ṭālib's wife. It is a fact that he had immigrated to Abyssinia with his wife and a group of Muslims several years before Hijrah. It is also known that Jaʿfar returned to Madīnah after the Muslims conquered Khaybar in 5 A.H. These findings are unanimously agreed upon by all historians.

We have seen that Asmā' was present when Sayyidah Khadījah passed away in Makkah and at Sayyidah Fāṭimah's wedding ceremony, according to many narrations, which state her name as Asmā' b. ʿUmays al-Khathʿamiya.

---

[207] Sayyid b. Ṭāwūs, *Iqbāl al-Aʿmāl*, on the authority of Shaykh Mufīd.

The following historians state that she was present at Sayyidah Fāṭimah's wedding ceremony: 'Alī b. 'Isā Hakkārī al-Irdibillī[208], Ḥaḍramī[209], Aḥmad b. Ḥanbal[210], al-Haythamī[211], Nisā'ī[212], and Muḥib al-Dīn al-Ṭabarī[213]. They depend on the narrations of Abū 'Abbās Khawārazmī from al-Ḥusayn b. 'Alī, Sayyid Jalāl al-Dīn Abū al-Ḥamīd b. Fakhr al-Mūsawī, and Dūlābī from Imām Bāqir and his father.

How can we comprehend the contradiction between these narrations and the fact that Sayyidah Fāṭimah's marriage took place after the battle of Badr, or even Uḥud in 2 A.H.?

This historical problem has not yet been solved despite the various attempts made by 'Allamah Majlisī[214].

More interesting is the following statement that was mentioned on the authority of Mujāhid[215] in which Asmā' was said to have been present at 'Ā'isha's marriage. In the statement, it was claimed that Asmā' said:

---

[208] Al-Irdibillī, 'Alī b. 'Isā Hakkārī, *Kashf al-Ghumma fī Ma'rifat al-A'imma*.

[209] Ḥaḍramī, *Rashfat al-Ṣādī*, p. 10.

[210] Ibn Ḥanbal, Aḥmad, *Musnad Aḥmad b. Ḥanbal*.

[211] 'Alī al-Haythamī, *Majma' al-Zawā'id*.

[212] al-Nasā'ī, Aḥmad b. Shu'ayb, *Khaṣā'iṣ Amīr al-Mu'minīn*, p. 31.

[213] al-Ṭabarī, Muḥib al-Dīn, *Dhakha'ir al-'Uqbī*.

[214] Majlisī, 'Allamah Muḥammad Bāqir, *Biḥār al-Anwār*, Vol. 10.

[215] Qummī, Shaykh 'Abbās, *Safīnat al-Biḥār*.

"I was the one who, in the company of other women, prepared 'Ā'isha and brought her to the Messenger of God. By God, he had not but a cup of buttermilk, which he drank and gave to 'Ā'isha, but she was too shy to take it, so I said to her:

> 'Do not reject it; it is from the hand of the Prophet.'

She then took it, and after drinking some, he ﷺ said:

> `Give some to your friends.'

But the women did not desire any. The Prophet ﷺ then said:

> 'Do not gather hunger and lying together.'

I said:

> `Messenger of God, is it considered lying if one of us says she does not like something?'

The Prophet replied:

> `Surely lying is counted (against the person) up to where even a small lie is recorded too."

As we said, this narration shows that Asmā' was present at 'Ā'isha's marriage, which took place before Sayyidah Fāṭimah's.

It is unanimously narrated that Asmā' was present when Imām Ḥusayn ؑ was born in 4 or 5 A.H. All these events are known to have taken place before conquering Khaybar and Ja'far b. Abū Ṭālib's return to Madīnah.

To clarify the issue concerning Asmā''s presence at Sayyidah Fāṭimah's wedding[216]:

> "This is an authentic finding, exactly as Ibn Battah narrated. But mentioning Asmā' b. 'Umays 's name is not accurate, for this Asmā' is Ja'far b. Abū Ṭālib's wife... Asmā', who attended Sayyidah Fāṭimah's wedding, is Asmā' b. Yazīd b. Sakan al-Ansārī. As for Asmā' b. 'Umays, she remained in the company of her husband in Abyssinia until he returned to Madīnah, the day Khaybar was conquered in 7 A.H. While Sayyidah Fāṭimah's marriage took place several days after the battle of Badr."

Regardless of this, I say that the narrations clearly state Asmā' b. 'Umays's name; therefore, this justification cannot be considered—besides, Asmā' b. Yazīd was an Ansāriyan woman and could not have been present at Sayyidah Khadījah's death. No other historian did not mention her presence in Makkah at that time.

In light of these findings, I deem it necessary to clarify that Asmā' b. 'Umays had immigrated with her husband to Abyssinia but repeatedly returned to Makkah and Madīnah. This becomes clear, especially when we realize that the distance between Jeddah and Abyssinia is limited to that of the width of the Red Sea, which is not so difficult for a journey. This historical confusion arose because her repeated trips were not adequately recorded, just as Abū Dharr's immigration to Abyssinia with Ja'far was not given enough attention.

---

[216] al-Shāfi'ī, Muḥammad b. Yūsuf al-Kanjī, *Kifāyat al-Ṭālib.*

Also found in Majlisī, 'Allamah Muḥammad Bāqir, *Biḥār al-Anwār*, Vol. 10.

This conclusion is supported by the following tradition[217]:

"Ibn Bābawayh said:

'The Prophet ordered 'Abd al-Muṭṭalib's daughters... (until he said): The Prophet, Hamza, 'Aqīl, Ja'far, and Ahl al-Bayt followed the caravan."

It is clearly stated in this narration that Ja'far, Asmā''s husband, was present, which, as we said, supports our conclusion. Besides this, the Prophet's immigration to Madīnah took place after Sayyidah Khadījah's death, and Ja'far traveled to Abyssinia twice. The second journey occurred before Hijrah and Sayyidah Khadījah's death. Thus, it becomes easy to understand how Asmā' was present at Sayyidah Khadījah's death.

There is confusion in historical findings regarding the reason for the presence of Umm Salamah's name in the events preceding Sayyidah Fāṭimah's marriage; i.e., the Prophet leaving some of Sayyidah Fāṭimah's dowry with her, and the women's consultation with her-although he married her in 4 A.H. In comparison, Sayyidah Fāṭimah's marriage took place in 2 A.H. Thus, the question arises as to what role she played in these events even though she was not yet married to the Prophet?

Two probable answers can be given to this question.

First, Perhaps there was a mistake in recording the year she married the Prophet. But this is based on something other than historical or scientific findings and, therefore, cannot be considered.

---

[217] Majlisī, 'Allamah Muḥammad Bāqir, *Biḥār al-Anwār*, Vol. 1, quoting *Mawlid Sayyidah Fāṭimah*.

Second: Since Lady Umm Salamah was the Prophet's ﷺ cousin, it was expected of her to take part in different stages of the wedding and to keep part of Sayyidah Fāṭimah's ﷺ dowry in her possession according to the Prophet's ﷺ wish.

I prefer the second opinion. Yet I leave it to God, for He is the Omniscient.

Sayyidah Fāṭimah's عليها السلام House

The contemporary civilized world realizes the importance of highlighting certain spots and structures connected to identified noble people or valuable entities. Thus, laws related to this matter have been legislated, such as diplomatic immunity for specific individuals and buildings and laws that regulate the use of public places, universities, temples, and so on, that are related to science, religion, and culture.

The importance of these actions and laws was known to God ﷻ and His chosen worshippers from the beginning. Rules and regulations that govern entering mosques, especially the Sacred Mosque in Makkah, such as preventing certain groups of people like the infidels, the junub, and menstruating women from entering them, reflect this. Other examples of such laws are the necessity to keep these places pure, respecting the sanctity of mosques, and forbidding hunting in and around Makkah during certain periods.

Sayyidah Fāṭimah's عليها السلام house is certainly one of these places, which is surrounded by sanctity, holiness, and exaltation. It was built on respect, honor, and righteousness. Those who realize know the value of her house.

ʿAllamah Majlisī رحمه الله reported on the authority of Anas b. Mālik that Buraydah said:

> "God's Messenger read the verse:
>
> ﴿فِي بُيُوتٍ أَذِنَ اللَّهُ أَنْ تُرْفَعَ وَيُذْكَرَ فِيهَا اسْمُهُ يُسَبِّحُ لَهُ فِيهَا بِالْغُدُوِّ وَالْآصَالِ﴾
>
> *﴿fī buyūtin ʾadhina llāhu ʾan turfaʿa wa-yudhkara fīhā smuhū yusabbiḥu lahū fīhā bi-l-ghuduwwi wa-l-ʾāṣāli*[1]*﴾*

﴾In houses God has allowed to be raised and wherein His Name is celebrated, He is glorified therein, morning and evening,﴿[218]

A man then exclaimed:

"Whose houses are these, O Messenger of God?" The Prophet ﷺ answered: "Prophet's houses."

Abū Bakr said:

"Messenger of God, is this one of these houses (He meant Sayyidah Fāṭimah's house)?"

The Prophet ﷺ replied:

"Yes, it is among the best of them."

Ibn ʿAbbās also said:

"I was in the Prophet's mosque when someone read:

'In houses which God hath permitted to be raised in honor;...'

So I said:

'Messenger of God, which houses?'

---

[218] Sūrat al-Nūr, Verse 36.

He said:

'Prophet's houses,' and pointed to Sayyidah Fāṭimah's house."

It has been narrated[219] that 'Abdullāh b. Ja'far al-Anṣārī said:

"Once, the Prophet of God proceeded towards Sayyidah Fāṭimah's house while I was with him; when we reached the door, he pushed the door (slightly) and said:

'As-salāmu 'alaykum'

Sayyidah Fāṭimah answered:

"Alayk as-Salām, Messenger of God.'

The Prophet then said:

'May I come in?'

She said:

'I do not have my veil on, O Messenger of God.'

He said:

'Sayyidah Fāṭimah, cover your head with your cloak.'

---

[219] Kulaynī, Shaykh Muḥammad b. Ya'qūb, *al-Kāfī*.

When she had done so, he said:

> 'As-salāmu 'alaykum.'

She answered:

> "Alayk as-Salām, Messenger of God.'

He repeated the request to enter the house with me, and she permitted us."

Sayyidah Fāṭimah's ﷺ Marital Life

Sayyidah Fāṭimah al-Zahrā' ﷺ moved from the home of Prophethood to the house of Imāmate, successorship, and guardianship. This turn in Sayyidah Fāṭimah's ﷺ life allowed her to become the companion of the father of the Imāms.

As days passed, Sayyidah Fāṭimah's ﷺ life became more beautiful, for she lived in an atmosphere of sanctity and chasteness, surrounded by modesty and humbleness. She aided her husband in worldly and religious affairs and cooperated with him to achieve his goals. The ideological tranquility they both enjoyed and the respect and glorification they held for each other perfected this harmony. Sayyidah Fāṭimah ﷺ realized the great rank her husband enjoyed. She respected him in the best manner as a Muslim woman should respect her Imām — for she recognized that 'Alī ﷺ was:

> The dearest person to God's Messenger ﷺ;
>
> The holder of the great guardianship;
>
> The possessor of absolute Imāmate;
>
> The Prophet's ﷺ brother, successor, and heir; The possessor of excellent talents;
>
> His long-standing service to Islām was also apparent to everyone.
>
> Likewise, 'Alī ﷺ respected Sayyidah Fāṭimah ﷺ, not only because she was his wife but also because she was:
>
> The most beloved to God's Messenger ﷺ;
>
> The mistress of all women;

And her sanctity was part of the Prophet's ﷺ.

Indeed, Sayyidah Fāṭimah ؑ enjoyed noble traits, which had any woman held, even one of them, she would be worthy of respect and exaltation.

Given such characteristics, you can imagine the tremendous marital happiness ʿAlī and Sayyidah Fāṭimah ؑ enjoyed. We can also realize that poverty or material deprivation did not disturb their life.

Imām ʿAlī ؑ said[220]:

"By God, I never angered Sayyidah Fāṭimah, or forced her to do something (she did not like), up to the day she died; nor did she ever anger or disobey me. When I looked at her, it would remove depression and sadness from my (heart)."

al-ʿAyyāshī reported[221] that Imām Bāqir ؑ said:

"Sayyidah Fāṭimah vouched to take care of the household work, make the dough, bake bread, and clean the house; in return, ʿAlī vouched to take care of the outside work (such as) gathering firewood and bringing food."

It is not precisely known how long ʿAlī ؑ and Sayyidah Fāṭimah ؑ lived in Ḥārithah b. al-Nuʿmān's house, but it is a fact that God's Messenger ﷺ constructed a home for them, which had a door to the mosque just like his own house.

---

[220] Majlisī, ʿAllamah Muḥammad Bāqir, *Biḥār al-Anwār*, on the authority of Ibn Shahrāshūb, Muḥammad b. ʿAlī, *Manāqib Āl Abī Ṭālib*.

[221] al-ʿAyyāshī, Muḥammad b. Masʿūd, *Tafsīr al-ʿAyyāshī*.

Historical Distortions Regarding Imām ʿAlī's ﷺ Right

We have previously spoken of the unjustified slandering and distortion of ʿAlī ﷺ and his noble life with Sayyidah Fāṭimah ﷺ We have also stated that Imām ʿAlī's ﷺ marriage to Sayyidah Fāṭimah ﷺ caused many people to show their hidden resentment and envy of them, by following every possible means to disturb Sayyidah Fāṭimah's life with her husband.

Among the many fabricated stories told against Imām ʿAlī ﷺ was that he had asked for Abū Jahl's (the chief of infidels) daughter's hand in marriage. When this news reached Sayyidah Fāṭimah ﷺ, she rushed to her father, who found out the falsity of the story.

Yet, let us review how some writers used this story to put down the Commander of the Faithful ﷺ and their attempt to tarnish his reputation.

An Egyptian writer, for instance, considered this story to be undoubtedly authentic and wrote the following[222]:

> "ʿAlī intended to marry a second wife besides Sayyidah Fāṭimah... without bearing in mind that the daughter of the Prophet of Islām would resent such action."

The invalidity of this statement is evident, for there is not a man in the world who does not realize that his wife prefers to be the only woman he marries.

---

222 *The Prophet's Daughters*, p.167.

The writer adds:

> "It would have been better if 'Alī had been satisfied with one wife,"

and filled up the pages of her book trying to show Abū Jahl's evil deeds and his long-standing enmity with Islām. She then compared the Prophet's daughter and Abū Jahl's daughter, intending to show the disadvantages of the fabricated would-be marriage.

Strangely enough, the writer also made clear her resentment and disapproval of fanatic Christian Orientalists who distorted the history of Islām, especially the famous Christian missionary La Manze. Yet, unfortunately, she was heedless of the need to verify such a story and considered its revelation undisputed. So, she used her imagination and fictitious writing style for this story, just as fable writers would.

Sayyid Ḥasan al-Amīn refuted such a story[223]:

> "It has been written[224] that 'Alī wanted to marry Abū Jahl's daughter and that the Prophet was angered by this act and ascended the minbar to speak with resentment and rejection about this matter."

The book also elaborates on the story in such a manner, which not only discredits 'Alī and Sayyidah Fāṭimah but also the Prophet himself.

---

223 al-Amīn, Sayyid Ḥasan, *The Shī'ī Islamic Encyclopedia*, Vol. 3.

224 al-Ṭabarī, Muḥib al-Dīn, *Dhakha'ir al-'Uqbī*.

This story makes Muḥammad appear as someone who refuses to practice what he preaches or does not accept to apply the Islamic law to himself and those related to him while requesting others to abide by it. Because he deems it lawful for others to marry more than one wife but refuses this law for his daughter... This, indeed, is a disastrous fabrication against the Prophet that the enemies of Islām could insert in the pages of our history books, depending on miscreant narrators who report such stories without reflecting upon them.

The story also defames ʿAlī ؑ by showing him as someone who angered both Sayyidah Fāṭimah ؑ and her father and defames Sayyidah Fāṭimah ؑ for refusing to practice God's commands, which He revealed to her father.

I shall not verify the veracity of the authority on which the narration was based, for it within is its sophistry. Yet, it is inevitable to ask: Why have the narrators, who fabricated this story, insisted on saying that he ؑ wanted to marry Abū Jahl's daughter, not any other woman? Why did they not claim that ʿAlī ؑ attempted to marry another woman? Surely, Abū Jahl's daughter did not enjoy beauty and perfection, which no other Arab girl enjoyed!

The fact is that they wanted their defamation of ʿAlī ؑ to be graver and more effective, for, in their story, ʿAlī ؑ specifically chose the daughter of the chief of the enemies of Islām.

This plot exposed itself and those who perpetuated it when they praised themselves while discrediting Muḥammad ﷺ, his daughter ؑ, and his cousin ؑ. They claimed in the same story that he mentioned his other son-in-law, who is a young man from Banī ʿAbd Shams, and praised him as "a noble son-in-law"; they claim the Prophet ﷺ said:

"He, the young man from Banī 'Abd Shams was truthful in his speech and executed his promises to me."

They want us to believe that the Prophet ﷺ praised his Umayyad son-in-law (the Umayyad belonged to the tribe of Banī 'Abd Shams), which means that he was trying to discredit his first son-in-law ['Alī ؑ] who, according to the story, lied to the Prophet ﷺ and violated his promises to him by being an unfaithful husband to his daughter.

Another aim for fabricating this story was to divert the attention from the actual people who angered Sayyidah Fāṭimah ؑ and put 'Alī ؑ under the spotlight as the one who did so. For this reason, they mentioned the following tradition at the story's beginning:

"The Prophet ﷺ said:

"Sayyidah Fāṭimah is part of me, discomforts me that which discomforts her, and harms me that which harms her."

They interpret it as:

The meaning of this tradition is that God ﷻ prohibited 'Alī ؑ from marrying another woman besides Sayyidah Fāṭimah ؑ, which would harm God's Messenger ﷺ.

Imām Ḥasan عليه السلام is Born

When Sayyidah Fāṭimah عليها السلام was twelve, she became pregnant with Imām Ḥasan عليه السلام. Thus, the light of Imāmate was carried on from ʿAlī عليه السلام to Sayyidah Fāṭimah عليها السلام. The day the child was to be born was approaching; the Prophet ﷺ had to go out of town, but before leaving, he ﷺ made several instructions about the would-be born child-including the order not to wrap the new baby in a yellow cloth.

On Ramaḍān 15, 3 A.H., Sayyidah Fāṭimah عليها السلام gave birth to her first son. On that great day, Asmāʾ b. ʿUmays was present with Sayyidah Fāṭimah عليها السلام. The women who attended the event unintentionally wrapped al-Ḥasan عليه السلام in a yellow cloth, unaware of the Prophet's ﷺ request.

When the Prophet ﷺ returned, he said:

> "Bring me my son; what have you named him?"

After al-Ḥasan was born, Sayyidah Fāṭimah asked ʿAlī عليه السلام to name the baby, but ʿAlī said:

> "I would not name him before God's Prophet".

When the Prophet ﷺ saw that al-Ḥasan عليه السلام was wrapped in a yellow cloth, he said:

> "Didn't I tell you not to wrap him in a yellow cloth?"

He then threw the yellow cloth away and wrapped the baby in a white one. When the Prophet ﷺ inquired about the name of the child, ʿAlī عليه السلام answered:

> "I would not name him before you."

The Prophet ※ replied:

"I, too, would not name him before my Lord, ※."

At that moment, God ※ revealed to Jibrā'īl ※,

'A son was born to Muḥammad, therefore descend and give him My blessings and congratulate him and say:

"Surely 'Alī is to you as Hārūn was to Mūsā, so give him (the newborn baby) the name of Hārūn's son:"'

When Jibrā'īl ※ revealed the message to the Prophet ※, he asked:

"What was Hārūn's son's name?"

Jibrā'īl ※ said:

"Shubbar."

The Prophet ※ then said:

"My tongue is Arabic."

Jibrā'īl ※ said:

"Name him al-Ḥasan."

Hence, the Prophet ※ gave him the name al-Ḥasan ※ and made Adhān in his right ear and Iqāmah in his left ear. On the seventh day, he ※ sacrificed two rams from which he gave the midwife a thigh and a dinar; he then shaved the baby's head and gave the weight of his hair in silver as charity. Finally, the Prophet ※ wiped the baby's head with "Khalou, " a special perfume made of saffron and other substances.

At that time in history, it was customary to cover newborn babies' heads with blood; with this in mind, the Prophet ﷺ told Asmā':

> "Asmā', using blood is an act performed by the ignorant."

He would embrace al-Ḥasan ﷷ and put his tongue in the baby's mouth, which would suckle it.

The Birth of Imām Ḥusayn عليه السلام

Six months after al-Ḥasan عليه السلام was born, Sayyidah Fāṭimah عليها السلام became pregnant with her second child.

Sayyidah Fāṭimah عليها السلام started noticing the signs that childbearing was near, but the Prophet ﷺ had already foretold of Imām Ḥusayn's عليه السلام birth.

Imām Ṣādiq عليه السلام said:

> "Once, Umm Ayman's neighbors came to the Prophet and said:
>
>> "Messenger of God, Umm Ayman did not sleep last night because of crying; she surely cried until morning. "
>
> The Prophet summoned her and said,
>
>> "Umm Ayman, your neighbors say that you spent the night crying. May God not cause your eyes to cry. What made you cry?"
>
> She answered:
>
>> "Messenger of God, I had a fearful dream which caused me to cry all night."
>
> The Prophet said:
>
>> "Tell me your dream, for surely God and His Messenger are most knowledgeable.

She said:

> "Last night, I saw a dream as if one of your limbs was thrown in my house."

The Messenger of God said:

> "Your eyes have slept, but you visioned a good thing. Umm Ayman, Sayyidah Fāṭimah will give birth to al-Ḥusayn, and you will bring him to me. So one of my limbs will be in your house."

When al-Ḥusayn ﷺ was born, Umm Ayman brought him to the Prophet ﷺ who said:

> "Both the carrier and he who is being carried are welcome. Umm Ayman, this is the interpretation of your dream."

Umm al-Faḍl, al-'Abbās's wife, had a similar dream.

Ṣafīyya b. 'Abd Muṭṭalib, Asmā' b. 'Umays and Umm Salamah were present when Imām Ḥusayn ﷺ was born. When the Prophet ﷺ asked Ṣafīyya (his aunt) to bring him the newborn child, she said:

> "We have not cleaned him yet."

When the Prophet ﷺ heard this, he said:

> "You clean him? Surely God ﷻ has cleaned and purified him."

After al-Ḥusayn ﷺ was born, Jibrā'īl ﷺ again descended to the Prophet ﷺ and revealed to him to give the new baby the name al-

Ḥusayn ﷵ. al-Ḥusayn is the Arabic version of the old Hebrew name Shabbīr, which was Hārūn's ﷵ second son's name. When Jibrā'īl ﷵ descended to the Prophet ﷺ, scores of angels accompanied him to congratulate and console the Prophet for Ḥusayn's ﷵ birth and expected martyrdom.

Imām Ḥusayn ﷵ was not nursed by any woman, including his mother ﷵ; instead, he suckled the Prophet's tongue until he grew old enough to eat. Because of this, his characteristics were precisely like the Prophet ﷺ.

Seven days after the birth, the Messenger of God ﷺ shaved Ḥusayn's ﷵ head and gave the weight of his hair as charity for him.

The Birth of Sayyidah Zaynab ﷺ

Sayyidah Zaynab ﷺ was (accurately) the third child born to Sayyidah Fāṭimah al-Zahrā' ﷺ. She was born directly after Imām Ḥusayn ﷺ, despite the false claim of some historians who hold the opinion that Zaynab ﷺ was born after the miscarriage, which Sayyidah Fāṭimah ﷺ had and resulted in the martyrdom of Muḥsin. These historians are motivated by their desire to divert attention from the merciless attack on Sayyidah Fāṭimah's ﷺ house, which not only resulted in Muḥsin's martyrdom but also the eventual death of Sayyidah Fāṭimah ﷺ herself.

Among these writers is the Egyptian Bint al-Shaṭi' who wrote[225]:

> "Zahrā', the Prophet's daughter was about to give birth to a new baby after bringing happiness unto Messenger's life by giving birth to his beloved sons: al-Ḥasan and al-Ḥusayn, and a third child, who was not destined to live and whose name was to be Muḥsin b. 'Alī..."[226]

Regardless of these unfounded claims, it has been established that Sayyidah Zaynab ﷺ was born in 5 A.H. and that she was the third child of the honorable 'Alawī household.

It is said that her grandfather, the Prophet ﷺ, named her Zaynab ﷺ, which is derived from two words: "Zayn" and "Ab," which together means "the embellishment of her father." Yet, Shaykh Muḥammad Jawād Mughnīyyah quoted the Egyptian newspaper[227] in his book[228] as saying:

---

225 Bint al-Shaṭi', *Baṭlat Karbalā.*

226 Majlisī, 'Allamah Muḥammad Bāqir, *Biḥār al-Anwār*, Vol. 10.

227 *al-Jamhūriyah*, October 31, 1972.

228 Mughnīyyah, Shaykh Muḥammad Jawād, *al-Ḥusayn Baṭala Karbalā'.*

"Zaynab was born in Shaʿbān 5 A.H. When her mother brought her to Imām ʿAlī ؏ and said:

"Name her"

He replied:

"I would not name her before God's Messenger."

The Prophet ﷺ was on a trip, and when he returned, he again refused to name her before her Lord. So Jibrāʾīl ؏ descended to inform the Prophet about God's blessings and said:

"The name of this baby is Zaynab; God chose this name for her."

Zaynab's ؏ history itself speaks of her honorable life and noble traits, as well as the miseries she encountered during her childhood, such as the death of her great grandfather, the martyrdom of her mother ؏, and the various inflictions which she lived through during the quarter of a century that her father, Imām ʿAlī ؏, was confined to his house because of his rights being usurped by others.

When Zaynab ؏ emigrated from Madīnah to Kufa, her father's ؏ capital, several misfortunes were destined for her, starting with the martyrdom of Imām ʿAlī ؏. Fierce battles between her brother, al-Ḥasan ؏, and Muʿāwiya, which resulted in the poisoning of the Imām ؏ followed this. After several years, Zaynab ؏ faced the greatest disaster in history when Imām Ḥusayn ؏, along with the prominent Hāshimīt men, was massacred at Karbalāʾ by the Umayyad. After slaughtering the men, they took Zaynab ؏ and the women to Sūrīyah, but she did not panic or give in to the enemy. From Sūrīyah, they sent her to Madīnah and then exiled her to Egypt to live the rest of her life.

Zaynab's ﷺ tomb[229] is well-known in Egypt today and is visited by believers worldwide.

229 There is disagreement about the location of Zaynab's tomb; most believe it to be in Sūrīyah.

Lady Umm Kulthūm

Sayyidah Fāṭimah's ﷺ household welcomed their second daughter and fourth child with happiness and glorification, as with the other children.

Lady Umm Kulthūm, like her sister, shared an honorable relationship with the Prophet, Imām ʿAlī, and Sayyidah Fāṭimah al-Zahrā' ﷺ in addition to her excellent upbringing.

She was also a victim of historical oppression and sorrowful inflictions and pains, which powerful men could barely handle.

Sayyidah Fāṭimah ﷺ in the Verse of Relationship

The verse of relationship, from the Qur'ān, says:

﴿قُل لا أَسأَلُكُم عَلَيهِ أَجرًا إِلَّا المَوَدَّةَ فِي القُربىٰ ۗ وَمَن يَقتَرِف حَسَنَةً نَزِد لَهُ فيها حُسنًا ۚ إِنَّ اللَّهَ غَفورٌ شَكورٌ﴾

﴿qul lā 'as'alukum 'alayhi 'ajran 'illā l-mawaddata fī l-qurbā wa-man yaqtarif ḥasanatan nazid lahū fīhā ḥusnan 'inna llāha ghafūrun shakūr^un^﴾

﴿Say, *'I do not ask you any reward for it except love of [my] relatives.' Whoever performs a good deed, We shall enhance for him its goodness. Indeed God is Forgiving, Appreciative*﴾[230]

This verse is an explicit command from God to His noble Prophet. It is:

> (Say) O Muḥammad, to your nation: (no reward do I ask of you for this) the message of Islām (except the love of those near of kin) to me. (i.e.) Ahl al-Bayt ﷺ.

It is unanimously agreed upon that the kin mentioned in this verse are Ahl al-Bayt ﷺ. There are many traditions narrated by both Shī'ī and Sunnī Scholars, which not only specify the kin mentioned

---

[230] Sūrat al-Shūrā, Verse 23.

in this verse but also state their names. Among the narrations mentioned by Sunnī scholars[231] are:

When this verse was revealed, someone said:

> "Messenger of God, who is the kin whose love is obligatory for us?"

The Prophet ﷺ replied:

> "'Alī, Sayyidah Fāṭimah, and her two children."

Ṭabarī and Ibn Ḥajar reported another narration similar to the one stated above; according to this narration, the Messenger of God ﷺ is reported to have said:

> "Surely God made it incumbent on you to love my kin, and I will ask you about them in the hereafter."

Moreover, the following narrations mentioned on the account of Ahl al-Bayt are a few of the many sayings of the Imāms in which they recite this verse as proof of the fact that loving them is a religious duty:

---

[231] al-Haythamī, Ibn Ḥajar, *al-Ṣawāʿiq al-Muḥriqah*.

Thaʿlabī.

al-Suyūṭī, Jalāl al-Dīn, *al-Durr al-Manthūr*.

al-Isfahānī, Aḥmad, *Ḥilyat al-Awliyaʾ wa-Ṭabaqāt al-Aṣfiyaʾ*.

al-Juwaynī, Ibrāhīm, *Farāʾid al-Simaṭayn*.

1. It is written[232] that Imām ʿAlī ﷺ said:

   "It is stated in Sūrat Fuṣṣilat that no one upholds our love save the faithful ones:"

﴿نَحْنُ أَوْلِيَاؤُكُمْ فِي الْحَيَاةِ الدُّنْيَا وَفِي الْآخِرَةِ ۖ وَلَكُمْ فِيهَا مَا تَشْتَهِي أَنفُسُكُمْ وَلَكُمْ فِيهَا مَا تَدَّعُونَ﴾

﴾*naḥnu 'awliyā'ukum fī l-ḥayāti d-dunyā wa-fī l-'ākhirati wa-lakum fīhā mā tashtahī 'anfusukum wa-lakum fīhā mā taddaʿūna*﴿

﴾*We are your friends in the life of this world and in the Hereafter, and you will have in it whatever your souls desire, and you will have in it whatever you ask for*﴿[233]

He then read:

﴿قُل لَّا أَسْأَلُكُمْ عَلَيْهِ أَجْرًا إِلَّا الْمَوَدَّةَ فِي الْقُرْبَىٰ ۗ وَمَن يَقْتَرِفْ حَسَنَةً نَّزِدْ لَهُ فِيهَا حُسْنًا ۚ إِنَّ اللَّهَ غَفُورٌ شَكُورٌ﴾

﴾*qul lā 'as'alukum ʿalayhi 'ajran 'illā l-mawaddata fī l-qurbā wa-man yaqtarif ḥasanatan nazid lahū fīhā ḥusnan 'inna llāha ghafūrun shakūrun*﴿

[232] al-Haythamī, Ibn Ḥajar, *al-Ṣawāʿiq al-Muḥriqah.*

[233] Sūrat Fuṣṣilat, Verse 31.

﴾Say, *'I do not ask you any reward for it except love of [my] relatives.' Whoever performs a good deed, We shall enhance for him its goodness. Indeed God is Forgiving, Appreciative*﴿[234]

2. It has also been reported[235] that Imām Ḥasan gave a speech in which he said:

   "Surely we are among the Ahl al-Bayt whose love and support were made incumbent (upon the faithful) by God."

   Imām Ḥasan then said the above verse.

3. Imām ʿAlī b. al-Ḥusayn (Zayn al-ʿĀbidīn) replied to the Syrian who said to him while he was a prisoner of the Umayyad in Dimashq (Damascus):

   "Praise be to God who killed you..etc."

   Then he said:

   "Haven't you read the [above-mentioned] verse?

4. Jābir b. ʿAbdullāh said[236]:

   "A beduin came to the Prophet and said:

   'Muḥammad, present Islām to me.'

[234] Sūrat al-Shūrā, Verse 23.

[235] al-Haythamī, Ibn Ḥajar, *al-Ṣawāʿiq al-Muḥriqah*.

[236] al-Shāfiʿī, Muḥammad b. Yūsuf al-Kanjī, *Kifāyat al-Ṭālib*, p. 31.

'The Prophet ﷺ replied:

`Bear witness that there is no God but God, to whom an associate does not exist; and that Muḥammad is the slave and Messenger of God. '

The Badawī said:

`Do you require any reward from me (for bringing me to Islām)?'

He ﷺ answered:

`No, save loving the nearest kin.'

The Badawī then asked,

`Mine or yours?'

The Prophet ﷺ said:

`My kin.'

The Badawī said:

`Let me pay allegiance to you, and may the curse of God be on those who do not love you and your kin.'

Thus he ﷺ said:

'Amīn.'"

Shaykh Amīnī listed forty-five (45) sources[237] stating that the verse was revealed regarding ʿAlī, Sayyidah Fāṭimah, al-Ḥasan, and al-Ḥusayn. The sources are Imām Aḥmad, Ibn al-Mundhir, Ibn Abū Ḥātim, Ṭabarī, Ibn Mardawayh, Thaʿlabī, Abū ʿAbdullāh al-Mullā, Abū Shaykh Nisāʾī, Wāḥidī, Abū Nuʿaym, Baghawī, Bazāz, Ibn al-Maghāzlī, Ḥaskānī, Muḥib al-Dīn, Zamakhsharī, Ibn Asākir, Abū al-Faraj, Hamūīnī, Nīsābūrī, Ibn Ṭalḥa, Rāzī, Abū al-Suʿūd, Abū Ḥayyān, Ibn Abi l-Ḥadīd, Bayḍawi, Nasafī, Haythamī, Ibn Ṣabbāgh, Kanjī, Manāwi, Qasṭallānī, Zarandi, Khāzin, Zarghanī, Ibn Ḥajar, Samhūdī, Suyūṭī, Safūrī, Saban, Shab Lanjī, Ḥaḍramī, and Nabawī.

---

[237] Amīnī, Shaykh ʿAbdul Ḥusayn Amīnī, *al-Ghadīr fī al-Kitāb wal-Sunna wal-Adab*, Vol. 3.

Sayyidah Fāṭimah عليها السلام in the Verse of Mubāhala

God ﷻ said:

﴿فَمَن حاجَّكَ فيهِ مِن بَعدِ ما جاءَكَ مِنَ العِلمِ فَقُل تَعالَوا نَدعُ أَبناءَنا وَأَبناءَكُم وَنِساءَنا وَنِساءَكُم وَأَنفُسَنا وَأَنفُسَكُم ثُمَّ نَبتَهِل فَنَجعَل لَعنَتَ اللَّهِ عَلَى الكاذِبينَ﴾

﴾fa-man ḥājjaka fīhi min baʿdi mā jāʾaka mina l-ʿilmi fa-qul taʿālaw nadʿu ʾabnāʾanā wa-ʾabnāʾakum wa-nisāʾanā wa-nisāʾakum wa-ʾanfusanā wa-ʾanfusakum thumma nabtahil fa-najʿal laʿnata llāhi ʿalā l-kādhibīna﴿

﴾Should anyone argue with you *concerning him, after the knowledge that has come to* you, say, *'Come! Let us call our sons and your sons, our women and your women, our souls and your souls, then let us pray earnestly and call down God's curse upon the liars.'﴿*[238]

This event is famous and is known to all Muslims. Muslim scholars all agree on the fact that it was revealed regarding the Christian delegation who came from Najrān to dispute the subject of ʿĪsā b. Maryam ﷺ with the Prophet ﷺ. Imām ʿAlī ﷺ mentioned[239] the event in the following manner:

A delegation of Najrāni Christians led by three prominent men, al-ʿAqīb, Muḥsin, and the Archbishop met along with two prominent Jews who came to the Prophet ﷺ. They intended to argue with him; the archbishop started:

"Abū al-Qāsim, who was Mūsā's father?"

---

[238] Sūrat Āl ʿImrān, Verse 61.

[239] Majlisī, ʿAllamah Muḥammad Bāqir, *Biḥār al-Anwār*, Vol. 6.

The Prophet ﷺ answered:

"ʿImrān."

The archbishop then said:

"Who was Yūsuf's father?"

The Prophet ﷺ answered:

"Yaʿqūb."

The archbishop continued:

"May I be your sacrifice; who is your father?"

The Prophet ﷺ answered:

"ʿAbdullāh b. ʿAbd al-Muṭṭalib."

Then the archbishop asked:

"Who is ʿĪsā's (ʿĪsā) father?"

The Prophet ﷺ waited a moment while Jibrāʾīl ﷺ revealed the following to him:

"(Say) he was the Spirit of God and His Word."

The archbishop asked,

"Can he be a spirit without a body?"

Again a revelation was sent to the Prophet ﷺ the revelation is as follows:

﴿إِنَّ مَثَلَ عِيسَىٰ عِندَ اللَّهِ كَمَثَلِ آدَمَ ۖ خَلَقَهُ مِن تُرَابٍ ثُمَّ قَالَ لَهُ كُن فَيَكُونُ﴾

⟨*inna mathala 'īsā 'inda llāhi ka-mathali 'ādama khalaqahū min turābin thumma qāla lahū kun fa-yakūn*⟩

⟨Indeed the case of 'Īsā with God is like the case of Ādam: He created him from dust, then said to him, 'Be,' and he was⟩[240]

When the archbishop heard this, he jumped in objection to the Prophet ﷺ saying that 'Īsā ؑ was created from dust and said:

"Muḥammad, We don't find this to be in the Tawrāt (Torah), the Bible, or in the Zabūr. You are the first one to say this."

This was the moment that the verse of Mubāhala[241] was revealed. After the delegation had heard the verse, they said,

"Assign for us a solemn meeting (in which every side supplicates to God to curse the other side if they are followers of falsehood)."

The Prophet ﷺ answered this:

"Tomorrow morning, if God wills."

---

[240] Sūrat Āl 'Imrān, Verse 59.

[241] The verse beginning this chapter.

The following day, the Prophet ﷺ finished his morning prayers and ordered 'Alī ؑ to follow him and Sayyidah Fāṭimah ؑ to follow 'Alī while holding al-Ḥasan and al-Ḥusayn ؑ.

The Prophet ﷺ then told them:

"When I supplicate, you should say: Amīn."

When the delegation saw the holy family ؑ and that the Prophet ﷺ had spread a mat for himself and his family, they said to each other:

"By God, he is a true Prophet; and if he curses us, surely God will answer his prayer and destroy us. The only thing that can save us is to ask him to relieve us from this meeting."

Rāzī states[242]:

'The Archbishop said:

"O Christians, I surely see faces of men, who if they were to ask God to move a mountain, He would surely do it. Do not hold this meeting, or you shall be destroyed, and no Christian will remain on Earth until the Day of Resurrection."

The delegation proceeded toward the Messenger ﷺ and said: "Abū al-Qāsim, relieve us (from this) solemn meeting."

The Prophet ﷺ said:

---

[242] ar-Rāzī, Fakhr ad-Dīn, *Mafātīḥ al-Ghayb* (*al-Tafsīr al-Kabīr*).

> "Indeed I will, but the One who sent me with righteousness is the witness that had I cursed you, God would not have left a Christian on the face of the earth."

This has been a summary of the story. What matters to us here is God's saying in the Mubāhala verse, "Our women and your women."

All Muslims have agreed that the Prophet ﷺ took ʿAlī ﷺ with him to represent "ourselves, "al-Ḥasan and al-Ḥusayn ﷺ represent "Our Sons, " and Sayyidah Fāṭimah al-Zahrāʾ ﷺ represents "Our Women, " It is also a given fact that he did not accompany any other woman including his wives, his aunts, or any other Muslim women.

This proves that there was no woman as excellent, holy, and chaste as Sayyidah Fāṭimah ﷺ. The Prophet ﷺ called Sayyidah Fāṭimah ﷺ alone to join him because she was the only woman capable of fulfilling the qualifications of the verse.

Sayyidah Fāṭimah ﷺ in Sūrat al-Insān

God ﷻ has said:

﴿إِنَّ الأَبرارَ يَشرَبونَ مِن كَأسٍ كانَ مِزاجُها كافورًا﴾

﴿*'inna l-'abrāra yashrabūna min ka'sin kāna mizājuhā kāfūran*﴾

﴿عَينًا يَشرَبُ بِها عِبادُ اللَّهِ يُفَجِّرونَها تَفجيرًا﴾

﴿*'aynan yashrabu bihā 'ibādu llāhi yufajjirūnahā tafjīran*﴾

﴿يوفونَ بِالنَّذرِ وَيَخافونَ يَومًا كانَ شَرُّهُ مُستَطيرًا﴾

﴿*yūfūna bi-n-nadhri wa-yakhāfūna yawman kāna sharruhū mustaṭīran*﴾

﴿وَيُطعِمونَ الطَّعامَ عَلىٰ حُبِّهِ مِسكينًا وَيَتيمًا وَأَسيرًا﴾

﴿*wa-yuṭ'imūna ṭ-ṭa'āma 'alā ḥubbihī miskīnan wa-yatīman wa-'asīran*﴾

﴿إِنَّما نُطعِمُكُم لِوَجهِ اللَّهِ لا نُريدُ مِنكُم جَزاءً وَلا شُكورًا﴾

﴿*'innamā nuṭ'imukum li-wajhi llāhi lā nurīdu minkum jazā'an wa-lā shukūran*﴾

﴿إِنّا نَخافُ مِن رَبِّنا يَومًا عَبوسًا قَمطَريرًا﴾

﴿*'innā nakhāfu min rabbinā yawman 'abūsan qamṭarīran*﴾

﴿فَوَقاهُمُ اللَّهُ شَرَّ ذٰلِكَ اليَومِ وَلَقّاهُم نَضرَةً وَسُرورًا﴾

﴿*fa-waqāhumu llāhu sharra dhālika l-yawmi wa-laqqāhum naḍratan wa-surūra*ⁿ﴾

﴿وَجَزاهُم بِما صَبَروا جَنَّةً وَحَريرًا﴾

﴿*wa-jazāhum bi-mā ṣabarū jannatan wa-ḥarīra*ⁿ﴾

﴿مُتَّكِئينَ فيها عَلَى الأَرائِكِ ۖ لا يَرَونَ فيها شَمسًا وَلا زَمهَريرًا﴾

﴿*muttaki'īna fīhā 'alā l-'arā'iki lā yarawna fīhā shamsan wa-lā zamharīra*ⁿ﴾

﴿وَدانِيَةً عَلَيهِم ظِلالُها وَذُلِّلَت قُطوفُها تَذليلًا﴾

﴿*wa-dāniyatan 'alayhim ẓilāluhā wa-dhullilat quṭūfuhā tadhlīla*ⁿ﴾

﴿وَيُطافُ عَلَيهِم بِآنِيَةٍ مِن فِضَّةٍ وَأَكوابٍ كانَت قَواريرا﴾

﴿*wa-yuṭāfu 'alayhim bi-'āniyatin min fiḍḍatin wa-'akwābin kānat qawārīr*ᵃ﴾

﴿قَواريرَ مِن فِضَّةٍ قَدَّروها تَقديرًا﴾

﴿*qawārīra min fiḍḍatin qaddarūhā taqdīra*ⁿ﴾

﴿وَيُسقَونَ فيها كَأسًا كانَ مِزاجُها زَنجَبيلًا﴾

﴿*wa-yusqawna fīhā ka'san kāna mizājuhā zanjabīla*ⁿ﴾

﴿عَينًا فيها تُسَمّىٰ سَلسَبيلًا﴾

﴿*ʿaynan fīhā tusammā salsabīla*ⁿ﴾

﴿وَيَطوفُ عَلَيهِم وِلدانٌ مُخَلَّدونَ إِذا رَأَيتَهُم حَسِبتَهُم لُؤلُؤًا مَنثورًا﴾

﴿*wa-yaṭūfu ʿalayhim wildānun mukhalladūna 'idhā ra'aytahum ḥasibtahum lu'lu'an manthūra*ⁿ﴾

﴿وَإِذا رَأَيتَ ثَمَّ رَأَيتَ نَعيمًا وَمُلكًا كَبيرًا﴾

﴿*wa-'idhā ra'ayta thamma ra'ayta naʿīman wa-mulkan kabīra*ⁿ﴾

﴿عالِيَهُم ثِيابُ سُندُسٍ خُضرٌ وَإِستَبرَقٌ ۖ وَحُلّوا أَساوِرَ مِن فِضَّةٍ وَسَقاهُم رَبُّهُم شَرابًا طَهورًا﴾

﴿*ʿāliyahum thiyābu sundusin khuḍrun wa-'istabraqun wa-ḥullū 'asāwira min fiḍḍatin wa-saqāhum rabbuhum sharāban ṭahūra*ⁿ﴾

﴿إِنَّ هٰذا كانَ لَكُم جَزاءً وَكانَ سَعيُكُم مَشكورًا﴾

﴿*'inna hādhā kāna lakum jazā'an wa-kāna saʿyukum mashkūra*ⁿ﴾

﴾Indeed the pious will drink from a cup seasoned with Kāfūr, a spring where the servants of God drink, which they make to gush forth as they please. They fulfill their vows and fear a day whose ill will be widespread. They give food, for the love of Him, to the needy, the orphan and the prisoner, [saying,] 'We feed you only for the sake of God. We do not want any reward from you nor any thanks. Indeed we fear from our Lord a day, frowning and fateful.' So God saved them from the ills of that day, and granted them freshness and joy. And He rewarded them for their patience with a garden and [garments of] silk, reclining therein on couches. They will find in it neither any [scorching] sun, nor any [biting] cold. Its shades will be close over them and its clusters [of fruits] will be hanging low. They will be served around with vessels of silver and goblets of crystal — crystal of silver**— [from] which they dispense in a precise measure. They will be served therein with a cup of a drink seasoned with Zanjabīl***, a spring in it, named Salsabīl. They will be waited upon by immortal youths, whom, when you see them, you will suppose them to be scattered pearls. As you look, you will see there bliss and a great kingdom. Upon them will be cloaks of green silk and brocade adorned with silver bracelets. Their Lord will give them to drink a pure drink. [They will be told]: 'This is indeed your reward, and your endeavour has been well-appreciated.'﴿*[243]

---

[243] Sūrat al-Insān, Verses 5-22.

* *Lit.*, camphor.

** According to *Tafsīr al-Qummī*, vol. 2, p. 399, the silver will be transparent.

*** *Lit.*, ginger.

These verses were revealed after 'Alī, Sayyidah Fāṭimah, Ḥasan, and Ḥusayn ﷺ gave charity to needy people. Zamakhsharī states this story[244]; it goes as follows:

> "Ibn 'Abbās said:
>
> > 'Once al-Ḥasan and al-Ḥusayn ﷺ were ill, the Messenger of God ﷺ and a group visited them. The visitors suggested to Imām 'Alī ﷺ to vow to God: if He were to relieve them, he would perform some good action. Therefore, Imām 'Alī ﷺ, together with Sayyidah Fāṭimah ﷺ and their servant Fidhdha, vowed to God that they would fast for three days if He would relieve Ḥasan and Ḥusayn.'
>
> 'When God had relieved them, Imām 'Alī ﷺ borrowed three aswu (a cubic measure) of barley from a Jew known as Shimon (Sim'ān). Sayyidah Fāṭimah ground one sa'a (singular of aswu) of the barley and baked five loaves of bread for her family's meal at sunset. As sunset approached, a needy man knocked on the door and said:
>
> > 'As-salāmu 'alaykum, Family of Muḥammad. I am a needy man from among the Muslims; feed me, may God feed you from the food of Paradise.'
>
> The holy family preferred the needy man over themselves and spent the night with nothing in their stomachs save water. They fasted the second day, and again at sunset, when they were waiting for their food, an orphan asked them for help, and they again preferred him over themselves. On the third evening, a captive (prisoner of war) asked them for help, and they

244 al-Zamakhsharī, *al-Kashshāf 'an Ḥaqā'iq at-Tanzīl.*

> repeated their preference for the needy above themselves.' "The following morning, Imām 'Alī ﷺ took al-Ḥasan and al-Ḥusayn ﷺ to the Messenger of God ﷺ who said the following when he saw them shaking like little chicks from hunger:
>
> The Prophet ﷺ said:
>
> > 'It displeases us to see you in this condition.'
>
> Then he went with them, wanting to see Sayyidah Fāṭimah ﷺ. When they arrived, Sayyidah Fāṭimah ﷺ was in the miḥrāb (prayer place), and her condition was such that it further displeased the Prophet ﷺ. At this time, Jibrā'īl ﷺ descended and said,
>
> > 'Take this chapter Muḥammad, - God surely congratulates you for having this family."

It is worthy to state that the Good ones mentioned here are 'Alī, Sayyidah Fāṭimah, Ḥasan, and Ḥusayn ﷺ, who deserve Paradise because of their act of feeding the needy, the orphan, and the captive.

Another point to remember here is that despite the detailed description of Paradise in the verses, God ﷻ does not mention the ḥūrīs. This is understood to be in honor and exaltation of Sayyidah Fāṭimah ﷺ, the wife of Imām 'Alī ﷺ, and the mother of Ḥasan and Ḥusayn ﷺ.

Spending in the Path of God ﷻ

Sayyidah Fāṭimah ؑ was very modest. Because as man's desire for the Hereafter increases, his worldly lusts decrease; when someone realizes the greatness and seriousness of the Day of Judgement, the worldly life becomes of little value to him. Besides, as man's reasoning and ability advance, his desire for lust decreases.

Have you not seen children play, have fun, become sad, and fight over worthless objects? As they grow up and their senses mature, they refrain from such actions because they consider them degrading to their personalities and contradict the rules of observing dignified conduct.

This is the case of righteous worshippers of God ﷻ who look down on the ephemeral things of this world, and their hearts cannot be attached to its vanities. They dislike this world for its worldly belongings; instead, they enjoy living to gain good deeds and further worship God ﷻ. They collect money to spend in the way of God, feed the hungry, and clothe and support the needy and deprived. These were also the fundamentals of modesty on which Sayyidah Fāṭimah al-Zahrā' ؑ depended. She deeply understood this worldly life and realized the extent of the Hereafter. It is not amazing to learn that Sayyidah Fāṭimah ؑ was satisfied with the minimum requirements of life; she chose the noble trait of preferring others over herself and aiding them, as we." as resenting extravagant living. It is a small wonder for Sayyidah Fāṭimah ؑ was the daughter of the most modest, whose religious and social life required him to live in modesty, and Sayyidah Fāṭimah ؑ was the first person expected to follow the steps of her father, the modest messenger.

Sayyidah Fāṭimah's ؑ marital life was also surrounded by modesty and satisfaction. Her husband 'Alī ؑ was a devout follower of the Prophet of Islām ﷺ, and there was not a man known who was more modest than ʿAlī ‎. Imām ʿAlī ‎ was the man who used to speak to the silver and gold in the treasury by saying:

> "O you yellow and white, deceive someone else besides me."

It has been reported that once a Badawī approached Imām ʿAlī ‎ for help. The Imām ‎ then ordered his agent to give the Badawī a grant of one thousand dinars, and the latter exclaimed:

> "Gold or silver dinars?"

Imām ʿAlī ‎ replied:

> "They are both just stones to me, so give the Badawī that which is more beneficial to him."

Here, we relate several narrations that speak of Sayyidah Fāṭimah's modesty and generosity:

1. Muḥammad b. ʿAlī al-Ṭabarī[245] was quoted[246] to have written:

   Imām Ṣādiq ‎ mentioned Jābir b. ʿAbdullāh al-Ansārī said:

   > "One day, when we had finished the ʿAṣr prayer with the Messenger of God, an old Arab immigrant man, who was wearing worn-out clothes and could barely walk because of his old age and weakness, came by. The Prophet asked the old man about his affair; the old man answered,

245 al-Ṭabarī, Muḥammad b. ʿAlī, *Bishārat al-Muṣṭafā li Shīʿat al-Murtaḍā*.

246 Majlisī, ʿAllamah Muḥammad Bāqir, *Biḥār al-Anwār*, Vol. 10.

> 'Prophet of God, I am starving, so feed me, I am naked, so clothe me, and poor, so help me.

The Prophet then said:

> 'Surely I find nothing to give you. Yet, he who guides to goodness is equal to him who performs it. So go to the house of she who loves God and His Messenger, and God and His Messenger love her. The one who prefers God over herself, I mean Sayyidah Fāṭimah.'

Sayyidah Fāṭimah's house was near the Prophet's house. He asked Bilāl to lead the man to her house. When the old man reached the house, he cried out:

> 'Peace be upon you, O household of prophethood, the (dwellers of the place where) angels frequently visit, where Jibrā'īl - the Holy Spirit - descends to bring what the Lord of the Worlds reveals.'

Sayyidah Fāṭimah said:

> 'Peace be upon you; who are you?'

The old Badawī answered,

> 'I am an old Arab man; I have immigrated to your father, The Master of mankind, from a distant place. Daughter of Muḥammad, I am hungry and need clothing, so console me-may God bless you.'

When this occurred, the Prophet, 'Alī, and Sayyidah Fāṭimah had not eaten for three days. Yet Sayyidah Fāṭimah gave him a tanned ram skin, which was used as al-Ḥasan and al-Ḥusayn's bed. Then Sayyidah Fāṭimah told the poor man:

'Take this, may God substitute it for you with a better gift by selling it.'

The old man replied:

'Daughter of Muḥammad, I complain of hunger, and you give me a ram's skin? How can I eat with this?'

When Sayyidah Fāṭimah heard what the old man had to say, she gave him the necklace, which was given to her by Fāṭimah b. Hamza b. 'Abd al-Muṭṭalib. The old man took the necklace and went to the Mosque to meet the Prophet, sitting in his companions' presence. He went to the Prophet and said:

'Messenger of God, Sayyidah Fāṭimah b. Muḥammad gave me this necklace and said: 'Sell it, for God will grant you a solution to your problem.'

When the Prophet heard what the man had to say, he cried:

'Indeed, God will grant you a solution, for Sayyidah Fāṭimah b. Muḥammad, the Mistress of all women, gave you this necklace.'

Meanwhile, 'Ammār b. Yāsir said:

'Messenger of God, do I have your permission to buy this necklace?'

The Prophet answered:

> 'Buy it, 'Ammār, surely if all of mankind and Jinn take part in buying it, God will not torture them in Hellfire.'

'Ammār said:

> 'How much do you want for it?'

The old Badawī said:

> 'A meal of bread and meat, a Yamani shirt to cover my private parts and to perform my prayers in front of my Lord, and a dinar so I can return to my family.'

'Ammār, who had just sold his share of the booty from the battle of Khaybar, told the man:

> 'I will give you twenty dinars, two hundred dirhams, a Yamani shirt, my horse to take you home, and your need of wheat bread and meat.'

The old man then said:

> 'What a generous man you are.'

When 'Ammār had fulfilled his promise to the old man, the latter came back to the Prophet ﷺ who said:

> 'Are you satisfied and clothed?'

The old man said:

> 'Yes, and I have become rich; may my father and mother be your sacrifice.'

The Prophet ﷺ then said:

> 'So reward Sayyidah Fāṭimah for her kindness.'

The old man supplicated,

> 'O God, surely You are our God whenever we ask You; 'We have no other God to worship besides you; 'You are the one who grants us beneficence in all conditions;' 'O God, grant Sayyidah Fāṭimah that which no eye has ever seen, and ear has ever heard ....'

During that time, 'Ammār had perfumed the necklace with parchment and wrapped it in a Yamani shirt, and gave it to one of his slaves by the name of Sahm, who he had bought with the money that he received for selling his share of the Khaybariyan booty. He told Sahm:

> 'Take this necklace and give it to the Messenger of God ﷺ and tell him I give you to him as well.'

When Sahm had delivered the message, the Prophet ﷺ said:

> 'Take the necklace to Sayyidah Fāṭimah, and I give you to her [as a slave] as well.'

When the slave told Sayyidah Fāṭimah the message, ﷺ took the necklace and told the slave that he was free. Upon hearing Sayyidah Fāṭimah, Sahm laughed, so Sayyidah Fāṭimah asked him about the reason that made him laugh. He answered:

'I smiled when I thought of the abundance of goodness put in this necklace; it fed a hungry man, clothed a naked man, satisfied a poor man, freed a slave, and returned to its original owner."

2. 'Allamah Majlisī quoting Furat[247] said[248]:

'Abū Saʿd al-Khudrī said:

One morning 'Alī b. Abū Ṭālib woke up very hungry and said:

'Sayyidah Fāṭimah, do you have anything to feed us?'

She answered:

'No, by Him who honored my father with Prophethood and honored you with successorship. We have nothing edible this morning, and we haven't had any food for two days save that which I have preferred to give you and our two children, Ḥasan and Ḥusayn.'

'Alī said:

'Sayyidah Fāṭimah! Why didn't you tell me so I could bring you some food?'

---

[247] Furat b. Ibrāhīm, *Tafsīr Furat*.

[248] Majlisī, 'Allamah Muḥammad Bāqir, *Biḥār al-Anwār*.

Sayyidah Fāṭimah answered:

'Abū al-Ḥasan, I surely become ashamed before my God to ask you to do something you cannot do.'

At this, ʿAlī b. Abū Ṭālib left Sayyidah Fāṭimah with complete trust that God would help him. He borrowed a dinar, and while he was holding the dinar and trying to buy food for his family, he came upon Miqdād b. al-Aswad. The sun had burned al-Miqdād's face and feet on that scorching day. When ʿAlī ؑ saw him, he exclaimed:

'Miqdād, what brings you out of your home at this hour?'

Miqdād answered:

'Abū al-Ḥasan, ask me not about what I have left behind in the house.'

ʿAlī ؑ said:

'My brother, I cannot leave you without knowing your problem.'

Miqdād said,

'Abū al-Ḥasan, for God's sake and your sake, leave me alone, and do not ask about my condition.'

Imām ʿAlī said:

> 'My brother, you should not hide your condition from me.'

Miqdād replied:

> 'Abū al-Ḥasan, now that you insist, by Him who honored Muḥammad with Prophethood and honored you with successorship, nothing forced me out of my house save poverty. I left my children starving; when I heard their cries, there remained no place for me to come out of my house in depression; this is my story.'

Imām ʿAlī ﷺ cried when he heard the story; he cried until his beard was wet from tears and said,

> 'By God, that which forced you out of your house and also forced me out of my house; I borrowed a dinar, but I prefer you to have it.'

When Imām ʿAlī ﷺ had given the dinar to Miqdād, he went to the Mosque and performed his Ẓuhr (noon), ʿAṣr (afternoon), and Maghrib (evening) prayers. When the Messenger of God had completed his prayers, he signaled ʿAlī, who was in the first line, to follow him. ʿAlī ﷺ obediently followed him out of the Mosque and, after the Prophet greeted him, said:

> 'Abū al-Ḥasan, do you have some food for dinner so that I can accompany you?'

Imām ʿAlī was too shy to answer the Messenger, but the Prophet of God ﷺ had detailed knowledge about the dinar and what had happened to it, for God ﷻ had revealed to His Prophet to have dinner at ʿAlī's house that night. When ʿAlī did not answer, the Prophet said,

> 'Abū al-Ḥasan, why don't you say no, so I may leave you; or yes, so I may accompany you?'

Imām ʿAlī ؑ said:

> 'Accompany me.'

The Prophet then took ʿAlī's hand and proceeded toward Sayyidah Fāṭimah's house. Sayyidah Fāṭimah was finishing her prayers when they arrived, and a pan oil fire was behind her. When she heard the Prophet coming, the dearest person to her, she greeted him, and he wiped his hand on her head and said:

> 'How is your evening, my daughter?'

She answered:

> 'Fine!'

He said,

> 'Give us some dinner. May God bless you, and surely He has.'

Sayyidah Fāṭimah ؑ placed the pan in front of the Prophet ﷺ and ʿAlī b. Abū Ṭālib...

At that moment, the Messenger of God put his hand on 'Alī's shoulder and said:

> "'Alī, this is a substitute for your dinar. This is a reward from God for the dinar; surely God grants whoever He wills without limit.'

The Prophet ﷺ cried and said:

> "Praise be to God, Who insisted on rewarding you in this world, too, and made you 'Alī — like Zakariyyā and Sayyidah Fāṭimah like Maryam b. 'Imrān, for whenever Zakariyyā entered the miḥrāb, he found Maryam with her subsistence."

3. It is quoted[249] that Imām Ḥusayn ؑ quoted Imām Ḥasan ؑ as saying:

"Once, on a Friday night, I watched my mother, Sayyidah Fāṭimah, pray all night long. She kept making rukūʿ and prostrating until dawn. I heard her supplicate for the believers by name, but she did not supplicate for herself, so I asked,

'Mother, why don't you supplicate for yourself as you supplicate for others?'

She answered:

`Son! Prefer your neighbor over yourself."'

[249] Majlisī, 'Allamah Muḥammad Bāqir, *Biḥār al-Anwār*, Vol. 10.

4. al-Ḥasan al-Basri said:

   "There was not a woman in this Ummah more submitting (to God) than Sayyidah Fāṭimah ﷺ. She used to pray until her feet became swollen."

5. 'The Messenger of God ﷺ said:

   "As for my daughter Sayyidah Fāṭimah, she is the mistress of all women from the beginning of history until the end. She is part of me, the light of my eye and the fruit of my heart. Sayyidah Fāṭimah is my spirit, which I hold in me; she is a human ḥūrī. Whenever she keeps up prayer in her miḥrāb before her Lord, her light illuminates to the angels in Heaven just as a star shines on mankind on Earth. So God, exalted is His name, says to the angels:

   > 'My angels, look at my servant, Sayyidah Fāṭimah, the mistress of all my female servants, keeping up prayers before Me. Her limbs shake from fear of Me, and she worships Me wholeheartedly. Bear witness that I have safeguarded her Shīʿī (followers) from Hellfire..."' [250]

6. Sayyidah Fāṭimah ﷺ used to breathe quickly while praying for fear of God. Speaking about Sayyidah Fāṭimah's worship is endless, especially her supplication to God ﷻ, for she realized the deep meaning of worship and supplication to God and came to enjoy keeping up prayers before the ﷻ. Yet, this is no

---

[250] Majlisī, 'Allamah Muḥammad Bāqir, *Biḥār al-Anwār*.

strange matter because it is regarding her father that the Qur'ān says:

﴿ما أنزلنا عليك القرآن لِتشقى﴾

﴾*mā 'anzalnā 'alayka l-qur'āna li-tashqā*﴿

﴾*We did not send down to* you *the Qur'ān that* you *should be miserable*﴿[251]

Because the Prophet would pray for long hours, God ﷻ revealed this verse to him as relief and comfort."[252]

---

[251] Sūrat Ṭā Ḥā, Verse 2.

[252] al-Ḥillī, Jamāl ad-Dīn Aḥmad b. Muḥammad b. Fahd, *Idāt ad-Dā'ī.*

Sayyidah Fāṭimah's ﷺ Glorification of God ﷻ

ʿAlī ؑ said to a man from Banī Saʿīd[253]:

> "Should I speak to you about Sayyidah Fāṭimah and myself? She was my spouse, who was the most beloved to the Prophet. Once, she carried water using a waterskin until it scarred her chest; she ground (grain) using a hand mill until blisters appeared on her hands; she swept the floor until her clothes became dusty and lit the fire under the cooking pot until her clothes became mud colored from the smoke.

Because of this, significant pain was inflicted on Sayyidah Fāṭimah ؑ, so I told her,

> 'Why don't you ask your father for a servant to relieve you from these jobs?'

When Sayyidah Fāṭimah ؑ went to the Prophet, she found he had company and was too shy to talk to him, so she left the house. But the Prophet ﷺ knew that she had come for something."

Imām ʿAlī ؑ continued:

> "The next morning, the Prophet came to the house while we were still under our quilt and said:
>
> > 'As-salāmu ʿalaykum!' Yet because we were ashamed (of being under the quilt), we preferred to remain silent.

---

253 Majlisī, ʿAllamah Muḥammad Bāqir, *Biḥār al-Anwār*.

The Prophet ﷺ once again said,

'As-salāmu 'alaykum!'

Once again, we remained silent.

Then, the Prophet said,

'As-salāmu 'alaykum' for the third time.

We feared he would depart, for it was the prophet's habit to say As-salāmu 'alaykum three times and then wait for permission to enter or leave.

So I said:

'Wa 'Alayk as-Salām, Messenger of God! Come in.'

He ﷺ sat near our heads and said:

'Sayyidah Fāṭimah, what was your need when you came to Muḥammad yesterday?'

Imām 'Alī ؑ added: "I was afraid that she (Sayyidah Fāṭimah) would not tell him, so I pulled my head from under the cover and said:

"I will inform you, Messenger of God! Surely, she carried water using a water skin until her chest was scarred, she ground (grain) using a hand mill until blisters appeared on her hands, she swept the floor until her clothes became dusty and lit the fire under the cooling pot until her clothes were mud colored from the smoke. So I said to her: 'Why don't ask your father for a servant to relieve you from these jobs?'"

The Prophet ﷺ upon hearing this, said:

> 'Shall I teach you something better for you than a servant and a world with everything in it? After every prayer, say: Allāhu Akbar thirty-four times, Alḥamdulilāh thirty-three times, and Subḥān Allāh thirty-three times, then conclude that with lā ilāha illā-llāh. Surely this is better for you than what you wanted and the world and its belongings.'

Thus, Sayyidah Fāṭimah ﷺ adhered to this glorification after every prayer, and it came to be known as '*Tasbīḥ Sayyidah Fāṭimah* ﷺ.'

'Abū Hārūn says:

> "Surely we command our children to adhere to '*Tasbīḥ Sayyidah Fāṭimah* ﷺ' the same way we command them to perform prayers. So perform the tasbīḥ, for whoever adheres to it shall never be miserable.'"

Regarding Sayyidah Fāṭimah's beads, it was reported[254] that it was made of woven wool threads which had knots by the number of Takbīr (Allāhu Akbar) until Hamza b. Abdal Muṭṭalib was martyred; she made them from the mud of his grave.

254 Ṭabrisī, Shaykh Faḍl b. Ḥasan, *Makārim al-Akhlāq*.

Since the martyrdom of Imām Ḥusayn, people have been using the mud surrounding his tomb to make beads for its great blessings.

Imām Ṣādiq said:

> "Beads should be made with blue thread and thirty-four beads, which was the way Sayyidah Fāṭimah's beads were made after Hamza's martyrdom."

There are various narrations, which were reported about "Tasbīḥ Sayyidah Fāṭimah's" importance and order. Yet, the most famous order on which our jurisprudents agree is to start with Allāhu Akbar, then Subḥān Allāh, and end with Alḥamdulilāh.

When we review the narrations above, it becomes clear that Sayyidah Fāṭimah al-Zahrā' performed her housework by herself, despite her honor and nobility, and that 'Alī helped her to do the housework.

Imām 'Alī said[255]:

> "Once, the Messenger of God came to us while Sayyidah Fāṭimah was sitting near the pot and I was cleaning some lentils; when the Prophet saw us, he said: 'Abū al-Ḥasan!' I said: 'At your service! O Messenger of God!' He then said: 'Listen to me, for I say not save that which is the word of the Lord: There is not a man who helps his wife in her housework, save that with every hair on his body a whole year of worship during which he fasted the days and kept up the nights in prayer is counted for him....'

[255] Majlisī, 'Allamah Muḥammad Bāqir, *Biḥār al-Anwār*.

The Prophet's ﷺ Love for Sayyidah Fāṭimah عليها السلام

It is difficult to define the extent of the Prophet's ﷺ love for Sayyidah Fāṭimah عليها السلام, for she occupied a special place in his heart as no other person did. His love for Sayyidah Fāṭimah عليها السلام was mixed with respect and exaltation. Besides being motivated by the father/daughter relationship, this love was granted to her for the special talents and noble traits Sayyidah Fāṭimah عليها السلام enjoyed. Perhaps we can go to the extent of saying that the Prophet was commanded to love and respect Sayyidah Fāṭimah عليها السلام. This matter led him to speak openly about her greatness and talents and her nearness to God ﷻ and His Messenger ﷺ on every occasion.

This reality is supported by the fact that the Prophet ﷺ did not pay this much attention to Zaynab, Ruqayyah, and Umm Kulthūm. Thus, we can again conclude that some reason other than fatherhood motivated his love and respect for Sayyidah Fāṭimah عليها السلام. Besides Sayyidah Fāṭimah's عليها السلام noble traits and special talents, the Prophet ﷺ knew what would happen to her after his death and the great miseries and sorrows that some so-called Muslims would inflict on her after his departure to the Heavens. So the Prophet ﷺ intended to make clear to his Ummah the greatness and excellence of Sayyidah Fāṭimah عليها السلام to clarify the falsity of those who would oppose Sayyidah Fāṭimah عليها السلام in the future.

The following reports illustrate the love and respect the Prophet ﷺ held for Sayyidah Fāṭimah عليها السلام.

1. Imām Ṣādiq reported[256] that Sayyidah Fāṭimah said:

"When the following verse was revealed:

﴿لَا تَجْعَلُوا دُعَاءَ الرَّسُولِ بَيْنَكُمْ كَدُعَاءِ بَعْضِكُم بَعْضًا ۚ قَدْ يَعْلَمُ اللَّهُ الَّذِينَ يَتَسَلَّلُونَ مِنكُمْ لِوَاذًا ۚ فَلْيَحْذَرِ الَّذِينَ يُخَالِفُونَ عَنْ أَمْرِهِ أَن تُصِيبَهُمْ فِتْنَةٌ أَوْ يُصِيبَهُمْ عَذَابٌ أَلِيمٌ﴾

❃lā tajʻalū duʻāʼa r-rasūli baynakum ka-duʻāʼi baʻḍikum baʻḍan qad yaʻlamu llāhu lladhīna yatasallalūna minkum liwādhan fa-l-yaḥdhari lladhīna yukhālifūna ʻan ʼamrihī ʼan tuṣībahum fitnatun ʼaw yuṣībahum ʻadhābun ʼalīm^{un}❃

❃Do not consider the Apostle's summons amongst you to be like your summoning one another. God certainly knows those of you who slip away under cover. So let those who disobey his orders beware lest an ordeal should visit them or a painful punishment should befall them❃[257]

'I feared to call the Messenger of God, 'Father'; so I began calling him Messenger of God. He ignored me two or three times and finally said:

'Sayyidah Fāṭimah, this verse was not revealed about you or your family, nor does it include your progeny; for you are from me, and I am from you. Rather, this verse was revealed regarding the vain and crude Qurayshīs who are arrogant and spendthrifts. Call me father; it surely is better for the heart and more satisfying to the Lord.'"

---

[256] Majlisī, ʻAllāmah Muḥammad Bāqir, *Biḥār al-Anwār*, Vol. 10.

[257] Sūrat al-Nūr, Verse 63.

2. ʿĀʾisha b. Ṭalḥa quoted ʿĀʾisha as saying:

   "I have seen no one more similar to the Messenger in speech and dialogue than Sayyidah Fāṭimah. Whenever she entered the house, he would greet her, kiss her hands, and ask her to sit near him. Likewise, when he entered the house, she would greet him, kiss his hands, etc....."

3. Bazl al-Harawī said to al-Ḥusayn b. Rūḥ:

   "How many daughters did the Messenger of God have?"

   Ibn Rūḥ said:

   > "Four."

   Bazl then asked:

   > "Who was the best of them?"

   He said:

   > "Sayyidah Fāṭimah"

   Bazl said:

   > "Why was she the best while she was the youngest and least company to the Prophet of God ﷺ?"

   Ibn Rūḥ then said:

   > "(She was the best) because she possessed two special characteristics:

1. She inherited the Messenger of God.

2. The Prophet's progeny are her children. Besides, God gifted her with these traits because He knew her sincere adherence and pure intention (to worship Him)."

4. Khawārazmī wrote[258] that Ḥudhayfa said:

"The Messenger of God used to kiss Sayyidah Fāṭimah all over her face before he went to sleep ...."

5. Ibn ʿUmar said: "

Once the Prophet ﷺ kissed Sayyidah Fāṭimah's head and said:

`May your father be your sacrifice; stay as you are ...."

6. Āʾisha said[259]:

"Once the Messenger of God kissed Sayyidah Fāṭimah's throat, so I said,

"Messenger of God! You have done something which you have not done before!"

The Prophet answered:

"ʿĀʾisha, whenever I long for Paradise, I kiss Sayyidah Fāṭimah's throat."

---

[258] al-Khawārazmī, *Maqtal al-Ḥusayn*.

[259] al-Ṭabarī, Muḥib al-Dīn, *Dhakhaʾir al-ʿUqbī*.

7. 7. Qundūzī reported that 'Ā'isha said:

"Whenever the Prophet returned from a trip, he would kiss Sayyidah Fāṭimah's throat and say:

"From her, I do smell the fragrance of Paradise."

Both Shī'ī and Sunnī scholars have reported the following narrations[260]:

1. The Messenger of God ﷺ said:

   "The best of women of Paradise are Sayyidah Khadījah b. Khuwaylid, Sayyidah Fāṭimah b. Muḥammad, Āsiya b. Muzāḥim (Pharaoh's wife), and Maryam b. 'Imrān."

2. He also said:

   "The best of the women of the world are four: Maryam b. 'Imrān, Āsiya b. Muzāḥim, Sayyidah Khadījah b. Khuwaylid, and Sayyidah Fāṭimah b. Muḥammad."

3. The Prophet ﷺ also said:

   "Among the world's women, the following are among (the best): Maryam b. 'Imrān, Sayyidah Khadījah b. Khuwaylid, Sayyidah Fāṭimah b. Muḥammad, and Āsiya-Pharaoh's wife."[261]

---

[260] Ibn Ḥanbal, *Aḥmad, Musnad Aḥmad b. Ḥanbal*, Vol. 2, p. 293.

[261] 'Abd al-Barr, Al-Ḥāfiẓ Abū 'Umar, *al-'Istī'āb fī Ma'rifat al-Aṣḥāb*.

al-'Asqalānī, Ibn Ḥajar, *al-Iṣābah fī Tamyīz al-Ṣaḥābah*.

These three narrations name the four best women but do not specify the best of them. However, many authentic narrations clearly state that Sayyidah Fāṭimah was the best of all women, including these honorable ladies. This is an indisputable fact, which both Shīʿī and Sunnī scholars unanimously agree. Among the sayings of Sunnī scholars who reported narrations to this effect are:

1. Masrūq reports that ʿĀʾisha told him:

   "We, the Prophet's wives, were gathered around him when Sayyidah Fāṭimah walked towards us; by God, her walk is the same as that of the Messenger of God when he saw her, he greeted her by saying:

   > `Welcome my daughter.'

   He then asked her to sit to his right or left. He then whispered something to her that caused her to cry; when he saw her sadness, he whispered something else to her, which caused her to laugh. (When I saw this) I told her,

   > 'The Messenger of God favored you with a special secret, yet you cry?'

   When the Prophet left, I exclaimed:

   > "What did he whisper to you?"

   Sayyidah Fāṭimah answered:

   > `I would not announce the secret of the Messenger of God!'

The Prophet's ﷺ Love for Sayyidah Fāṭimah ؑ

After the Prophet's death, I told her:

'I insist on you my right over you tell me (what he told you)!'

She said:

'Yes, I will tell you now. The first time he whispered to me, he told me that Jibra'īl used to review the Qur'ān with him once a year, but this year, he reviewed it twice. So, he said, I think my departure is near. Therefore, fear God and be patient, for I will be a good (person) to precede you.'

Sayyidah Fāṭimah added:

'So I cried, as you saw. When he noticed my sadness, he once again said to me:

'Sayyidah Fāṭimah, is it not satisfying to you to be the Mistress of believing women (or the Mistress of the women of my Ummah)?"

2. Baghawī writes[262] that the Prophet ﷺ said to Sayyidah Fāṭimah:

"Is it not satisfying to you to be the Mistress of the women of the world?"

3. Ḥakīm Nīsābūrī reported[263] that that the Prophet ﷺ said to Sayyidah Fāṭimah ؑ:

---

[262] al-Baghawī, Abū Muḥammad al-Ḥusayn, *Maṣābīḥ as-Sunnah*.

[263] al-Ḥakim al-Nīshābūrī, *al-Mustadrak 'ala al-Ṣaḥīḥayn*.

"Is it not satisfying to you to be the Mistress of the women of the world, this Ummah and believing women?"

Although many narrations state that Sayyidah Fāṭimah was the Mistress of all women. Aḥmad b. Ḥanbal mentions at the end of the first narration that the Prophet also informed Sayyidah Fāṭimah that she was the first to follow him after his death.

4. Bukhārī reported[264] that God's Messenger said:

"Sayyidah Fāṭimah is part of me; he who harms her harms me."

This narration has been reported with various words with the same meaning; over fifty narrators said it. For instance[265]:

"When 'Abdullāh b. al-Ḥasan was still young, he visited 'Umar b. 'Abd Azīz sat him in an honorable place, paid much attention to him, and fulfilled his wishes. Ibn 'Abd Azīz pinched the boy's stomach and said:

"Remember this when it is time for interceding."

When 'Abdullāh b. al-Ḥasan left, 'Umar's family blamed him for doing so with a young boy. But 'Umar said:

'A trustworthy man informed me that the Messenger of God said:

"Surely Sayyidah Fāṭimah is a part of me, pleases me that which pleases her."

---

[264] Bukhārī, Muḥammad b. Ismāʿīl, *Ṣaḥīḥ Bukhārī*, Vol. 5, p. 21 & p. 29.

[265] al-Isfahānī, Abu l-Faraj, *Kitāb al-Aghānī*, Vol. 8, p. 307.

'Umar then added:

'And I know that had Sayyidah Fāṭimah been alive, what I did with her descendant ('Abdullāh) would have pleased her.'

His Family said,

"But why did you pinch his stomach and say what you said to him?"

'Umar b. 'Abd Azīz then said:

"There is not a man from Banī Hāshim who does not have the right to intercede, and I hope to be included among those through this boy."

Samhūdī comments on this narration by saying:

"This proves that anyone who hates or harms a descendant of Sayyidah Fāṭimah makes himself subject to harming the Prophet. On the contrary, if someone pleases them, he also pleases the Prophet."

Moreover, Suhaylī added:

"This narration leads us to the conclusion that he who curses her (Sayyidah Fāṭimah) becomes an infidel, and he who praises her praises her father."

5. Imām Jaʿfar b. Muḥammad and Jābir b. ʿAbdullāh al-Anṣārī said[266]:

"Once the Prophet saw Sayyidah Fāṭimah wearing a cloak of camel skin while grinding (grain) with her hands and holding her child. Tears came from the Prophet's eyes, and he said,

> 'Daughter! Bear with the hardships of this world, and later, you will enjoy the blessings of the Hereafter.'

Sayyidah Fāṭimah replied:

> 'Messenger of God, praise be to God for His benefactions, and thanks be to Him for his gifts.'

(It was then that) God revealed:

$$\text{﴿وَلَسَوْفَ يُعْطِيكَ رَبُّكَ فَتَرْضَىٰ﴾}$$

❁*wa-la-sawfa yuʿṭīka rabbuka fa-tarḍā*❁

❁*Soon your Lord will give you [that with which] you will be pleased*❁[267]

In conclusion, we can derive from the above narrations that Sayyidah Fāṭimah al-Zahrā' was the nearest of all to God's Messenger. The love, affection, and harmony that they shared were unique. Thus, we realize it was not strange that he taught

---

[266] Majlisī, ʿAllāmah Muḥammad Bāqir, *Biḥār al-Anwār*, Vol. 10.

[267] Sūrat al-Ḍuḥā, Verse 5.

Sayyidah Fāṭimah ؓ the best deeds and guided her to the noblest traits and best conduct.

Sayyidah Fāṭimah's ﷺ Knowledge

Sayyidah Fāṭimah ﷺ acquired her divine knowledge from the clear spring of Prophethood and received the excellence of truth from the house of revelation. So it embellished her attentive heart with wisdom, brilliant reason, and brightness, realizing the real meaning of every fact to the fullest extent.

Yet, although Sayyidah Fāṭimah ﷺ heard abundant narrations from her father, what has been reported on her authority is limited to certain issues. I will explain later the reason for this.

Among the narrations reported on Sayyidah Fāṭimah's ﷺ account are:

1. Imām Askari ﷺ said[268]:

   "A woman came to Sayyidah Fāṭimah al-Zahrā' ﷺ and said:

   > 'I have a weak mother who has become confused about a matter related to her prayer; she sent me to inquire from you about it.'

   Sayyidah Fāṭimah al-Zahrā' ﷺ answered her; the woman repeatedly came with questions for Sayyidah Fāṭimah, and she ﷺ kindly answered her every time. One day, the lady again approached Sayyidah Fāṭimah ﷺ with another question from her mother and said to Sayyidah Fāṭimah:

   > 'I shall not inconvenience you (anymore), daughter of God's messenger.'

[268] Majlisī, 'Allamah Muḥammad Bāqir, *Biḥār al-Anwār*.

Sayyidah Fāṭimah replied,

> 'Ask me about anything that comes to your mind. Because if a man had been hired to transport a heavy load to the top of a mountain for a reward of one thousand dinars, do you think it would bother him?'

The woman said:

> 'No.'

Sayyidah Fāṭimah continued:

> 'My reward for (answering) every inquiry is more than that which fills (the space) between the ground and the Throne with pearls; thus, I should be more apt to answer your questions. Surely I heard my father say:
>
>> 'When the scholars of our Shī'ī (followers) are gathered (on the Day of Resurrection), they will be bestowed with garments of honor equal in quantity to their knowledge and struggle to guide God's worshippers, up to where anyone of them will be gifted with one million garments of light.'
>
> Then the caller of our Exalted and Glorified Lord will say:
>
>> 'O you guardians of the orphans of Muḥammad. (You) who inspire them when they are separated from their fathers, who are their Imāms; these are your pupils and the orphans whom you guarded and inspired; therefore, give them garments of knowledge in life. Thus, they will give each orphan corresponding to the knowledge he received

from them (the scholars), up to where some orphans are given one million garments. Like-so, the orphans give those who learned from them.' Then God ﷻ said: `Repeat upon these scholars, the guardians of the orphans, the bestowment and double and complete it for them and those who follow them."

Sayyidah Fāṭimah ﷺ then added:

'Worshipper of God, surely a thread of those garments is better than that on which the sun rises."'

2. Yazīd b. 'Abdul Mālik (Nawfalī) quoted his father, who cited his grandfather as saying[269]:

"Once, I entered the house of Sayyidah Fāṭimah ﷺ who was the first to greet me; she then said:

'What brings you here?'

I said:

"I have come in search of blessing."

Sayyidah Fāṭimah ﷺ said:

"My father (who was present) said:

'He who greets him or me for three consecutive days, will be granted Paradise by God.'

[269] Majlisī, 'Allamah Muḥammad Bāqir, *Biḥār al-Anwār*, Vol. 10.

I said:

'While you are living?'

She answered:

'Yes, and after we are dead.'"

3. Imām 'Alī quoted Sayyidah Fāṭimah as saying[270]:

"The Messenger of God said: .

'Sayyidah Fāṭimah, God will forgive him who praises you; who will make him my companion where ever in Paradise I may be."

4. Swayd b. Ghafla said[271]:

"Once, 'Alī was inflicted with hardship; so Sayyidah Fāṭimah knocked on the Messenger of God's door, who said:

'I hear the movement of my beloved one near the door, Umm Ayman get up and see!'

Umm Ayman opened the door, and Sayyidah Fāṭimah entered the house. The Prophet said:

'You have come to us at a time that you have not previously come!'

---

[270] Al-Irdibillī, 'Alī b. 'Isā Hakkārī, *Kashf al-Ghumma fī Ma'rifat al-A'imma*.

[271] Rāwandī, Quṭb al-Dīn, *al-Da'awāt*.

Sayyidah Fāṭimah said:

> 'Messenger of God, what is the angels' food near our Lord?'

The Messenger of God said:

> 'By Him Who holds my soul in His hand, fire has not been lit (in our house) for an entire month; yet, I will teach you five statements which Jibrā'īl taught me.'

She ﷺ said:

> 'Messenger of God, what are these five statements?'

The Prophet ﷺ said:

> 'O Lord of the First and Last;
>
> O You Possessor of Might, and Strength;
>
> O You Who is Merciful with the poor;
>
> O You most Beneficent, most Merciful."'
>
> (Note: It appears the fifth statement was mistakenly erased.)[272]

After that, Sayyidah Fāṭimah ﷺ returned, and 'Alī ﷺ saw her and exclaimed,

[272] This is how the hadith was mentioned in the consulted work.

"May my father and mother be your sacrifice, Sayyidah Fāṭimah; what have you to tell me?"

She said:

"I went seeking worldly things but have returned (with the goodness of) the hereafter."

'Alī then said:

"Expect goodness, expect goodness!"

5. It is reported[273] that Imām Ṣādiq said:

'Once, Sayyidah Fāṭimah approached God's Messenger with a problem. The Prophet listened to her problem, gave her a wrapped piece of material, and said:

'Learn what is written in it.'

(When she opened it) she found written in it:

"He who believes in God and the Last Day shall not harm his neighbor.

He who believes in God and the Last Day shall honor his guest.

He who believes in God and the Last Day shall say that which is useful or keep silent.'"

---

[273] Majlisī, 'Allāmah Muḥammad Bāqir, *Biḥār al-Anwār*, Vol. 10, citing Kulaynī, Shaykh Muḥammad b. Ya'qūb, *al-Kāfī*.

Islamic Dress, a Societal Necessity

Among the Islamic teachings to which Sayyidah Fāṭimah al-Zahrā' ﷺ gave special attention was protecting women's honor and beauty through observing the Islamic way of dress. Sayyidah Fāṭimah realized that crimes, social disasters, and humiliations were rampant because of unveiling, debasement, dissoluteness, and the mixture of the sexes. These social crimes are now called freedom and civilization by various publications scattered throughout Muslim and non-Muslim countries.

It shouldn't be forgotten that less than one-tenth of such crimes and debasements used to occur to Muslim women when they observed the Islamic covering and exalted themselves from exhibiting their bodies to men. That day, they used to honor themselves in the garments of honor and modesty when they truly believed in what was forbidden and permitted. But as time passed, they exhibited their privacy to thousands of men from all walks of life and with many faiths; Muslim women lost their honor and dignity... and reached the point of disgrace where they stand today.

The following are two reports which explicitly present the Messenger's admiration of Sayyidah Fāṭimah's ﷺ stands regarding women:

1. Anas b. Mālik said[274]:

   "The Messenger of God ﷺ asked:

   'What is best for women?'

---

[274] al-Isfahānī, Aḥmad, *Ḥilyat al-Awliya' wa-Ṭabaqāt al-Aṣfiya'*, Vol. 2, p. 40.

We did not know how to answer the Prophet, so 'Alī asked Sayyidah Fāṭimah about the Prophet's question. Sayyidah Fāṭimah answered:

'It is best for them not to see men and not to let men see them.'

'Alī returned to God's Messenger and conveyed Sayyidah Fāṭimah's answer to him. When the Prophet had heard the answer, he said:

'Surely she has spoken the truth, for she is part of me.'

2. 'Alī b. al-Ḥusayn b. 'Alī said[275]:

"Once a blind man asked for permission to enter Sayyidah Fāṭimah's house, but she kept a veil between them. The Messenger of God noticed her actions and asked:

'Why did you keep a veil between you when he cannot see you?'

Sayyidah Fāṭimah answered:

'Messenger of God, it is true that he cannot see me, but I can see him, and he can smell my fragrance.'

At this, the Prophet said:

'I bear witness you are part of me.'

---

[275] Ibn al-Maghāzlī, *Manāqib al-Imām 'Alī b. Abī Ṭālib*.

Besides these narrations, many prayers and supplications have been reported on Sayyidah Fāṭimah's account; among them is the famous supplication for relieving fever and headaches. This supplication is mentioned below as an example of Sayyidah Fāṭimah's prayers.

Sayyidah Fāṭimah taught the following supplication to Salmān al-Fārisī and said to him:

> "If it pleases you not to be inflicted with fever as long as you live in this world, then read these words, which my father, Muḥammad, taught me, and I say every morning and evening:
>
> > 'In the name of God, the Most Beneficent, Most Merciful
> >
> > In the Name of God the light; In the Name of God the light of light
> >
> > In the Name of God, light upon light
> >
> > In the Name of God, the planner of affairs
> >
> > In the Name of God, Who created light from light
> >
> > And
> >
> > Revealed light upon the Ṭūr
> >
> > By a decree inscribed
> >
> > In a scroll unfolded
> >
> > According to a decree fore-ordained

Unto a Learned Prophet

Praise be to God, Who is known with Might

Whose Glory is established

Who is praised during times of prosperity and infliction

May God's grace be upon our Master, Muḥammad

And his purified progeny.'

Salmān later said:

"By God, I have taught this supplication to more than a thousand souls in Makkah and Madīnah who were inflicted with fever, and they were all relieved by the will of God."

God's Messenger ﷺ taught Sayyidah Fāṭimah ؑ the following supplication[276]:

'O God, Our Lord and the Lord of Everything

(He) Who revealed Ṭawrāt, Injīl and Furqān (Qur'ān)

(He) Who causes the seed grain and the date stone to split and sprout

I seek refuge in You from every beast that you shall seize by its forelock

---

[276] Sayyid b. Ṭāwūs, *Muhaj al-Daʿawāt wa Manhaj al-ʿIbādāt*.

Indeed, You are the First, where nothing has succeeded (You)

And the last, where nothing shall come after (You)

You are the Evident; there is nothing more Manifest than You

And the Eminent, there is nothing more Eminent than You

Send your grace upon Muḥammad and his Ahl al-Bayt

May Peace be upon them

And settle my debts for me

Make me free from poverty

And decree easy for me all my affairs

O You! Most Merciful of all

In conclusion, we can easily state that had Sayyidah Fāṭimah al-Zahrā' been given a chance to manifest her knowledge and had she lived for fifty or sixty years; we would have been able to inherit a treasure of knowledge and information of various subjects and sciences. Unfortunately, Sayyidah Fāṭimah was neither given the chance to teach us nor did she live over twenty years — as you will come to know.

God's Messenger ﷺ Reveals Sayyidah Fāṭimah's ؑ Future

It was natural for the Prophet ﷺ who knew and foretold future events to reveal to his family, especially his beloved daughter Sayyidah Fāṭimah ؑ, the circumstances they would face. He ﷺ undoubtedly informed Sayyidah Fāṭimah ؑ that she would suffer from the harsh treatment of some so-called Muslims after his death and that she would be the first to follow him to the blessings of Paradise after his departure.

There are many traditions reported to this effect; the following are just a few samples:

1. Shaykh Mufīd is quoted[277] as writing[278] that ʿAbdullāh b. ʿAbbās said:

    "When God's Messenger was on his deathbed, he cried until tears overtook his beard.

    So he was asked:

    'What makes you cry, Messenger of God?'

    The Prophet answered:

    'I am crying for my progeny, for the crimes that will be committed against them by the evildoers of my nation after my death. It is as if I (can see) my daughter, Sayyidah Fāṭimah, being oppressed and crying:

---

[277] Majlisī, ʿAllamah Muḥammad Bāqir, *Biḥār al-Anwār*, Vol. 10.

[278] Mufīd, Shaykh Muḥammad, *al-Amālī*.

"O Father!" But no one will come to help her among my Ummah.'

Sayyidah Fāṭimah began weeping when she heard this, so the Prophet said,

'Do not cry, my daughter.'

She said:

'I am not crying because of that which will be done to me after you; rather, I am crying because I will be separated from you, Messenger of God.'

He then said:

'Rejoice, O daughter of Muḥammad, at the close succession of me, for you will be the first one to follow me from among my Ahl al-Bayt.'

2. Shaykh Mufīd is also quoted[279] as writing in his book[280]:

"The Prophet said:

'When I saw her (Sayyidah Fāṭimah), I remembered what would happen to her after my death. It is as if I (could see) humiliation entering her house, her sanctity violated, her right seized, her inheritance usurped, her side broken, and her unborn child is caused to be aborted, all while she is crying:

---

[279] Majlisī, ʿAllamah Muḥammad Bāqir, *Biḥār al-Anwār*, Vol. 10.

[280] Mufīd, Shaykh Muḥammad, *al-Amālī*.

"Mohammad!"'

But she will not be answered; she asks for help but will not be helped. Surely, she will remain afflicted, sad, and crying after me, remembering the cease of revelation from her father's house at one time and being separated from me another time. She became estranged at night when she spent time listening to me reciting the Qur'ān. She then will see herself humiliated after she was honored during the days of her father...'"

3. According to interpreting the Qur'ān written by Furāt b. Ibrāhīm, Jābir b. 'Abdullāh Ansārī reported that God's Messenger said[281] to Sayyidah Fāṭimah during the illness, which caused him to pass away:

"May my father and mother be your sacrifice! Call your husband for me."

Sayyidah Fāṭimah then told al-Ḥasan and al-Ḥusayn:

"Go tell your father to come and that your grandfather summons him."

Thus, al-Ḥusayn went and called him to come. When 'Alī b. Abū Ṭālib entered the house, and he found Sayyidah Fāṭimah sitting near God's Messenger and saying:

'How distressed I am for your agony, father.'

---

[281] Majlisī, 'Allāmah Muḥammad Bāqir, *Biḥār al-Anwār*, Vol. 6.

The Prophet ﷺ said:

> 'There is no agony for your father after this day, Fāṭimah. Yet, do as your father did when (his son) Ibrāhīm passed away:

Then I said:

> 'Eyes spill tears, and the heart may be affected, but we shall not say that which angers the Lord. Yet, surely we are saddened by (your death) Ibrāhīm.'"

4. Another reported tradition states[282]:

'Once, the Prophet ﷺ summoned ʿAlī, Sayyidah Fāṭimah, al-Ḥasan, and al-Ḥusayn ؏ and ordered everyone present in the house to leave. He then ordered Umm Salamah to stand at the door so no one could come near it.

The Prophet ﷺ then said to ʿAlī ؏:

"Come near me."

ʿAlī came near as the Prophet asked; he then held Sayyidah Fāṭimah's hand and put it on his chest for a long time, and held ʿAlī's hand in his other hand. When the Prophet tried to speak, he was overtaken by tears and could not do so. Therefore, ʿAlī, Sayyidah Fāṭimah, al-Ḥasan, and al-Ḥusayn cried when they saw him ﷺ crying.

---

[282] Majlisī, ʿAllamah Muḥammad Bāqir, *Biḥār al-Anwār*, Vol. 10.

God's Messenger ﷺ Reveals Sayyidah Fāṭimah's ؑ Future

Sayyidah Fāṭimah ؑ then said,

"Messenger of God! You have broken my heart and brought sorrow to me with your crying. You are the Master of all Prophets and the trusted Prophet of your Lord; you are the beloved Prophet of God! Who do I have for my children after you? Who do I have to protect me from the humiliation which will inflict me after you? Who does 'Alī, your brother and the helper of your religion, have after you? Who is to (attend to) God's revelation and affair?"

Sayyidah Fāṭimah ؑ then broke down crying and embraced him together with 'Alī, Ḥasan, and Ḥusayn ؑ. The Prophet ﷺ raised his head. While holding Sayyidah Fāṭimah's hand, he placed it in 'Alī's hand and said:

'Abū al-Ḥasan, she is God's and His Messenger's, Muḥammad, trust to you. Therefore, keep God's and His Messenger's trust by protecting her. Surely, I know you will.'

"Alī, this (Sayyidah Fāṭimah) by God, is the Mistress of all women of Paradise; this, by God, is (like) Maryam al-Kubra.'

'By God, before I reached this state, I asked God (certain things) for you and me, and He surely has given me what I asked.'

"Alī, execute that which Sayyidah Fāṭimah commands you to do, for I have commanded her to (perform certain affairs) which Jibrāʾīl ordered me to do. Be informed, 'Alī,

> that I am satisfied with him whom my daughter is satisfied with, and so are my Lord and the angels.
>
> 'ʿAlī, Cursed is he who oppresses her;
>
> Cursed is he who usurps her right;
>
> Cursed is he who violates her sanctity..."

The Prophet then embraced Sayyidah Fāṭimah ﷺ, kissed her hand, and said:

> "May your father be your sacrifice, Sayyidah Fāṭimah."

At that moment, the Messenger of God ﷺ was putting his head on ʿAlī's chest, but his love for Sayyidah Fāṭimah kept driving him to embrace and kiss her repeatedly. He cried until his tears made his beard and shirt wet.

Imām Ḥasan and Imām Ḥusayn ﷺ began crying and kissing his feet; when Imām ʿAlī ﷺ tried to separate them, the Prophet ﷺ said:

> "Let them smell me, and let me smell them;
>
> Let them be near me. Indeed, they will be afflicted with sorrows and difficult problems after me. May God curse him who abuses them.' O God! I commend them to your protection and the protection of the righteous believers."

Meanwhile, Sayyidah Fāṭimah ﷺ was speaking to her father in a crying voice and saying,

"May my soul be your sacrifice!

May my face prevent harm from your face!

Father, can you not speak a word to me?

Indeed, I see the knights of death attacking you fiercely."

God's Messenger ﷺ then said:

"Daughter, I am leaving you;

thus, peace be upon you from me."

The Prophet's ﷺ Death

It was eleven years after Hijrah. God's Messenger ﷺ was about to conclude establishing the main pillars on which the Islamic law, ordained to be everlasting for being the final faith, was to depend.

His noble soul was compelled to return with satisfaction and comfort to One Who Created it after it had attained the goal of bringing about the most significant change in the history of humanity. Yes, indeed, it was inevitable for the Prophet's soul to depart towards Him, who it truly knew, for so many years, called mankind to worship, and courageously struggled in the path of elevating His Word. And as it was said: "Death was written to fit man just as a necklace was made to fit a girl's neck."

The Prophet ﷺ, along with the rest of the Muslims, had made his final morning prayer. It was the last time they (the people) were to see the Divine light come upon them. By the time the sun had reached the middle of the sky, the Prophet's sun had made its eternal set.

By noon, he was lying dead between his family ؏; they could do nothing save shed tears of sorrow for the most significant affliction of history.

What a day it was. Greatness, perfection, honor, and exaltation had been lost. Muslims were so saddened that whenever they were afflicted with great sorrow after that, they said:

> "Surely this is a day like when the Messenger of God died."

The house was crowded with crying people, but Sayyidah Fāṭimah's ؑ weeping was the greatest. She had lost her noble father, and with him went her happiness and joy; with his death came sadness and pain.

When the Muslims heard of the Prophet's ﷺ death, they rushed towards the Mosque. The people were overwhelmed and did not realize what had happened... They became like scattered sheep on a rainy night without their shepherd. What were they to do? ʿAlī ؓ was busy attending to washing the Prophet's ﷺ body and could not speak to them in detail.

It was undoubtedly true! He had died! Yet, ʿUmar b. al-Khaṭṭāb refused to allow people to believe what had happened. He began shouting in their faces and threatening them by saying, 'God's Messenger did not die, nor will he die until his religion reigns over all other religions. He shall return to amputate the hands and legs of the men who believed in his death. I will not hear a man say:

'The Messenger of God died save I will cut off his head."

ʿUmar's call was decisive and rebellious... he, the speaker, used the most effective method of speech to persuade his listeners to believe him...

ʿUmar sought to distract the Muslims from considering the matter of succession until the events of the Saqīfah concluded.

He put fear in the hearts of the Muslims by telling them that the Prophet ﷺ would come to amputate the hands and legs of those who believed in his death.

ʿUmar threatened them by saying,

"I will cut off the neck of anyone who says: God's Messenger died."

Fear and hope were the tools that 'Umar used to control the Muslims' nerves. Because of the people's great love for the Prophet, the call to refuse to accept his death quickly found its way into their minds. Hence, no one objected to 'Umar and the belief that the Messenger had not died; this overtook all other news.

The Muslims lived several hours in total suspense and confusion. They were prevented from believing in the Prophet's ﷺ death until Abū Bakr returned from a nearby village.

As soon as Abū Bakr returned, he proceeded toward the prophet's house and uncovered his face to ensure he was dead. He then went to the Mosque and found 'Umar still stating that the Prophet had not died. Abū Bakr ordered 'Umar to sit down; 'Umar refused until he ordered him three times, yet 'Umar still refused. Thus, Abū Bakr stood in another corner of the Mosque and addressed the people:

> "He who worships Muḥammad should be informed that Muḥammad has died. He who worships God should know that God is ever-living and does not die."

Abū Bakr then recited the following verse:

﴿وَمَا مُحَمَّدٌ إِلَّا رَسُولٌ قَدْ خَلَتْ مِن قَبْلِهِ الرُّسُلُ ۚ أَفَإِن مَاتَ أَوْ قُتِلَ انقَلَبْتُمْ عَلَىٰ أَعْقَابِكُمْ﴾

﴾wa-mā muḥammadun 'illā rasūlun qad khalat min qablihi r-rusulu 'a-fa-'in māta 'aw qutila nqalabtum 'alā 'a'qābikum﴿

﴾Muḥammad is but an apostle; [other] apostles have passed before him. If he dies or is slain, will you turn back on your heels?﴿[283]

When the Muslims heard this, they submitted to the fact... Even ʿUmar believed he had died, and as ʿUmar himself said,

> "I only believed that he died after I had made sure that the verse was from the Noble Qur'ān."

Abū Bakr and ʿUmar's story was sad. Right? Yet even the simplest minds cannot be convinced that these events can be interpreted...

Look!

ʿUmar shouts, swears, and threatens those who say that the Messenger of God ﷺ has died... But when Abū Bakr recites a verse from the Qur'ān — which ʿUmar himself did not recognize — the latter suddenly collapses and believes that Muḥammad ﷺ died.

How did ʿUmar know the Prophet ﷺ will not die until his religion reigns over all other religions?

Did he inform ʿUmar that he would return to cut off the arms and legs of those who said he was dead?

Didn't ʿUmar know that the verse recited by Abū Bakr was a Qur'ānic verse so that he could claim to believe in the Prophet's ﷺ death?

But indeed, "still waters run deep!"

---

[283] Sūrat Āl ʿImrān, Verse 144.

By behaving in such a way, 'Umar could suspend the Muslims and hold them back for several hours until Abū Bakr returned. Then, they (Abū Bakr and 'Umar) immediately started the execution of their premeditated plan to seize power.

Can't you see 'Umar was overreacting to the Prophet's death? Still, simultaneously with Abū Bakr's speech, he turned around, forgetting all about his supposedly broken heart to announce his allegiance to Abū Bakr as the new leader of the Muslims.

At any rate, Abū Bakr's and 'Umar's success in seizing power from 'Alī عليه السلام after the Prophet's ﷺ death can only be the first of premeditated planning to do so long before the death of God's Messenger ﷺ. Thus, this show, which 'Umar and Abū Bakr put on, can only be part of this planning. We can verify the authenticity of this statement when hands are set free to search the pages of history books.

After the Prophet's ﷺ Death

After the Prophet's ﷺ death, events continued to occur. When studying the era following the Prophet's ﷺ death, history speaks of the wonders which occurred.

Indeed, history tells us about "Apostasy," which included most Muslims who objected to Abū Bakr's seizure of power from its righteous candidate, 'Alī b. Abū Ṭālib ؑ.

It also tells us how Sayyidah Fāṭimah's ؑ rights were usurped, especially in Fadak, and how 'Alī ؑ was dragged to the Mosque to pay allegiance to Abū Bakr!

History tells us how Sayyidah Fāṭimah's ؑ house was set on fire by him, who pretended not to believe in her father's death yesterday.

Yes, history tells us how the Prophet ﷺ died, and with him died his repeated warnings to those who would oppress his family members and that they will be met with the wrath of God ﷻ. It also tells us of Sayyidah Fāṭimah's ؑ sadness and misery, which she suffered after the death of her dear father.

Fidhdha, Sayyidah Fāṭimah's ؑ helper, spoke of Sayyidah Fāṭimah's ؑ sadness; she said: "It was on the eighth day after the Prophet's ﷺ death that Sayyidah Fāṭimah ؑ revealed the extent of her sorrow and inability to bear life without her father. She ؑ came to the Mosque and, while crying, said:

> `Oh! Father
>
> Oh! My sincere friend
>
> Oh! Abū al-Qāsim

Oh! The helper of the widowed and the orphans

Who do we have for Ka'bah and the Mosque?

Who does your saddened and grieved daughter have?"

Fidā' added:

"Sayyidah Fāṭimah ؑ then proceeded towards the tomb of the Prophet; it was difficult for her to walk because her tears covered her eyes. She passed out when she saw the mi'ḍanah (minaret), so the women rushed to rescue her. After putting water on her face, she regained consciousness.

Sayyidah Fāṭimah then said,

'My strength has been eradicated

My endurance has betrayed me

My enemies have rejoiced at my misfortune

And my grief will kill me

Father! I remain bewildered and lonely

Confused and lonesome

My voice is subdued

My back is broken

My life is disturbed

I find no one, Father, after you to attend to my loneliness

Neither to stop my tears

Nor to support me in times of weakness

Indeed, precise revelations, the place of Jibrā'īl's landing, and Mīkā'īl's location have vanished after you, Father,

Motives (of others) have changed

And gates have been shut in my face

Thus, I detest this world after you

And my tears shall be shed for you as long as I breathe.

My longing for you shall not cease.

My sadness for (being separated from) you shall not vanish, Sayyidah Fāṭimah then cried out loudly, Father.

With you went the light of the world

Its flowers wither away after blossoming in your presence

Father.

I will forever be sorrowful for you until we are reunited

Father.

Sleeping has left me since we have been separated

Father!

Who is there for the widows and the orphans?

Who will we have for the Ummah until the Day of Rising?

Father!

We became after you among the oppressed

Father.

People shun us after you.

After your presence among men glorified us,

Thus, what tear shall not spill on your departure?

What sadness (after you) shall not continue to exist?

Which eyelid shall be smeared with slumber?

You are the spring of faith and the light of Prophets

So, how can mountains not sway?

And seas not dry out?

How can the Earth not tremble?

Father! I have been afflicted with the greatest sorrow; my disaster is not minor!

Father.

I have been inflicted with the greatest misfortune and the biggest calamity.

Angels cry for you, and stars cease to move because of you

Your minbar (after you) is gloomy; your minbar is empty

Of your secret conversation (with your Lord)

Your grave is joyful for holding you

And Paradise is delighted with your presence

Supplication and prayers

Father!

How gloomy are your meeting places (without your presence)?

How pained I am for you until I soon join you!

How bereaved is Abū al-Ḥasan, the entrusted one!

The Father of your two sons, al-Ḥasan and al-Ḥusayn, your beloved one

He whom you brought up as a youth and made your brother a man (Abū al-Ḥasan)

The most beloved of your companions to you

Abū al-Ḥasan, who was the first to immigrate and help you

Sadness has overtaken us; Crying will kill us

And distress will always accompany us.'

Sayyidah Fāṭimah ﷺ then returned to her house and lived in misery and sadness until she joined her beloved father not long after he passed away."

Following Imām ʿAlī ﵊ to the Mosque

After the Messenger of God ﷺ, Abū Bakr seized the Caliphate. He and his followers claimed that since the Muslims unanimously elected him, he was the righteous leader of the Ummah.

Yet, with a bit of reflection upon the matter of the Caliphate, one realizes it is an extension and continuation of the Prophethood without revelation. Since Prophethood can only be assigned to someone through divine decree, the Caliphate cannot be given to anyone by people; instead, it is a divine decree given to specific men by God.

This consensus that Abū Bakr and his followers claim to have achieved is not valid because the Ansār, Banī Hāshim, ʿAmmār, Salmān, Miqdād, Abū Dharr, and many other companions opposed the takeover by Abū Bakr of this divine post, which was previously granted to Imām ʿAlī ﵊. Abū Bakr could seize power and eradicate ʿAlī's ﵊ and his followers' attempts to regain his righteous position.

Why was Abū Bakr elected?

We can cite several factors that have motivated some Muslims to choose Abū Bakr as their leader:

1. Resentment to see both prophethood and Imāmate posts occupied by Banī Hāshim. ʿUmar revealed this factor in a long conversation with Ibn ʿAbbās: According to ʿUmar, (If prophethood and Imāmate posts were both occupied by Banī Hāshim) then they would constantly brag about them!

2. ʿAlī's ﵊ youthful age

3. The Arabs, especially the Qurayshīs, envy of ʿAlī ﷺ

4. ʿAlī ﷺ would lead and judge people according to righteousness and the right path had they chosen him as the leader, as ʿUmar stated.

After Abū Bakr seized power, ʿAlī ﷺ should inevitably pay allegiance to him, for it is the natural path of every coup to force the opposition to announce its support to the new regime. But what can they do with ʿAlī ﷺ, who refused to pledge allegiance to Abū Bakr?

Can they threaten him? But he is the famous hero who could extinguish the Arab heroes, kill their brave men, and compete with their "wolves"!

Can they deceive him ﷺ into doing so? But ʿAlī ﷺ is that cautious man who is aware of such matters!

Nevertheless, allegiance must be taken from ʿAlī ﷺ at any rate.

But behold! What would Sayyidah Fāṭimah's ﷺ stand be had ʿAlī ﷺ been forced to pledge allegiance to Abū Bakr? In other words, what can they do if Sayyidah Fāṭimah ﷺ defends her husband?

Should they ignore all these obstacles? Or what should they do?

This created an unsolvable problem for the coup leaders, who spent long hours reflecting on the issue. Meanwhile, Imām ʿAlī ﷺ confined himself to his house to compile the Noble Qurʾān after realizing the fruitlessness of his efforts to regain his rights. He virtually secluded himself from the outside world. This situation was disadvantageous to the coup leaders, for in ʿAlī's ﷺ refusal to pledge allegiance to Abū Bakr lies a deep meaning and an excuse for others to object to Abū Bakr's seizure of power.

Yet, opinions met of the necessity of bringing ʿAlī ﷺ by force to the Mosque, whatever the price. Mainly because they later came to realize that he was more concerned about Islām's interests than his own. Therefore, a commissioned force led by ʿUmar's slave boy, Qunfud, was sent to ʿAlī's ﷺ house. When this force reached the house, Qunfud requested permission to enter so they may speak to him regarding the issue, but ʿAlī ﷺ refused them permission to enter, after which they returned to the Mosque and said to Abū Bakr and ʿUmar:

> "They refused us permission to enter."

ʿUmar said:

> "Go back, and if you are denied permission again, then enter (the house) with force."

So the group once again asked for permission, but Sayyidah Fāṭimah ﷺ said:

> "You are prohibited from entering my house without permission."

Upon hearing this, the force members went back except for Qunfud. They informed ʿUmar that they were not allowed to enter the house. This angered ʿUmar, who said:

> "What do women have in this?"

Events continued to occur, and two pictures were drawn in front of us:

First:

'Umar orders his slave boy to start Sayyidah Fāṭimah's ﷺ house on fire! A man objects by saying:

> "But Sayyidah Fāṭimah is in it."

Yet 'Umar replied:

> "So what!"

Second[284]:

The Prophet ﷺ assigned 'Alī ﷺ as his successor. All the companions had full knowledge of this assignment. Yet 'Umar forgets this fact for the sake of Abū Bakr and strikes Sayyidah Fāṭimah's ﷺ womb, which causes her to miscarry Muḥsin.

At any rate, 'Alī ﷺ was forced to come to the Mosque. When Sayyidah Fāṭimah al-Zahrā' ﷺ saw this, she followed him and addressed Abū Bakr by saying:

> "Do you wish to make me a widow? By God, if you do not let him go, I will uncover my head, rip my shirt, and go to my father's tomb and cry to my Lord..."

---

[284] According to Jāḥiẓ and the author of *'Abaqāt al-Anwār*.

So she took al-Ḥasan and al-Ḥusayn's hands and proceeded towards her father's tomb!

When Imām 'Alī saw the seriousness of the situation, he immediately interfered and said to Salmān:

> "Prevent Muḥammad's daughter (from reaching her father's grave) for surely I can see the outskirts of Madīnah being sunk into the earth."

Salmān later said:

> "I was near Sayyidah Fāṭimah when, by God, I saw the foundations of the Mosque's walls being elevated up to the point that had a man wanted to go from under them, he would have been able to do so. So I said:
>
> > 'My Mistress, surely God sent your father to be mercy, thus do not become the cause of His wrath.'"

These noble stands of Sayyidah Fāṭimah forced Abū Bakr and 'Umar to release 'Alī; Sayyidah Fāṭimah returned home after setting the most honorable example of devotion to her husband.

Encounters in the Mosque:

As we have already mentioned, Abū Bakr sent 'Umar to Sayyidah Fāṭimah's house with orders to compel 'Alī and his friends to come and pledge allegiance to him. If these means could not persuade them, 'Umar would set the house on fire. When Sayyidah Fāṭimah asked him what he meant, he told her he would undoubtedly burn the house down unless they were content to do as the rest of the people had done.

Knowing 'Umar's temper, 'Alī ‎ and his friends exited the house. Imām 'Alī ‎, whom 'Abbās and Zubayr accompanied, approached 'Umar's party saying,

> "O you, Muhājirs! You claim the succession to the Prophet of God, citing your priority in Islām and your kinship to him before the Ansārs. Now, I put forward the same arguments in preference to you. Am I not the first who believed in the Prophet before any of you embraced his faith? Am I not the nearest to the Prophet than any of you? Fear God, if you are true believers, do not snatch away the Prophet's authority from his house to your own."

Standing behind the door, Sayyidah Fāṭimah ‎ reproachfully addressed the raiding people thus:

> "O, people! You left behind the Prophet's dead body to us and proceeded to wring the Caliphate for yourselves, extinguishing our rights."

She ‎ then burst into tears and cried:

> "O Father! O Prophet of God! How soon after you are troubles pouring on us at the hands of the son of Khaṭṭāb ('Umar) and the son of Abū Quḥāfah (Abū Bakr)! How soon they ignored your words at Ghadīr al-Khum and your saying that 'Alī was to you as Hārūn was to Mūsā."

Hearing Sayyidah Fāṭimah's ‎ wailing, most people in 'Umar's party turned back. 'Alī ‎ was, however, taken to Abū Bakr and was asked to swear allegiance to him.

Imām ʻAlī عليه السلام said:

> "What if I do not do him homage?"

He was answered:

> "By God, we shall kill you if you do not do as others have done,"

Upon hearing this, ʻAlī عليه السلام said:

> "What! Will you kill a man who is a servant of the Lord and a brother of the Prophet of the Lord?"

Hearing this, ʻUmar said,

> "We do not acknowledge you as a brother of the prophet of the Lord"

and addressed Abū Bakr, who was silent, requesting him to speak out about ʻAlī's عليه السلام fate, but (it was claimed) Abū Bakr said that so long as Sayyidah Fāṭimah عليها السلام was alive, he would not compel her husband to do so. So ʻAlī عليه السلام departed and proceeded directly to the tomb of the Prophet ﷺ where he cried out:

> "O, my brother! Your people now treat me contemptuously and are bent on killing me."

Abū Bakr Versus Sayyidah Fāṭimah ﷺ

Sayyidah Fāṭimah ﷺ, the only surviving child of the Prophet, his most beloved, claimed the inheritance of the property which could be apportioned to her in the lands of Madīnah and Khaybar, as also Fadak, which were gained without the use of force, the Prophet had given to her for her maintenance, under the commands of God ﷻ.[285]

Yet, Fadak became an arena for political games when Abū Bakr refused to transfer it to Sayyidah Fāṭimah ﷺ. It is appropriate here to speak about Fadak before clarifying the corresponding events that occurred in its regard:

Fadak was a village at a two-day walking distance from Madīnah. It was inhabited by Jews who refused to submit to Islām initially, but they later realized the might of the Muslims, especially after they were led by ʿAlī b. Abū Ṭālib ﷺ conquered Khaybar; the Jews yielded to the Messenger of God ﷺ without fighting. So he took possession of the village.

The village was valued at 100,000 dirhams by ʿUmar's appraisers when he expelled its inhabitants to Sūrīyah. ʿUmar took possession of the village and paid half the price to the Jews.

Fadak becomes the Prophet's ﷺ personal property

Since the reason that motivated the inhabitants of Fadak to transfer its possession to God's Messenger ﷺ was fear of the Muslims after they had conquered Khaybar, this property became the sole possession of the Prophet ﷺ. This conforms to God's decree in the Noble Qurʾān:

---

285 Ṣadūq, Shaykh Muḥammad b. ʿAlī, *Man Lā Yaḥḍuruh al-Faqīh*.

﴿وَمَا أَفَاءَ اللَّهُ عَلَىٰ رَسُولِهِ مِنْهُمْ فَمَا أَوْجَفْتُمْ عَلَيْهِ مِنْ خَيْلٍ وَلَا رِكَابٍ وَلَٰكِنَّ اللَّهَ يُسَلِّطُ رُسُلَهُ عَلَىٰ مَن يَشَاءُ ۚ وَاللَّهُ عَلَىٰ كُلِّ شَيْءٍ قَدِيرٌ﴾

﴿wa-mā 'afā'a llāhu 'alā rasūlihī minhum fa-mā 'awjaftum 'alayhi min khaylin wa-lā rikābin wa-lākinna llāha yusalliṭu rusulahū 'alā man yashā'u wa-llāhu 'alā kulli shay'in qadīr^un^﴾

﴿The spoils that God gave to His Apostle from them, you did not spur any horse for its sake, nor any riding camel, but God makes His apostles prevail over whomever He wishes, and God has power over all things﴾[286]

There was no dispute between the Muslims that Fadak belonged to the Prophet ﷺ; instead, the disagreement was related to how much Fadak the Jews granted him as part of the peace settlement. Thus, it is strange to hear Abū Bakr narrate a tradition from the Prophet:

> "We, the group of Prophets, do not inherit, nor are we inherited; what we leave is for alms!"

Because, had the Prophet said so (which is not true), how did Abū Bakr understand from this saying that Fadak did not belong to him? There is an apparent contradiction in Abū Bakr's arguments.

Therefore, after realizing beyond doubt that Fadak was the personal property of God's Messenger ﷺ, it is appropriate to inquire about what he did with it. But the answer is obvious. He granted it to Sayyidah Fāṭimah ﷺ before his death. Fadak became the personal property of Sayyidah Fāṭimah al-Zahrā' ﷺ. It is not

[286] Sūrat al-Ḥashr, Verse 6.

for anyone to object to the Prophet ﷺ for granting his property to anyone, including his daughter.

We can cite the following factors as proofs of the Prophet's ﷺ granting Fadak to his noble daughter ؏:

1. Sayyidah Fāṭimah's ؏ saying to Imām 'Alī ؏:

"This is Ibn Abū Quḥāfah snatching away my father's grant to me."

2. Sayyidah Fāṭimah al-Zahrā"s ؏ saying to Abū Bakr:

"Surely Fadak was granted to me by my father, the Messenger of God ﷺ."

Her infallibility prevents her from uttering falsehood or demanding that which does not belong to her.

3. 'Alī ؏, the infallible Imām, would not allow his wife to demand something that did not belong to her.

4. Imām 'Alī ؏ wrote in his letter to 'Uthmān b. Ḥunayf:

"Yes! Fadak was the only land from that which was under the heavens, in our hands, but the inclinations of certain men lusted for it, and the souls of others relinquished it."

Hence, had it been part of the Prophet's ﷺ inheritance, he ﷺ would not have said that it belonged to them ('Alī and Sayyidah Fāṭimah ؏).

5. Imām ʿAlī عليه السلام, together with Umm Ayman, testified to the fact that God's Messenger ﷺ granted it to Sayyidah Fāṭimah al-Zahrāʾ عليها السلام when Abū Bakr requested Sayyidah Fāṭimah to summon witnesses that he ﷺ gave it to her.

Yet, despite these indisputable proofs, Abū Bakr denied Sayyidah Fāṭimah's عليها السلام possession of Fadak and brought the following as proof of the correctness of his action:

1. According to Abū Bakr, Fadak did not belong to the Messenger of God ﷺ; it instead was the property of all Muslims.

2. Besides, according to Abū Bakr, even if it belonged to the Prophet of God ﷺ, he had heard him saying:

   "We, the group of prophets, do not inherit, nor are we inherited."

3. Abū Hurayrah narrated that the Prophet ﷺ said:

   "My inheritance is not to be divided after me, even if it is one dinar or dirham. That which I leave is alms, save what is to maintain my wives and dependents."

However, when these hypothetical points made by Abū Bakr are put on the board for discussion, free from ideological or emotional prejudgments, and far from blind sanctification of the early followers of Islām, we can record the following points against them:

1. He denied the Prophet's ﷺ ownership of Fadak. Still, all the Muslims—whether early Muslims or present-day ones-

unanimously agree that Fadak was the sole possession of God's Prophet ﷺ. This fact is also supported by the Qur'ānic verse we have already mentioned. Therefore, Abū Bakr's claim is invalidated for merely attempting to nullify the effect of the Qur'ān.

2. Abū Bakr's claim that he heard the Prophet of God ﷺ say:

"We, the group of prophets, do not inherit, nor are we inherited; what we leave is for alms,"

It is disputable because,

a. This narration is irrelevant regarding this issue; we have already stated that Fadak was a grant from the Prophet ﷺ to his daughter before he died. So, quoting a narration related to inheritance is inappropriate to deny Sayyidah Fāṭimah ؑ her property.

b. This narration was only reported by one man — who is Abū Bakr himself — and since the Noble Qur'ān stated a general rule concerning inheritance, the Prophets and their heirs are included in this rule. So, Abū Bakr's claim cannot be considered proof from the Noble Qur'ān, nor can it be proof of excluding the prophets and their families from the Qur'ānic rule.

c. Yet, the actual reasons that provoked Abū Bakr and his followers to deprive Sayyidah Fāṭimah al-Zahrā' ؑ of her property, even though the Prophet ﷺ said:

"Sayyidah Fāṭimah is a part of me, he who loves her loves me, and he who angers her anger me,"' had more dangerous and implicit motives behind them; they were directly related to the political events of that time.

3. As for Abū Hurayrah's narration, it is sufficient for us to remember that he was famous for forging Prophetic traditions. Even he, himself, admitted this[287].

The real motives led Abū Bakr to usurp Fadak from Sayyidah Fāṭimah.

The history books at hand need thorough examination and revision, for they have been recorded according to the wishes and satisfactions of despotic rulers throughout history. Given this, and because Sayyidah Fāṭimah al-Zahrā' was a strong supporter of her husband in his quest to regain the Caliphate, her views were proof that the followers of Imām 'Alī could use Fadak to verify his claims against Abū Bakr easily; we can easily understand how Abū Bakr was successful in depriving Sayyidah Fāṭimah al-Zahrā' of her rights, and how his moves corresponded to his adopted political thinking. So, not only was Abū Bakr able to persuade the Muslims to dismiss Sayyidah Fāṭimah's stands as those of a woman who can be depended upon even in such a secondary issue like Fadak, but he also aimed at convincing them that since she was not to be believed in such a matter, she was also to be abandoned with the most critical issue of that time (i.e., Caliphate).

Yet, more motives can be spotted to have led Abū Bakr to usurp Sayyidah Fāṭimah al-Zahrā''s property. Among them are:

---

[287] Anyone wishing to study more about his life should refer to Abū Rayyah, Maḥmūd, *Shaykh al-Madhirah: Abū Hurayrah Dawsī*.

1. Since Fadak brought enormous profits to its owners, 'Alī ﷺ could use this profit in his fight against Abū Bakr just as Sayyidah Khadījah ﷺ was able to use her wealth against the infidels.

2. The political challenge that Abū Bakr created here was aimed at proving to 'Alī and Sayyidah Fāṭimah al-Zahrā' ﷺ that the nation was not ready to aid them in an emotional issue in which he was successful in downgrading 'Alī and Sayyidah Fāṭimah ﷺ by controlling and directing public opinion. Listen to Abū Bakr as he speaks to the people after Sayyidah Fāṭimah's ﷺ speech in the Mosque:

"O, people!

What is this attentiveness to every aimless speech?

Where were these claims at the time of God's Messenger ﷺ?

He who heard something should say so!

He who witnessed anything should speak out!

Indeed, they are ('Alī and Sayyidah Fāṭimah ﷺ) like foxes who have no witnesses save their tails!

They instigate every dissension!

And say: Renew (trouble) after it has cooled down

They seek help from the weak and gain support from women

They are like Umm Tahal (a woman who was a prostitute during the era of ignorance) whose family chose prostitution for her

Indeed, if I wish, I can say a lot and had I said (something), I would have revealed (much).

But I will remain silent as long as I am left alone."

3. Abū Bakr's drive to deprive Sayyidah Fāṭimah al-Zahrā' ﷺ of her property had another underlying motive. Had Abū Bakr admitted Sayyidah Fāṭimah's ﷺ words regarding Fadak as indisputable facts, she could also claim her husband's right to leadership, which would force Abū Bakr to hand it back to 'Alī ﷺ.

Ibn Abī l-Ḥadīd said:

I asked 'Alī b. Fariqi, a distinguished teacher of Madrassa-Gharbia, Baghdad:

"Was Sayyidah Fāṭimah truthful in making a claim (regarding Fadak)?"

He answered:

"Yes!"

I said:

"Did Abū Bakr know she was a truthful woman?"

Again, he answered:

> "Yes."

I asked:

> "Then why did the Caliph not give that she was entitled to back to her?"

At that moment, the teacher smiled and said with great dignity:

> "If he had accepted her word on that day and had returned Fadak to her on account of her being a truthful woman and without asking for any witnesses, she could very well use this position for the benefit of her husband on the following day and say: 'My husband, 'Alī, is entitled to the Caliphate, ' and then the Caliph would have had to surrender the Caliphate to 'Alī on account of his having acknowledged her to be a truthful woman. However, to obviate any such claim or dispute, he deprived her of her undisputed right!"

4. Several emotional factors led Abū Bakr to refuse Sayyidah Fāṭimah, Sayyidah Khadījah's daughter, her rights. Some of these factors are:

   a. Once, the Prophet of God ﷺ sent Abū Bakr to the Muslims, during Hajj season, to recite for them the newly revealed Sūrat al-Tawbah, but before reaching his destination, Abū Bakr was stopped by 'Alī b. Abū Ṭālib ﷺ informed him that the Messenger commanded him to deliver the Sūrah himself because according to the Prophet:

"No one can take the Messenger's place save him or someone from him."

This undoubtedly creates a feeling of envy in a man's heart! A matter that can be said to have influenced Abū Bakr himself.

b. When the Prophet was too ill to lead the prayers, Abū Bakr was asked by his daughter, 'Ā'isha, to do so. But as soon as God's Messenger ﷺ learned what was going on, he, supported by Imām 'Alī and 'Abbās, came out and removed Abū Bakr and led the prayers himself. The author of *Sayyidah Fāṭimah Umm Abiha* says:

"This event might have led Abū Bakr to think that Sayyidah Fāṭimah was the one who informed the Prophet ﷺ of Abū Bakr's actions, just as 'Ā'isha told him (Abū Bakr) to lead the prayers!"

c. 'Ā'isha, the Prophet's ﷺ wife, and Abū Bakr's daughter had uncalled-for feelings towards Sayyidah Fāṭimah ؏ and her mother, Sayyidah Khadījah ؏.

For instance, 'Ā'isha said:

"Although Sayyidah Khadījah died three years before the Prophet married me, I did not have a feeling of envy" for anyone as much as I had for her. This was because he (the Prophet) constantly mentioned her name, and His ﷻ Lord ordered him to give her the good news of a house made of brocade in Paradise. He also slaughtered sheep and distributed their meat among her (Sayyidah Khadījah's) friends."

This undoubtedly led Abū Bakr to join his daughter in her feelings towards Sayyidah Khadījah عليها السلام, her daughter (Sayyidah Fāṭimah عليها السلام), and her son-in-law ('Alī عليه السلام).

d. 'Ā'isha, Abū Bakr's daughter, was sterile. Yet Sayyidah Khadījah عليها السلام was the only wife of the Prophet who had children who survived. That child of Sayyidah Khadījah عليها السلام was 'Ā'isha's principal adversary, Sayyidah Fāṭimah عليها السلام. So the Messenger of God's ﷺ descendants would only come from his daughter عليها السلام and her husband, 'Alī عليه السلام. This surely was an unwelcome fact to 'Ā'isha and her father, Abū Bakr.

Sayyidah Fāṭimah's ﷺ Protest Against Abū Bakr's Actions

Sayyidah Fāṭimah ﷺ felt grieved by Abū Bakr's actions and was so displeased with him that when she knew of his attempt to seize Fadak, she accompanied a group of women to the mosque. There, she sat down and delivered the following speech:

> 'Praise be to God for that which He gave us, and thanks be to Him for all that which He inspired and commended in His Name for that which He Provided: Form prevalent favors which He created, And abundant benefactions which He offered and perfect grants which He presented; (such benefactions) that their number is much too plentiful to compute; Bounties too vast to measure; Their limit was too distant to realize; He recommended to them (His creatures) to gain more (of His benefaction) by being grateful for their continuity; He ordained Himself praiseworthy by giving generously to His creatures; I bear witness that there is no God but God One without a partner, a statement which sincere devotion is made to be its interpretation; hearts guarantee its continuation, and illuminated in the minds is its sensibility. He Who cannot be perceived with vision; neither can He be described with tongues; nor can imagination surround His state.
>
> He originated things but not from anything before them and created them without examples. Rather, He created them with His might and dispersed them according to His will; not for a need did He create them; nor for a benefit (for Him) did He shape them, But to establish His wisdom, bring attention to His obedience, manifest His might, lead His creatures to venerate Him humbly, and to exalt His decrees. He then made the reward for His obedience and punishment for His

disobedience to protect His creatures from His Wrath and amass them into His Paradise.

I, too, bear witness that my father, Muḥammad, is His Slave and Messenger, Whom He chose before sending him, named him before sending him when creatures were still concealed in that which was transcendental, guarded against that which was appalling, and associated with the termination and nonexistence. For God ﷻ knew what was to follow, comprehended what would come to pass, And realized the place of every event. God has sent him (Muḥammad) as perfection for His commands, a resolution to accomplish His rule, and an implementation of the decrees of His Mercy. So he found the nations to vary in their faiths: Obsessed by their fires, Worshipping their idols, And denying God despite their knowledge of Him. Therefore, God illuminated their darkness with my father, Muḥammad, uncovered obscurity from their hearts and cleared the clouds from their insights. He revealed guidance among the people, So he delivered them from being led astray, led them away from misguidance, guided them to the proper religion, and called them to the straight path.

God then recalled him back in mercy, love, and preference. So, Muḥammad is in comfort from the burden of this world; devoted angels surround him, the Merciful Lord's satisfaction, and the mighty King's nearness.

So may the praise of God be upon my father, His Prophet, the Trusted one, the chosen one from among His creatures, and His sincere friend, and may peace and blessings of God be upon him.'

Sayyidah Fāṭimah ﷺ then turned to the crowd and said: 'Surely you are God's slaves at His command Prohibition; You are the bearers of His religion and revelation; You are God's trusted ones with yourselves; and His messengers to the nations. Amongst you does He have righteous authority; A covenant He brought unto you, and an heir He left to guard you; That is The eloquent book of God; The truthful Qur'ān; The brilliant light; The shining beam; Its insights are indisputable; Its secrets are revealed; Its indications are manifest; and its followers are blessed by it. (The Qur'ān) leads its adherents to goodwill, and Hearing it leads to salvation; with it are the bright divine authorities achieved, His manifest determination gained, His prohibited decrees avoided, His manifest evidence recognized, His satisfying proofs made apparent, His permissions granted, and His laws written.

So, God ﷻ made belief to be purification for you from polytheism.

Prayer — exaltation for you from conceit.

Giving alms — a purification for the soul and a (cause of) growth in subsistence.

Fasting — implantation of devotion.

Pilgrimage — a construction of religion.

Justice — a harmony of the hearts.

Obeying us (Ahl al-Bayt) — management of the nation.

Our leadership (Ahl al-Bayt) — safeguard from disunity.

Jihād (*struggle*)— a strengthening of Islām.

Patience — a helping course for deserving (divine) reward.

Ordering goodness (a*mr bil ma'rūf*) — public welfare.

Kindness to the parents — safeguard from wrath.

Maintaining close relations with one's kin — a cause for a longer life and multiplying the number of descendants.

Retaliation (*Qiṣāṣ*) — For sparing blood (souls).

Fulfillment of vows— subjecting oneself to mercy.

Completion of weights and measures — a cause for preventing the neglect of others' rights. Forbiddance of drinking wines an exaltation from atrocity.

Avoiding slander — a veil from a curse.

Abandoning theft — a reason for deserving chastity.

Prohibited polytheism — so that one can devote himself to His Lordship.

Therefore, Fear God as He should be feared, and die not except in a state of Islām; obey God in what He has commanded you to do and that which He has forbidden, for indeed those truly fear among His servants, who know.'

Sayyidah Fāṭimah al-Zahrā' ﷺ then added:

> 'O People! Be informed that I am Sayyidah Fāṭimah, and my father is Muḥammad. I say that repeatedly and initiate it continually; I say not what I say mistakenly, nor do I do what I do aimlessly. Now hath come unto you an Apostle from amongst yourselves; It grieves him that you should perish; Ardently anxious is he over you; To the believers he is most kind and merciful. Thus, if you identify and recognize him, you shall realize that he is my father and not the father of any of your women, the brother of my cousin ('Alī ﷺ) rather than any of your men. What an excellent identity he was. May the peace and blessings of God be upon him and his descendants. Thus, he propagated the Message by coming out openly with the warning, and while inclined away from the path of the polytheists, (whom he) struck their strength and seized their throats. At the same time, he invited (all) to the way of his Lord with wisdom and beautiful preaching. He destroyed idols and defeated heroes until their group fled and turned their backs. So night revealed its dawn; righteousness uncovered its genuineness; the voice of the religious authority spoke out loud; the evil discords were silenced; The crown of hypocrisy was diminished; the tightening of infidelity and desertion were untied, So you said the statement of devotion amongst a band of starved ones, and you were on the edge of a hole of fire; (you were) the drink of the thirsty one; the opportunity of the desiring one; the firebrand of him who passes in haste; the step for feet; you used to drink from the water gathered on roads; eat jerked meat.[288]

---

[288] Sayyidah Fāṭimah ﷺ was stating their lowly situation before Islām.

You were despised outcasts, continually fearing abduction from those around you. Yet, God rescued you through my father, Muḥammad, after much ado, and after he was confronted by mighty men, the Arab beasts, and the demons of the people of the Book Who, whenever they ignited the fire of war, God extinguished it. Whenever the thorn of the devil appeared, or a mouth of the polytheists opened wide in defiance, he would strike its discords with his brother ('Alī, ﷺ), who comes not back until he treads its wing with the sole of his feet and extinguishes its flames with his sword. ('Alī is) diligent in God's affair, near to the Messenger of God, A master among God's worshippers, setting to work briskly, sincere in his advice, earnest and exerting himself (in service to Islām); While you were calm, gay, and feeling safe in your comfortable lives, waiting for us to meet disasters, awaiting the spread of news, you fell back during every battle. You took to your heels at times of fighting. Yet, When God chose His Prophet from the dwelling of His prophets and the abode of His sincere (servants), The thorns of hypocrisy appeared on you, the garment of faith became worn out, The misguided ignorant spoke out, the sluggish, ignorant came to the front and brayed. The male camel of the vain wiggled his tail in your courtyards, and the Devil stuck his head from its hiding place and called upon you; he found you responsive to his invitation and observing his deceits. He then aroused you, found you quick (to answer him), and invited you to wrath; therefore, you branded other than your camels and proceeded to other than your drinking places. Then, while the era of the Prophet was still near, the gash was still wide; the scar had not yet healed, and the Messenger was not yet buried. A (quick) undertaking, as you claimed, aimed at preventing discord (trial); surely, they have fallen into trial already! And indeed, Hell surrounds the unbelievers. How preposterous! What an idea!

What a falsehood! For God's Book is still amongst you; its affairs are apparent; its rules are manifest; its signs are dazzling; its restrictions are visible, and its commands are evident. Yet, indeed, you have cast it behind your backs! What! Do you detest it? Or according to something else you wish to rule? Evil would be the exchange for the wrongdoers! And if anyone desires a religion other than Islām (submission to God), it will never be accepted by him, And in the hereafter, he will be in the ranks of those who have lost. Surely, you have not waited until its stampede seized and it became obedient. You then started arousing its flames, instigating its coal, complying with the call of the misled devil, quenching the light of the manifest religion, and extinguishing the light of the sincere Prophet. You concealed sips on froth and proceeded toward his (the Prophet) kin and children in swamps and forests (meaning you plot against them in deceitful ways). Still, we are patient with you as if we are being notched with knives and stung by spearheads in our abdomens, yet now you claim that there is no inheritance for us! What!

﴿أَفَحُكْمَ الْجَاهِلِيَّةِ يَبْغُونَ ۚ وَمَنْ أَحْسَنُ مِنَ اللَّهِ حُكْمًا لِقَوْمٍ يُوقِنُونَ﴾

﴾'a-fa-ḥukma l-jāhiliyyati yabghūna wa-man 'aḥsanu mina llāhi ḥukman li-qawmin yūqinūna﴿

﴾Do they seek the judgement of [pagan] ignorance? But who is better than God in judgement for a people who have certainty?﴿[289]

---

[289] Sūrat al-Mā'idah, Verse 50.

Don't you know? Yes, indeed, it is obvious to you that I am his daughter. O Muslims! Will my inheritance be usurped? O son of Abū Quḥāfah! Where is it in the Book of God that you inherit your father, and I do not inherit mine? Indeed, you have come up with an unprecedented thing. Do you intentionally abandon and cast the Book of God behind your back? Do you not read where it says:

﴿وَوَرِثَ سُلَيْمَانُ دَاوُودَ﴾

﴿wa-waritha sulaymānu dāwūda﴾

﴿Sulaymān inherited from Dāwūd﴾[290]

And when it narrates the story of Zakariyyā and says:

﴿وَإِنِّي خِفْتُ الْمَوَالِيَ مِن وَرَائِي وَكَانَتِ امْرَأَتِي عَاقِرًا فَهَبْ لِي مِن لَدُنكَ وَلِيًّا﴾

﴿wa-'innī khiftu l-mawāliya min warā'ī wa-kānati mra'atī 'āqiran fa-hab lī min ladunka waliyya^n﴾

﴿يَرِثُنِي وَيَرِثُ مِنْ آلِ يَعْقُوبَ ۖ وَاجْعَلْهُ رَبِّ رَضِيًّا﴾

﴿yarithunī wa-yarithu min 'āli ya'qūba wa-j'alhu rabbi raḍiyya^n﴾

﴿Indeed I fear my kinsmen, after me, and my wife is barren. So grant me from Yourself an heir who may inherit from me and

---

[290] Sūrat al-Naml, Verse 16.

inherit from the House of Ya'qūb, and make him, my Lord, pleasing [to You]!'﴿[291]

And:

﴿وَأُولُو الْأَرْحَامِ بَعْضُهُمْ أَوْلَىٰ بِبَعْضٍ فِي كِتَابِ اللَّهِ﴾

﴿*wa-'ulū l-'arḥāmi ba'ḍuhum 'awlā bi-ba'ḍin fī kitābi llāhi*﴾

﴿*but the blood relatives are more entitled to inherit from one another in the Book of God**﴾[292]

And:

﴿يُوصِيكُمُ اللَّهُ فِي أَوْلَادِكُمْ لِلذَّكَرِ مِثْلُ حَظِّ الْأُنثَيَيْنِ﴾

﴿*yūṣīkumu llāhu fī 'awlādikum li-dh-dhakari mithlu ḥaẓẓi l-'unthayayni*﴾

﴿*God enjoins you concerning your children: for the male shall be the like of the share of two females*﴾[293]

---

[291] Sūrat Maryam, Verses 5-6.

[292] Sūrat al-Anfāl, Verse 75.

* Cf. 33:6.

[293] Sūrat al-Nisā', Verse 11.

And,

﴿كُتِبَ عَلَيْكُمْ إِذَا حَضَرَ أَحَدَكُمُ الْمَوْتُ إِن تَرَكَ خَيْرًا الْوَصِيَّةُ لِلْوَالِدَيْنِ وَالْأَقْرَبِينَ بِالْمَعْرُوفِ ۖ حَقًّا عَلَى الْمُتَّقِينَ﴾

﴿kutiba 'alaykum 'idhā ḥaḍara 'aḥadakumu l-mawtu 'in taraka khayran-i l-waṣiyyatu li-l-wālidayni wa-l-'aqrabīna bi-l-ma'rūfi ḥaqqan 'alā l-muttaqīna﴾

﴿Prescribed for you, when death approaches any of you and he leaves behind any property, is that he make a bequest for his parents and relatives, in an honourable manner, —an obligation on the Godwary﴾[294]

You claim that I have no share! And that I do not inherit my father! What! Did God reveal a (Qur'ānic) verse regarding you, from which He excluded my father? Or do you say: 'These (Sayyidah Fāṭimah and her father) are the people of two faiths; they do not inherit each other?' Are we not, me and my father, a people adhering to one faith? Or is it that you have more knowledge about the specifications and generalizations of the Qur'ān than my father and my cousin (Imām 'Alī)? So, here you are! Take it! (Ready with) its nose rope and saddled! But if it shall encounter you on the Day of Gathering; (thus) what a wonderful judge is God, a claimant is Muḥammad, and a day is the Day of Rising. At the time of the Hour shall the wrongdoers lose, and it shall not benefit you to regret (your actions) then! For every message, there is a time limit; soon shall ye know who will be inflicted with torture that will

---

[294] Sūrat al-Baqarah, Verse 180.

humiliate him and who will be confronted by an everlasting punishment.

(Sayyidah Fāṭimah then turned towards the Ansārs and said:)

O, you people of intellect! The strong supporters of the nation! And those who embraced Islām, what is this shortcoming in defending my right? And what is this slumber (while you see) injustice (being done toward me)? Did not the Messenger of God, my father, used to say: A man is upheld (remembered) by his children? Oh, how quickly have you violated (his orders)? How soon have you plotted against us? But you still are capable (of helping me in) my attempt and powerful (to help me) in that which I request and (in) my pursuit (of it). Or do you say:

"Muḥammad has perished"?

Indeed, this is a great calamity; Its damage is excessive, its injury is significant, and Its wound (is much too deep) to heal. The Earth became darkened with his departure; the stars eclipsed for his calamity; hopes were seized; mountains submitted; sanctity was violated, and holiness was encroached upon after his death. Therefore, this, by God, is the great affliction and the grand calamity; there is not an affliction which is the like of it, nor will there be a sudden misfortune (as surprising as this). The Book of God ﷻ announced in the courtyards (of your houses) where you spend your evenings and mornings: a call, a cry, a recitation, and (verses) in order. It had previously come upon His (God's) Prophets and Messengers; (for it is) a decree final, and predestination fulfilled:

﴿وَمَا مُحَمَّدٌ إِلَّا رَسُولٌ قَدْ خَلَتْ مِن قَبْلِهِ الرُّسُلُ ۚ أَفَإِن مَّاتَ أَوْ قُتِلَ انقَلَبْتُمْ عَلَىٰ أَعْقَابِكُمْ ۚ وَمَن يَنقَلِبْ عَلَىٰ عَقِبَيْهِ فَلَن يَضُرَّ اللَّهَ شَيْئًا ۗ وَسَيَجْزِي اللَّهُ الشَّاكِرِينَ﴾

﴿wa-mā muḥammadun ʾillā rasūlun qad khalat min qablihi r-rusulu ʾa-fa-ʾin māta ʾaw qutila nqalabtum ʿalā ʾaʿqābikum wa-man yanqalib ʿalā ʿaqibayhi fa-lan yaḍurra llāha shayʾan wa-sa-yajzī llāhu sh-shākirīna﴾

﴿Muḥammad is but an apostle; [other] apostles have passed before him. If he dies or is slain, will you turn back on your heels? Anyone who turns back on his heels will not harm Allah in the least, and soon Allah will reward the grateful﴾[295]

O you people of reflection, will they usurp me the inheritance of my father while you hear and see me? (And while) You are sitting and gathered around me? You hear my call and are included in the (news of the) affair? (But) You are many and well-equipped! (You have) the means and the power, and the weapons and the shields. Yet, the call reaches you, but you do not answer; the cry comes to you, but you do not come to help. All of this while you are characterized by struggle, known for goodness and welfare, the selected group (chosen), and the best ones chosen by the Messenger for us, Ahl al-Bayt. You fought the Arabs, bore with pain and exhaustion, struggled against the nations, and resisted their heroes. We were still, so were you in ordering you, and you in obeying us. So that Islām became triumphant, the accomplishment of the days came near, the fort of polytheism was subjected, the outburst of was subjected, the outburst of infidelity calmed down, and the

[295] Sūrat Āl ʿImrān, Verse 144.

system of religion was well-ordered. Thus, (why have you) become confused after clearness? Conceal matters after announcing them? Turned on your heels after daring? Associated (others with God) after believing? Will you not fight people who violated their oaths? Plotted to expel the Apostle and became aggressive by being the first (to assault) you? Do ye fear them? Nay, it is God Whom ye should more justly fear if you believe!

Nevertheless, I see you are inclined to easy living; dismissed he who is more worthy of guardianship ('Alī ﷺ); You secluded yourselves with meekness and dismissed that which you accepted. Yet, if you show ingratitude, ye and all on earth together, God is free of all wants, worthy of all praise. Indeed, I have said all that I have said, knowing that you intend to forsake me and knowing the betrayal that your hearts sensed. But it is the state of soul, the effusion of fury, the dissemination of (what is) the chest, and the presentation of the proof. Hence, Here it is! Bag it (leadership and) put it on the back of an ill she-camel, which has a thin hump with everlasting grace, marked with the wrath of God, and the blame of ever (which leads to) the Fire of (the wrath of God kindled (to a blaze), that which doth mount (right) to the hearts; For God witnesses what you do, and soon will the unjust assailants know what vicissitudes their affairs will take! And I am the daughter of a warner (the Prophet) to you against a severe punishment. So, act, and so will we, and wait, and we shall wait.'[296]

It appears from recorded historical events that Sayyidah Fāṭimah ﷺ was successful at the beginning in persuading Abū Bakr to hand back Fadak to her to listen to part of a speech he (according to

296 The end of Sayyidah Fāṭimah's speech.

some historians) delivered after hearing Sayyidah Fāṭimah's ﷺ speech. He said:

> 'O daughter of the Messenger of God... Indeed, the Prophet is your father, not anyone else's, the brother of your husband, not any other man's; he certainly preferred him over all his friends and ('Alī ﷺ) supported him in every important matter; no one loves you save the lucky, and no one hates you save the wretched. You are the blessed progeny of God's Messenger, the chosen ones, our guides to goodness, our path to Paradise, and you, best of women, the daughter of the best of prophets, truthful is your sayings, excelling in reason. You shall not be driven back from your right...But I heard your father saying: 'We, the group of prophets, do not inherit, nor are we inherited. Yet, this is my situation and property; it is yours (if you wish); it shall not be concealed from you, nor will it be stored away from you. You are the Mistress of your father's nation and the blessed tree of your descendants. Your property shall not be usurped against your will, nor can your name be defamed. Your judgment shall be executed in all that which I possess. This, do you think I violate your father's (will)?"

Sayyidah Fāṭimah ﷺ then refuted Abū Bakr's claim that the Prophet had stated that prophets could not be inherited and said:

> "Glory be to God! Surely, God's Messenger did not abandon God's Book or violate His commands. Instead, he followed its decrees and adhered to its chapters. So, do you unite with treachery, justifying your acts with fabrications? Indeed, after his departure, similar to the disasters plotted against him during his lifetime. But behold! This is God's Book, a just judge and a decisive speaker, saying:

﴿يَرِثُنِي وَيَرِثُ مِنْ آلِ يَعْقُوبَ ۖ وَاجْعَلْهُ رَبِّ رَضِيًّا﴾

﴾*yarithunī wa-yarithu min 'āli ya'qūba wa-j'alhu rabbi raḍiyyan*﴿

﴾*who may inherit from me and inherit from the House of Ya'qūb, and make him, my Lord, pleasing [to You]!'*﴿[297]

﴿وَوَرِثَ سُلَيْمَانُ دَاوُودَ﴾

﴾*wa-waritha sulaymānu dāwūda*﴿

﴾*Sulaymān inherited from Dāwūd*﴿[298]

Thus, He ﷻ made clear that He made share of all heirs, decreed from the amounts of inheritance, allowed for males and females, and eradicated all doubts and ambiguities (about this issue which existed with the) bygones. Nay! But your minds have made up a tale (that may pass) with you, but (for me) patience is most fitting against that which ye assert; it is God (alone) whose help can be sought."

After delivering her speech, Abū Bakr changed the mode with which he addressed Sayyidah Fāṭimah ﷺ. Read his following speech, his reply to Sayyidah Fāṭimah's ﷺ just reported speech.

Abū Bakr said: "Surely God and His Apostle are truthful, and so has his (the Prophet's) daughter told the truth. Surely, you are the source of wisdom, the element of faith, and the sole

---

[297] Sūrat Maryam, Verse 6.

[298] Sūrat al-Naml, Verse 16.

> authority. May God not refute your righteous argument nor invalidate your decisive speech. But these are the Muslims between us who have entrusted me with leadership, and it was according to their satisfaction that I received what I have. I am not being arrogant, autocratic, or selfish, and they are my witnesses."

Upon hearing Abū Bakr speak of the people's support for him, Sayyidah Fāṭimah al-Zahrā' ﷺ turned towards them and said:

> "O people, who rush towards uttering falsehood and are indifferent to disgraceful and losing actions! Do you not earnestly seek to reflect upon the Qur'ān, or are your hearts isolated with locks? But on your hearts is the stain of the evil you committed; it has seized your hearing and sight; evil is what you justified. Cursed is that which you reckoned, and wicked is what you have taken for an exchange! You shall, by God, find bearing it (to be a great) burden and its consequence disastrous. (That is) on the day when the cover is removed and appears to you what is behind it of wrath. When God confronts you with what you could never have expected, there will perish, there and then, those who stood on falsehoods." (the end).

Although parts of Abū Bakr's speeches cannot be verified with authentic evidence, and although we have already mentioned part of the actual speech, which Abū Bakr delivered after Sayyidah Fāṭimah's ﷺ arguments, it appears certain that Abū Bakr was finally persuaded to submit Fadak to her.

Nevertheless, when Sayyidah Fāṭimah ﷺ was leaving Abū Bakr's house, 'Umar suddenly appeared and exclaimed:

"What is it that you hold in your hand?"

Abū Bakr replied:

> 'A decree I have written for Sayyidah Fāṭimah in which I assigned Fadak and her father's inheritance to her."'Umar said, " What will you spend on the Muslims if the Arabs decide to fight you?"

'Umar then seized the decree and tore it up!

Fadak in the Political Arena

In addition to being a reason for encouraging others to be unjust to Ahl al-Bayt ﷺ, the usurping of Fadak by Abū Bakr ignited political unrest throughout history. Āyatullāh Ja'far Subḥānī, a leading historian, wrote regarding Fadak throughout history[299]:

> "The foundation of the deprivation of the descendants of Sayyidah Fāṭimah's claim of Fadak was laid in the time of the First Caliph. After the martyrdom of 'Alī, Mu'āwīya assumed the reins of government and divided Fadak amongst three persons (Marwān, 'Amr b. 'Uthmān and his son, Yazīd).
>
> During the Caliphate of Marwān period, he assumed all three shares and gifted them to his son, 'Abd Azīz. He, in turn, gave the same to his son, 'Umar, since 'Umar b. 'Abd Azīz was an upright person from amongst Banī Umayyah; the first heresy that he removed was that he returned Fadak to the descendants of Sayyidah Fāṭimah. After his death, however, the succeeding Umayyad Caliphs removed Fadak from the Banī Hāshim and remained in their possession until their rule ended.
>
> During the Caliphate of Banī 'Abbās, the question of Fadak vacillated strangely. For example, Saffah gave it to 'Abdullāh Bin Ḥasan, and after him, Manṣūr Dawānīqī took it back, but his son Mahdī returned it to the descendants of Zahrā'. After him, Mūsā and Hārūn took it away from them on account of some political considerations. When Ma'mūn assumed the office of caliph, he handed it over formally to its owner. After his death, the conditions of Fadak vacillated once again, and it was returned at one time to the descendants of Sayyidah Fāṭimah and then taken away from them again.

---

[299] Subḥānī, Āyatullāh Ja'far, *The Message*, p. 601.

During the periods of the Caliphate of Banī Umayyah and Banī 'Abbās, Fadak assumed a largely political aspect as compared with its pecuniary aspect. And even if the First Caliphs needed income from Fadak, the later Caliphs and nobles were so rich that they did not need it. Hence, when 'Umar Bin 'Abd Azīz handed over Fadak to the descendants of Sayyidah Fāṭimah, Banī Umayyah reproached him and said,

> `By this act of yours, you have found fault with the two venerable men (Abū Bakr and 'Umar).'

They, therefore, persuaded him to distribute the income from Fadak among the descendants of Sayyidah Fāṭimah but to keep its ownership with himself."

The House of Grief

When political opposition fails, silent protest begins. This kind of protest can be more effective than the first because, in addition to having the benefits of offending and disapproving of the opponent's acts, it also gives the person the chance to keep calm and tranquil.

Sayyidah Fāṭimah al-Zahrāʾ ﷺ acted in such a manner when she realized that with the weaknesses which afflicted her, she could not prevail. So she took refuge in a house in Baqīʿ near the tombs of martyrs to cry for her father and complain to him about that which grieved her. Sayyidah Fāṭimah ﷺ used to visit her father's great tomb, take a handful of dirt from his grave, smell it, and then begin weeping. Sayyidah Fāṭimah ﷺ would then return to her home and cry day and night. The elderly men of Madīnah came to Imām ʿAlī ﷺ complaining and said:

> 'Abū al-Ḥasan! Sayyidah Fāṭimah cries day and night so none of us can sleep comfortably. Hence, we demand you ask her to either cry during the day or at night."

Imām ʿAlī ﷺ replied:

> "Most gladly."

He then proceeded towards Sayyidah Fāṭimah ﷺ, who was crying; when she saw him approaching, she stopped, and Imām ʿAlī ﷺ said:

> "Daughter of God's Messenger, the elderly men of Madīnah have asked me to ask you to either cry during the day or the night."

Sayyidah Fāṭimah ﷺ answered:

> "Abū al-Ḥasan, how short will my stay among them be? And soon, I will depart from them. Therefore, by God, I join my father — God's Messenger ﷺ."

When Imām ʿAlī ﷺ saw her insistence, he built a house for her behind Baqīʿ, which later became known as "the House of Grief". After that, with every sunrise, Sayyidah Fāṭimah ﷺ would take al-Ḥasan and al-Ḥusayn ﷺ to that house and cry until sunset, when Imām ʿAlī ﷺ would come and bring them back home.

Once, Sayyidah Fāṭimah al-Zahrā' ﷺ longed for the sound of Adhān, which Bilāl performed. But Bilāl had sworn never to perform it again after the Prophet's death; nevertheless, he decided to do so concerning Sayyidah Fāṭimah's request. Yet, as soon as Bilāl said:

> 'Allāhu Akbar',

Sayyidah Fāṭimah ﷺ remembered the era of her great father ﷺ and started weeping, so that when Bilāl said:

> "I bear witness that Muḥammad is His worshipper and Messenger, "

Sayyidah Fāṭimah took a deep breath and fell unconscious. When Sayyidah Fāṭimah ﷺ fell, the people requested Bilāl to stop Adhān because they believed that Sayyidah Fāṭimah ﷺ had died.

Now that the voice of rejection seized to reveal that which was in Sayyidah Fāṭimah's ﷺ heart, the language of tears spoke out for her, and as it is correctly said:

"The language of tears, is more painful to the heart and sadder to the eyes"!

The Withering Rose

It was a short life... As short as the lives of fragrant roses...

A life that Sayyidah Fāṭimah ﷺ endured and now is ending... even before it was given the chance to blossom fully!

Indeed, the successive calamities and severe hardships that befell Sayyidah Fāṭimah al-Zahrā' ﷺ, while she was still young, left her with a broken rib and confined to bed, suffering from her broken rib and remembering what had come to pass against her and her devoted husband who was her safe refuge. She remembered her usurped rights...

She remembered her oppressed husband and his stolen position...

She remembered him being led by his turban to the Mosque while she followed him...

She remembered all this, and a gloomy picture appeared before her tired eyes... then a sigh became imprisoned deep in her heart...That heart which longs for the great Messenger ﷺ who gave her the good news of her speedy departure after him...

Oh! How forsaken she was?

But she was the Prophet's ﷺ daughter!

She was his favorite child!

She whom the Prophet ﷺ repeatedly expressed the importance of observing her rights!

And as he said: "Man is observed by respecting his children".

Yet, this did not stop the arrogant ones from encroaching on her rights, nor did it stop the sinful hands from reaching out to strangle the beautiful rose before it fully blossomed!

Thus, the branch, which the Prophet ﷺ left among his nation, withered away, its flowers scattered, and its branches wilted.

Sayyidah Fāṭimah ﷺ appeared pale and faint!

God is with you, Umm al-Ḥasan.

You shall depart towards a generous Lord and a great father... then you shall complain to him about what you have encountered...

Yes! Umm al-Ḥasan... only ninety days are left...

But you, Muḥammad's Ummah, remember her...

Write this in the pages of history... and tell the generations about Sayyidah Fāṭimah's ﷺ sad story!

On her Death Bed

The moment when eternal separation starts is anguishing. This is a fact known to everyone who has experienced it, for it is the last opportunity for the beloved to be with his dear ones... then the inevitable, the predestined, happens. At such a moment, one earnestly needs calmness and tranquility. Yet, many are the ones who mourn and break apart instead.

Sayyidah Fāṭimah al-Zahrā' ﷺ was calm and patient when the women of Muhājirūn and Ansār came to visit her.

Swayd b. Ghafla said:

> "When Sayyidah Fāṭimah was inflicted with her illness, the women of the Muhājirūn and Ansār gathered around her and said:
>
> 'How are you doing, daughter of God's Messenger?'

Sayyidah Fāṭimah praised God ﷻ, prayed for her father ﷺ, and said:

> "I have become, by God, to have feelings of resentment for your world, detesting your men; I have cast them after testing them, hated them after examining them. Thus, shameful is the defiling of honor, playing after being serious, striking the soft rocks, the slackening of spears, the foolishness of judgments, and the misguidance of wants".
>
> "Evil indeed is which their souls have sent forward before them (with the result) that God's wrath is on them, and in torment will they abide".
>
> "Certainly, it (God's wrath) has control of their affairs, held them responsible (for deserving it), and launched its disagreement on them".
>
> "So, may the unjust ones be done away with, cursed, and damned. Woe unto them! How have they snatched it away from the foundations of the Message, the fundamentals of prophethood and guidance, the place of descent for the Devoted Spirit, and he who is clever in the affairs of this world and the hereafter?

(She means that they usurped ʿAlī's ﷺ right)

> Surely; (their action) is an apparent loss. Why were they hostile to Abū al-Ḥasan? They took vengeance, by God, from him for his unbiased sword, his carelessness about his death (i.e., his unprecedented courage), his deadly assaults, his severe encounters, and his anger for the sole sake of God ﷻ.
>
> "By God, had they prevented each other from assuming the reigns of power, which God's Messenger entrusted to him, he would have held it and led them smoothly; he would not have harmed them the size of a thread, Nor would his followers' stammer, (meaning they would have lived in harmony under his rule). He surely would have delivered them to a pure, lush, abundant spring flowing over its banks, yet its sides are not muddy. He certainly would have brought them back satisfied and advised them secretly and publicly without providing himself with any availing thing. Nor would he favor himself with the worldly things with any gain, save that which would quench the thirst of the thirsty and feed the hungry. Indeed, the abstinent would have been distinguished from the desirous and the truthful from the liar.

﴿وَلَو أَنَّ أَهلَ القُرىٰ آمَنوا وَاتَّقَوا لَفَتَحنا عَلَيهِم بَرَكاتٍ مِنَ السَّماءِ وَالأَرضِ وَلٰكِن كَذَّبوا فَأَخَذناهُم بِما كانوا يَكسِبونَ﴾

﴿wa-law ʾanna ʾahla l-qurā ʾāmanū wa-ttaqaw la-fataḥnā ʿalayhim barakātin mina s-samāʾi wa-l-ʾarḍi wa-lākin kadhdhabū fa-ʾakhadhnāhum bi-mā kānū yaksibūn[a]﴾

﴾*If the people of the towns had been faithful and Godwary, We would have opened to them blessings from the heaven and the earth. But they denied; so We seized them because of what they used to earn*﴿[300]

﴿فَأَصابَهُم سَيِّئاتُ ما كَسَبوا ۚ وَالَّذينَ ظَلَموا مِن هٰؤُلاءِ سَيُصيبُهُم سَيِّئاتُ ما كَسَبوا وَما هُم بِمُعجِزينَ﴾

﴾*fa-'aṣābahum sayyi'ātu mā kasabū wa-lladhīna ẓalamū min hā'ulā'i sa-yuṣībuhum sayyi'ātu mā kasabū wa-mā hum bi-mu'jizīna*﴿

﴾*So the evils of what they had earned visited them, and as for the wrongdoers among these, the evils of what they earn shall be visited on them and they will not thwart [God's might]*﴿[301]

Indeed... "Come to see!

"As long as you live, time shall show you amazing events!

"I wish I knew what proof they have for what they have done.

"On what foundation have they stood?

"On what reliable grip have they held?

"Upon whose progeny have they encroached and spoke against?

[300] Sūrat al-A'rāf, Verse 96.

[301] Sūrat al-Zumar, Verse 51.

"Evil, indeed, is the patron and evil the companion!

"They have exchanged, by God, the daring for the tales and the capable for the impotent.

﴿الَّذِينَ ضَلَّ سَعيُهُم فِي الحَياةِ الدُّنيا وَهُم يَحسَبونَ أَنَّهُم يُحسِنونَ صُنعًا﴾

﴿alladhīna ḍalla saʿyuhum fī l-ḥayāti d-dunyā wa-hum yaḥsabūna ʾannahum yuḥsinūna ṣunʿan﴾

﴿Those whose endeavour goes awry in the life of the world, while they suppose they are doing good.'﴾[302]

﴿أَلا إِنَّهُم هُمُ المُفسِدونَ وَلٰكِن لا يَشعُرونَ﴾

﴿ʾa-lā ʾinnahum humu l-mufsidūna wa-lākin lā yashʿurūna﴾

﴿Look! They are themselves the agents of corruption, but they are not aware﴾[303]

"Woe unto them!

﴿قُلِ اللَّهُ يَهدي لِلحَقِّ ۗ أَفَمَن يَهدي إِلَى الحَقِّ أَحَقُّ أَن يُتَّبَعَ أَمَّن لا يَهِدّي إِلّا أَن يُهدىٰ ۖ فَما لَكُم كَيفَ تَحكُمونَ﴾

[302] Sūrat al-Kahf, Verse 104.

[303] Sūrat al-Baqarah, Verse 12.

﴾*quli llāhu yahdī li-l-ḥaqqi 'a-fa-man yahdī 'ilā l-ḥaqqi 'aḥaqqu 'an yuttabaʿa 'am-man lā yahiddī 'illā 'an yuhdā fa-mā lakum kayfa taḥkumūna*﴿

﴾Say, *'God guides to the truth. Is He who guides to the truth worthier to be followed, or he who is not guided unless he is shown the way? What is the matter with you? How do you judge?'*﴿[304]

"But upon my life! it has already been conceived (meaning it is too late to do anything).

"So wait until its fruit comes about.

"Then shall ye fill your buckets with pure blood and fatal venom?

"That day, the dealers in falsehood will perish!

"And the ones who come to follow shall know the evil their successors have established!

"Then awaken the aversion in yourselves to your world!

"Prepare your hearts for calamities,

"Adapt yourselves to a sharp sword; an assault of a tyrant enemy, an overwhelming commotion, and atrocity from oppressors who shall leave your booty worthless, and your crops unharvested;

[304] Sūrat Yūnus, Verse 35.

﴿قالَ يا قَومِ أَرَأَيتُم إِن كُنتُ عَلىٰ بَيِّنَةٍ مِن رَبّي وَآتاني رَحمَةً مِن عِندِهِ فَعُمِّيَت عَلَيكُم أَنُلزِمُكُموها وَأَنتُم لَها كارِهونَ﴾

﴿qāla yā-qawmi 'a-ra'aytum 'in kuntu 'alā bayyinatin min rabbī wa-'ātānī raḥmatan min 'indihī fa-'ummiyat 'alaykum 'a-nulzimukumūhā wa-'antum lahā kārihūna﴾

﴿He said, 'O my people! Tell me, should I stand on a manifest proof from my Lord, and He has granted me His own mercy —though it should be invisible to you— shall we force it upon you while you are averse to it?﴾[305]

Swayd b. Ghaflah added:

> "The women informed their men what Sayyidah Fāṭimah al-Zahrā' ﷺ had said, then a group of men went to her and said:
>
> > 'O you Mistress of all women! Had Abū al-Ḥasan mentioned this to us before we made the oath and given the promise (to Abū Bakr), then surely we would not have exchanged him (Imām 'Alī ﷺ) for anyone else!'
>
> Sayyidah Fāṭimah ﷺ said:
>
> > "Leave me alone! Surely, there is no excuse for you after (I have already) spoken to you, and there shall be no command after (I have seen) your shortcomings. "

When we review Sayyidah Fāṭimah's ﷺ speech, it becomes clear to us that she blamed the people for accepting Abū Bakr's and

[305] Sūrat Hūd, Verse 28.

'Umar's leadership over Imām 'Alī ﵇. She also foretold of many calamities, which would take place as a result of this misdeed. Sayyidah Fāṭimah's predictions were confirmed; 'Umar seized power after Abū Bakr appointed him as his successor to the Caliphate. After 'Umar, 'Uthmān was appointed leader; this started the era of explicit oppression against the Muslims. Imām 'Alī ﵇, in his Sermon of Shiqshiqīyyah, pointed out the course of the Caliphate and how it was transferred from one person to another until, finally, he was appointed leader virtually by force. He ﵇ then explained how the same ones who paid allegiance to him turned against his rule, which triggered unrest among the Muslims that had everlasting adverse effects. In this sermon, Imām 'Alī ﵇ also added his view on the Caliphate and this world in several eloquent words. He ﵇ said:

"By God, the son of Abū Quḥāfah (Abū Bakr) dressed himself with it (the caliphate), and he certainly knew that my position about it was the same as the position of the axis about the handmill. The floodwater flows down from me, and the bird cannot fly unto me. I put a curtain against the Caliphate and kept myself detached from it. Then I began to think whether I should assault or endure calmly the blinding darkness of tribulations wherein the elders age and the young grow old, and the true believer acts under strain till he meets God (on his death). I found that endurance thereon was wiser. So I adopted patience although there was pricking in the eye and suffocation of my inheritance till the first one went his way but handed over the Caliphate to Ibn Khaṭṭāb after himself."

Then he quoted 'Ā'isha:

> "My days now are passed on the camel's back (in difficulty), while there were days (of ease) — when I enjoyed the company of Jābir's brother Ḥayyān.'
>
> "Strangely, during his lifetime, he wished to get rid of the Caliphate, but he straightened its way for the other after his death. No doubt these two shared their udders strictly among themselves. This one put the Caliphate in a tough enclosure where the utterance was haughty, and the tough was rough. Mistakes were plenty, and so were the excuses, therefore. One in contact with it was like the rider of an unruly camel. If he pulled up its rein, the very nostril would be slit, but if he let it loose, he would be thrown. Consequently, by God, people got involved in recklessness, wickedness, unsteadfastness, and deviation.
>
> Nevertheless, I remained patient despite the length of period and stiffness of trial till he went his way (by death); he put the matter (of Caliphate) in a group and regarded me as one of them. But good Heavens! What had I to do with this `consultation'? Where was any doubt about me concerning the first of them that I was not considered akin to these men? But I remained low when they were low and flew high. One of them turned against me because of his hatred, and the other got inclined the other way due to his in-law relationship and this thing and that thing, till the third man of these people stood up with heaving breasts between his dung and fodder. His cousins also stood up with him, swallowing God's wealth like a camel devouring spring foliage until his rope broke down. His actions finished him, and his gluttony brought him down

prostrate. At that moment, the crowd of people frightened me. It advanced towards me from every side like the mane of the hyena, so much so that Ḥasan and Ḥusayn were getting crushed, and both the ends of my shoulder garment were torn. They collected around me like a herd of sheep and goats. When I took up the reins of government, one party broke away, and another turned disobedient while the rest began acting wrongfully as if they had not heard the word of God saying:

﴿تِلْكَ الدَّارُ الْآخِرَةُ نَجْعَلُهَا لِلَّذِينَ لَا يُرِيدُونَ عُلُوًّا فِي الْأَرْضِ وَلَا فَسَادًا ۚ وَالْعَاقِبَةُ لِلْمُتَّقِينَ﴾

﴾tilka d-dāru l-ʾākhiratu najʿaluhā li-lladhīna lā yurīdūna ʿuluwwan fī l-ʾarḍi wa-lā fasādan wa-l-ʿāqibatu li-l-muttaqīn[a]﴿

﴾This is the abode of the Hereafter which We shall grant to those who do not desire to domineer in the earth nor to cause corruption, and the outcome will be in favour of the Godwary﴿[306]

Yes, they had heard and understood it by God, but the world appeared glittering in their eyes, and its embellishments seduced them. Behold, by Him, who split the grain (to grow) and created living beings; if people had not come to me and supporters had not exhausted the argument and if there had been no pledge of God with the learned to the effect that they should not acquiesce the gluttony of the oppressor and the hunger of the oppressed, I would have cast the rope of Caliphate on its shoulders. I would have given the last one the same treatment as the first. Then you would have seen that, in

[306] Sūrat al-Qaṣaṣ, Verse 83.

> my view, this world of yours is no better than the sneezing of a goat."

(It is said that when Amīr al-Mu'minīn ﷺ reached here in his sermon, a man from 'Irāq stood up and handed him a paper with something written on it. Amīr al-Mu'minīn ﷺ began looking at it when Ibn 'Abbās said,

> "O Amīr al-Mu'minīn, I wish you resumed your Sermon from where you broke it."

He ﷺ replied,

> "O Ibn 'Abbās, it was like the foam of a camel which gushed out but subsided."

Ibn 'Abbās says that he never grieved over any utterance as he did over this one because Amīr al-Mu'minīn ﷺ could not finish it as he wished to. Commenting on this sermon, 'Allamah Rāzī says:

> "The words in this sermon, `Like the rider of a camel,' mean to convey that when a camel rider is stiff in drawing up the rein, then in this scuffle the nostril gets bruised; but if he lets it loose despite the camel's unruliness, it would throw him somewhere and would get out of control. '*Ashnaq an-Nāqah*' is used when the rider holds up the rein and raises the camel's head upwards. In the same sense, the word `*Shannaq an-Nāqah*' is used. Ibn al-Sikayt has mentioned[307] this because he has used this word in harmony with '*Aslāsa lahā*', and harmony could be retained only by using both in the same form. Thus, Amīr al-Mu'minīn

307 Ibn al-Sikayt, *Iṣlāḥ al-Manṭiq*.

🕮 has used *'Ashnaq lahā'is'* though in place of *'In Rafa'a lahā Rāsahā,'* (i.e., 'if he stops it by holding up the reins.)"

An Apology too Late!

After Sayyidah Fāṭimah's 🕮 visit with women and then the men, which resulted in an emotional revolution in the hearts of the Muslims, Abū Bakr and 'Umar decided to visit the Mistress of women 🕮 and try to achieve her contentment with them. The story was reported[308] as follows:

> "When Sayyidah Fāṭimah 🕮 was suffering from her fatal illness, Abū Bakr and 'Umar came to visit her. They asked for permission to enter, but she refused to see them. Upon this, Abū Bakr vowed not to enter any house until he saw Sayyidah Fāṭimah and asked her to forgive him. Abū Bakr, because of his oath, was forced to spend that night in the cold with no cover. 'Umar then went to 'Alī 🕮 and addressed him by saying:
>
>> "More than once we have come to see Sayyidah Fāṭimah to ask her for requital, but she refuses to permit us to enter. If you see to it, you can get us permission from her to talk to her."
>
> Imām 'Alī 🕮 said:
>
>> "I surely will."

---

[308] Ṣadūq, Shaykh Muḥammad b. 'Alī, *'Ilal al-Sharāi'*.

Imām ʿAlī ؑ then entered the house and told Sayyidah Fāṭimah ؑ:

"Daughter of God's Messenger, you have seen what these two men have done. They have repeatedly come to see you, but you have not permitted them to enter; now, they have asked me to ask you to give them that permission."

She said:

"By God, I shall not give them permission, nor will I speak to them until I meet my father and complain to him about what they have done and committed against me."

ʿAlī ؑ said,

"But I have assured them that I will (acquire your permission)."

Now Sayyidah Fāṭimah ؑ replied:

"Now that you have assured them of something, the house is yours, and women follow men (in their commands); I shall not disagree with you in anything, so allow whoever you wish (to enter the house)."

When ʿAlī ؑ heard Sayyidah Fāṭimah's ؑ reply, he left the house and permitted them to enter. The two men entered the house; when they saw Sayyidah Fāṭimah ؑ, they submitted their greetings to her, but she did not reply, only turned her face away; in turn, they followed her face, and she constantly turned away from them. The two parties repeated this action several times until Sayyidah Fāṭimah ؑ said:

"ʿAlī, cover me with your garment."

She then said to some women who were present:

"Turn me towards them!"

When this was done, Abū Bakr said:

"Daughter of God's Messenger, we have only come to you in an attempt to achieve your satisfaction and avoid your wrath; we ask you to requite and forgive us for the misdeed which we have committed against you."

Sayyidah Fāṭimah ﷺ said:

"I shall not speak a word to either of you until I meet my Lord and complain to Him about you. I shall then complain about your actions and everything you have committed against me."

Sayyidah Fāṭimah ﷺ then turned towards ʿAlī ﷺ and said:

"I shall not speak to them until I ask them about something which they heard from God's Messenger. If they tell the truth, I will speak to them."

They said:

"By God, she has the right to do so. Besides, we only speak that which is right and testify to that which is true."

She said:

"I ask you by God, do you remember when the Messenger of God called you out in the middle of the night regarding a matter which came up with 'Alī?"

They answered:

"Yes, By God."

Sayyidah Fāṭimah then said:

"I ask you by God, did you hear him say:

'Sayyidah Fāṭimah is part of me and I am from her; he who offends me offends God. He who offends her after my death is the same as he who offends her during my life, and he who offends her during my life is the same as he who offends her after my death'?'

They both answered:

"Yes, by God, we remember."

She said:

"Praise be to God. O God, I hold you witness, so you who are present testify to this; surely they have offended me when I am living and after my death. By God, I shall not speak to you until I meet my Lord and complain to Him about you and that which you have inflicted me with."

When Abū Bakr heard this, he wailed and burst into loud laments, saying:

"I wish that my mother had not given birth to me".

'Umar said:

"It is strange how people appointed you as guardian of their affairs while you are not but a foolish old man! You become anxious at a woman's anger and rejoice at her satisfaction. What is wrong with him who angers a woman?"

They then left the house.

Commenting on this story, Sayyid Qazwīnī ؒ writes:

"There was no need for Abū Bakr to wail and apologize when he had the opportunity to amend his mistakes, nor was there a reason for him to burst into loud laments when he had the chance to return her estate to her. But surely the Caliph wished to achieve Sayyidah Fāṭimah's ؑ satisfaction at the same time he was keeping her property and rights usurped."

Abū Bakr's Family Versus Sayyidah Fāṭimah's ؑ Progeny

The early injustices done by Abū Bakr against Sayyidah Fāṭimah al-Zahrā' ؑ paved the way for his offspring to do the same against the Prophet's progeny. Sayyid Ṣafdar Ḥusayn summarized[309] the wrongdoings committed by the Bakrs (the descendants of Abū Bakr) against Sayyidah Fāṭimah ؑ and her descendants ؑ in several points. He wrote: "History shows that Abū Bakr himself and his whole family (excepting Asmā' and her son Muḥammad) were hostile to the Prophet's family, in utter disregard to what the Qur'ān ordained or what the Prophet had said relating to the respect and love for his family. The following is the list of those whose hostility was distinctively marked:

1. Abū Bakr, on his accession to the Caliphate, sent 'Umar to Sayyidah Fāṭimah's house to compel 'Alī, by force, to come in and do fealty to him. 'Umar threatened to burn the house down upon Sayyidah Fāṭimah and brought 'Alī under escort to Abū Bakr, where he was so humiliated and insulted that he cried bitterly at the tomb of the Prophet complaining about the treatment he had received. Subsequently, Sayyidah Fāṭimah was so much grieved by Abū Bakr that as long as she survived her father, she never spoke a word to Abū Bakr, and on her deathbed, she forbade him from joining her funeral.

2. Abū Bakr's daughter, 'Ā'isha, revolted against 'Alī, the Caliph, and at the head of thirty thousand soldiers, she fought the battle of Jamal, but she was discomfited with heavy loss.

3. Abū Bakr's son-in-law, Zubayr b. al-'Awwām, the husband of Asmā', the eldest daughter of Abū Bakr, was the Commander

---

[309] Ḥusayn, Sayyid Ṣafdar, *The Early History of Islām*, p. 242.

of 'Ā'isha's armies; during the heat of the battle, he withdrew and took the road towards Makkah but was slain only at a short distance from the field of battle.

4. Abū Bakr's grandson, 'Abdullāh, the son of Zubayr by Asmā', was the commander of 'Ā'isha's infantry. He was the adopted son of 'Ā'isha. After the battle, he was pulled out from under a heap of the slain lying on the battlefield.

5. Abū Bakr's cousin, Ṭalḥa, and the husband of Abū Bakr's daughter, Umm Kulthūm, was a Commander of 'Ā'isha's Troops. In the heat of the battle, Marwān (the Secretary and the evil genius of Caliph 'Othmān), an officer in the same forces, seeing Ṭalḥa busily engaged, said to his slave:

   'It was but the other day that Ṭalḥa was busily instigating the murderers of 'Othmān and now he busily seeks to revenge his blood. What a hypocrisy to gain worldly grandeur!' So saying, he shot an arrow, which pierced through Ṭalḥa's leg and struck his horse, which flew wildly off the ranks, and Ṭalḥa fell to the ground. He was instantly taken to Basra, where he died after a while.

6. Abū Bakr's cousin, Abū al-Rahman, a brother of Ṭalḥa, also fell fighting in the same battle.

7. Muḥammad, the son of Ṭalḥa, also fell in the same battle.

8. Abū Bakr's sister, Umm Farwah's daughter, Ja'dah b. al-Ash'ath poisoned al-Ḥasan, the son of 'Alī, to death. She was suborned for committing wickedness by Yazīd, the son of Mu'āwīya, or by Mu'āwīya himself.

9. Abū Bakr's sister's (Umm Farwah's) son Isḥāq, both brothers, the sons of Ashʿath, appeared among the armies of Yazīd, fighting against Ḥusayn, the son of ʿAlī, at the Karbalāʾ tragedy. Later on, the former was killed fighting against Mukhtār, who was avenging the murder of Ḥusayn, while the latter, who had taken off the dead body of Ḥusayn some of his clothes, was torn to death by dogs.

10. Muṣʿab, a son of Zubayr, the son-in-law of Abū Bakr, fought against Mukhtār, who was killed avenging the murder of Ḥusayn."

Sayyidah Fāṭimah al-Zahrā"s ﷺ Will to Imām ʿAlī ؑ

Imām ʿAlī ؑ was surprised to find that his dear wife had left her bed and had started doing the housework; he asked her about it, and she replied:

> "This is the last day of my life. I want to wash my children's hair and clothes because they will soon be orphans without a mother!"

Imām ʿAlī ؑ then asked her about the source of knowledge of this news (the day of her departure). She ؑ told him that she had seen the Messenger of God ﷺ in her dream, and he had told her that she would join him that night. She then asked Imām ʿAlī ؑ to execute her will.

He said:

> "Instruct me to do anything you wish, daughter of God's Messenger." ʿ

Alī ؑ then asked everyone to leave the house, and he sat next to her.

Sayyidah Fāṭimah ؑ started:

> "Cousin, you are not accustomed to me being a False-teller, undevoted, or have I disobeyed you since I have become your companion?"

ʿAlī ﷺ said:

> "God forbid! You know more about God, devoted, pious, honorable, and fearing God than (to give me a reason) to reprimand you for disobeying me. Surely, it is excruciating for me to be separated from you and to lose you, but it is an inevitable destination. By God, you have renewed the sorrow I have just encountered with the death of God's Messenger; surely your death and departure will be a great calamity, but
>
> ﴿إِنَّا لِلَّهِ وَإِنَّا إِلَيهِ راجِعونَ﴾
>
> ﴿*ʾinnā li-llāhi wa-ʾinnā ʾilayhi rājiʿūna*﴾
>
> ﴿*'Indeed we belong to God, and to Him do we indeed return'*﴾[310]
>
> What a painful, bitter, and sad calamity. Indeed, this is a calamity for which there is no consolement and a disaster for which there is no compensation."

Then they both cried, and Imām ʿAlī ﷺ embraced her head and said:

> "Instruct me to do anything you wish; you certainly will find me devoted and execute everything you command me to do. I shall also put your matters over mine."

---

[310] Sūrat al-Baqarah, Verse 156.

She ‎ﷺ said:

> "May God reward you with the best of goodness. Cousin, firstly, I ask you to marry after my death; surely she will be to my children as I was. Besides, men cannot do without women."

Sayyidah Fāṭimah ‎ﷺ then added:

> "I ask you not to let anyone who did injustice to me witness my funeral, for they certainly are enemies of mine and the enemy of God's Messenger. Also, don't give them the chance to pray over me, nor to any of their followers. Bury me at night when eyes are rested, and sight is asleep."

Commenting on Imām ‘Alī's ‎ﷺ speech after Sayyidah Fāṭimah's burial ‎ﷺ, the commentator on *Nahjul Balagha*[311] wrote:

> "The treatment meted out to the daughter of the Prophet after his death has been excruciating and sad. Although Sayyidah Sayyidah Fāṭimah ‎ﷺ did not live in this world more than a few months after the death of the Prophet ‎ﷺ, even this short period has a long tale of grief and woe (about her). In this connection, the first scene that strikes the eyes is that the arrangements for the funeral rites of the Prophet ‎ﷺ had not yet been made when the contest for power started in the Saqīfah of Banī Sa‘īdah. Naturally, their leaving the body of the Prophet (without burial) must have injured Ḥaḍrah Sayyidah Fāṭimah's ‎ﷺ grief-stricken heart to see that those who claimed love and attachment (to the Prophet ‎ﷺ) during his life became so engrossed in their machinations for power that instead of

311 Sharīf Raḍī, Muḥammad b. al-Ḥusayn, *Nahj al-Balāgha*, Sermon/Letter/Saying 2, Ansariyan Publications print, p. 347.

consoling his only daughter, they did not even know when the Prophet ﷺ was given a funeral bath and when he was buried. The way they condoled her was that they crowded her house with material to set fire to it and tried to secure allegiance by force with the display of oppression, compulsion, and violence. All these excesses were intended to obliterate the prestigious position of this house so that it might not reclaim its lost prestige on any occasion. With this aim in view, to crush her economic position, her claim for (the estate of) Fadak was turned down by dubbing it as false, the effect of which was that Ḥaḍrah Sayyidah Fāṭimah ؑ made the dying will that none of them should attend her funeral."

Sayyidah Fāṭimah ؑ was ready to meet her Lord. She bathed then lay down in her garment... She then instructed Asmā' b. 'Umays to wait awhile and then to call her name; if there were no answer, this would mean that she ؑ had departed towards her Lord.

Asmā' waited awhile, then called Sayyidah Fāṭimah's ؑ name... but there was no answer;

Asmā' repeated the call:

"O daughter of the chosen Muḥammad!

O daughter of the most honorable of them whom women bore!

O daughter of the best of those who have walked on gravel! O daughter of him who was:

﴿فَكَانَ قَابَ قَوْسَيْنِ أَوْ أَدْنَىٰ﴾

﴾*fa-kāna qāba qawsayni ’aw ’adnā*﴿

﴾*until he was within two bows’ length or even nearer*﴿[312]

...There is no answer... silence overwhelms the house ...Asmā’ then proceeds toward Sayyidah Fāṭimah ﷺ and finds her dead.

At that point, Ḥasan and Ḥusayn ﷺ entered and asked:

> "Where is our mother?"

Yet Asmā’ uttered not a word!

Ḥasan and Ḥusayn ﷺ proceeded toward their mother and found her dead. At this, Ḥusayn ﷺ turned towards Ḥasan ﷺ and said:

> "May God console you for our mother!"

Imām ‘Alī ﷺ was at the Mosque. Ḥasan and Ḥusayn ﷺ went to the Mosque and broke the news to their father. As soon as he ﷺ heard their words, he fell unconscious. When he regained consciousness, he said:

> "Who will console me now, daughter of Muḥammad? You used to console me, so who will take your place now?"

The Hāshimīt women were then gathered to receive the news of the great calamity... Yes, the calamity befell them once more, while the blood still flowed from the wound of losing the Prophet ﷺ...

---

[312] Sūrat al-Najm, Verse 9.

Madīnah shakes...

Everyone came to console ʿAlī ﷺ and his two children ﷺ... God is with you, Sayyidah Zahrā'’s children... It was just yesterday that you were inflicted with the death of your great father — the Prophet of God ﷺ — and your new calamity is no less than that! But take patience, for this is the will of the Mighty Lord ﷻ.

A Quiet Funeral

In the darkness of the jet-black night, when eyes were asleep and voices were silent, a Heavenly procession left ʿAlī's ﷺ house while carrying the Messenger of God's ﷺ daughter ﷺ to her final abode.

This was on the night of the third (3rd) of Jumādā ath-Thāniyah (the second), 11 A.H.

The heartbreaking procession moved towards an unknown location, followed by a few devoted ones...

They were ʿAlī, Ḥasan, Ḥusayn, and Zaynab ﷺ, along with Umm Kulthūm... Abū Dharr, ʿAmmār, Miqdād, and Salmān were following them.

Where are the thousands who inhabited Madīnah? One asked, and the answer came: Sayyidah Fāṭimah ﷺ requested they may not be present at her funeral!

The family and their friends hurry to bury Sayyidah Fāṭimah ﷺ... then they rush back to their own homes so that no one would know where Sayyidah Fāṭimah ﷺ was buried!

In such a matter, the first start from Ahl al-Bayt ﷺ set after the sun (the Prophet ﷺ) and left everyone with the only light of Imāmate!

I was asked:

> "What do you think about the end of Sayyidah Fāṭimah's life?
>
> What will be the position of those who oppressed her in the hereafter?"

I waved my hand to him...

So long... with no word... dead silence...

So long!

But wait... can't you hear the Commander of the Faithful ‎ﷺ... the known hero... ʿAlī ‎ﷺ... Don't you realize he is crying? Yet, who would not cry for being separated from the Mistress of Women ‎ﷺ?

Listen to him, he is speaking to the Prophet ‎ﷺ:

> "O Prophet of God, peace be upon you from me and your daughter who has come to you and hastened to meet you. O Prophet of God! My patience about your chosen (daughter) has been exhausted, and my power of endurance has weakened, except that I have ground for consolation in having endured the great hardship and heart-rending event of your separation. I laid you down in your grave while your last breath had passed (when your head) was between my neck and chest.`

﴿إِنَّا لِلَّهِ وَإِنَّا إِلَيهِ راجِعونَ﴾

﴾*ʾinnā li-llāhi wa-ʾinnā ʾilayhi rājiʿūn*[a]﴿

﴾*ʿIndeed we belong to God, and Him do we indeed return.*ʾ﴿[313]

> "Now the trust has been returned, and what had been given has been taken back. My grief knows no bounds, and my nights will remain sleepless till God chooses for me the house in which you are now residing. Certainly, your daughter would apprise you of the joining together of your Ummah (people)

[313] Sūrat al-Baqarah, Verse 156.

> for oppressing her. You ask her in detail and get all the news about the position. This happened when a long time had not elapsed, and your remembrance had not disappeared. My salām be on you both, the salām of a grief-stricken not of a disgusted or a hateful person; for if I go away, it is not because I am weary (of you); and if I stay, it is not due to lack of belief in what God has promised the endurers."

Failing Attempts

At sunrise, people gathered to participate in Sayyidah Fāṭimah's ﷺ funeral, but they were informed that the darling of God's Messenger ﷺ had been secretly buried during the night.

Meanwhile, ʿAlī ﷺ made the shapes of four fresh graves in Baqīʿ to conceal the location where Sayyidah Fāṭimah ﷺ was buried. When the people entered the graveyard, they were confused as to which spot was Sayyidah Fāṭimah al-Zahrā''s ﷺ grave; the people turned towards each other and, with feelings of guilt, said:

> "Our Prophet ﷺ has not left behind, but one daughter, yet she has died and was buried without our participation in the funeral or the prayer rituals. We do not even realize the place where she has been buried."

Noticing that a revolt might be ignited because of the emotional atmosphere this event created, the governing party announced:

> "Select a group of Muslim women and ask them to dig these graves so that we may find Sayyidah Fāṭimah ﷺ and perform prayers on her."

Yes! They attempted to execute the plan, violating Sayyidah Fāṭimah's ﷺ will and causing ʿAlī's ﷺ attempts to hide the grave to lie vainly.

Have they forgotten ʿAlī's ﷺ sharp sword and his well-known courage? Did they think that ʿAlī ﷺ would remain indifferent to their outrageous actions up to the point of letting them dig Sayyidah Fāṭimah's ﷺ grave?

Imām ʿAlī ﷺ did not fight back after the Prophet's ﷺ death because he considered the Muslim's unity and overall interests. Yet, this did not mean he would ignore their villainous crimes against Sayyidah Fāṭimah ﷺ even after her death. In other words, ʿAlī ﷺ was asked by the Prophet ﷺ to have patience, but only to a certain extent; when ʿAlī ﷺ received the news of the about-to-be-executed plot, he put on his fighting gear and rushed towards Baqīʿ. A man from among the people called out:

> "This is ʿAlī b. Abū Ṭālib leveling his sword and saying:
>
> > If anyone moves even a mere stone from these graves, I shall strike even the "back of the last follower of the unjust."

People who realized ʿAlī's ﷺ seriousness took his threats with complete belief that he would do just as he said if anyone were to oppose him. Yet, a man from the governing ones addressed ʿAlī ﷺ by saying:

> "What is the matter, Abū al-Ḥasan? By God, we shall dig her grave out and perform prayers on her."

ʿAlī ﷺ then grabbed the man by his clothes, shook him, threw him to the ground, and said,

> "Son of the Sawadah! I have abandoned my right to prevent people from forsaking their faith, but as regards Sayyidah Fāṭimah's grave, by Him in whose hand is my soul, if you and your followers attempt to do anything to it, I will irrigate the ground with your blood."

At this, Abū Bakr said,

> "Abū al-Ḥasan, I ask you by the right of God's Messenger, and by Him Who is above the Throne: leave him alone, and we will not do anything which you would not approve of..."

Thus, until this day, the location of Sayyidah Fāṭimah's عليها السلام grave remains a secret.

Sayyidah Fāṭimah al-Zahrā' ﷺ on the Last Day

On the Day when the oppressed shall bite their hands (in fear); when the oppressors shall be gathered in humiliation and lowliness, remembering their disgraceful deeds:

Then, each of them shall review his file, packed with oppression against his chosen worshippers. On that Day shall every human, whatever color, creed, faith, and his deeds may be, shall be gathered... no one will be left behind... even the fetus who was the victim of abortion shall come that Day to present his case...

Then Sayyidah Zahrā' ﷺ's great personality shall manifest to every soul...

Following are several narrations reported by Ahl al-Bayt ﷺ regarding Sayyidah Fāṭimah ﷺ on the Last Day:

1. 'Alī ﷺ said[314]:

   "I heard the Prophet say: "On the Day of Rising, a caller shall announce from beyond the veil: "O gathered people, lower your eyes so that Sayyidah Fāṭimah, the Daughter of Muḥammad, may pass,"[315]

---

[314] al-Ḥakim al-Nīshābūrī, *al-Mustadrak 'ala al-Ṣaḥīḥayn*, Vol. 2, p. 153.

[315] Also reported in al-Jazarī, Ibn al-Athīr, *Usd al-Ghābah fī Ma'rifat al-Ṣaḥāba*, Vol. 5, p. 523.

al-Shāfi'ī, Muḥammad b. Yūsuf al-Kanjī, *Kifāyat al-Ṭālib*, p. 212.

adh-Dhahabī, Shams ad-Dīn, *Mizān al-I'tidāl*, Vol. 2, p. 18.

Qundūzī added the following to it[316]:

> 'Alī ﷺ reported that the Prophet ﷺ said:
>
> > "On the Day of Rising, a caller shall call from the sole of the Throne:
> >
> > > "O people of Resurrection, cast your eyes down so that Sayyidah Fāṭimah b. Muḥammad may pass while holding al-Ḥusayn's shirt, which will (still) be saturated with blood.'
> >
> > She will then embrace the leg of the Throne and say:
> >
> > > "O (God), You are the Omnipotent and Just; pass the judgment between me and those who killed my son."
> >
> > (The Prophet ﷺ added):
> >
> > > "Then He shall judge according to my Sunnah, by the Lord of Ka'bah, Sayyidah Fāṭimah will then say:
> > >
> > > > "O God! grant me intercedence for everyone who cried for his disaster; God will then grant her intercedence for them."

[316] al-Balkhī, Sulaymān b. Ibrāhīm al-Qundūzī, *Yanābīʿ al-Mawaddah lī-Dhawī l-Qūrbā*, p. 104.

2. Others have reported[317] that Abū Ayyūb Ansārī said:

"The Messenger of God ﷺ said:

A caller shall call from the sole of the Throne: O gathered people, lower your heads and cast your eyes down so that Sayyidah Fāṭimah b. Muḥammad may pass on the Path. '

He added:

'She then passes accompanied by seventy thousand Ḥūrī al-'Ayn as if they were a flashing light."

3. Many Sunnī Scholars have reported that God's Messenger ﷺ stated that Sayyidah Fāṭimah al-Zahrā' ﷺ shall arrive at the gathering place (while) riding Gadha' or Gusau female camel.

4. Jābir b. 'Abdullāh Ansārī said:

"I said to Abū Ja'far (al-Bāqir ﷺ):

'May I be your sacrifice son of God's Messenger; narrate to me a ḥadīth regarding the noble traits of your grandmother Sayyidah Fāṭimah so that if I report it to your Shī'ī (followers), they will rejoice at (hearing) it!'

[317] al-Iṣbahānī, Abū Nu'aym, *Dalā'il al-Nubuwwah.*

al-Haythamī, Ibn Ḥajar, *al-Ṣawā'iq al-Muḥriqah.*

Abū Jaʿfar ﷺ said:

`My father told me that my grandfather reported that God's Messenger said:

"On the Day of Rising, minbars of light shall be erected for the prophets and messengers, of which my minbar shall be the highest among all minbars on that day. God will then say: Deliver a speech, ' so I will deliver a speech that none of the prophets or messengers have heard. Then, for the successors (of prophets) shall be erected minbars of light, and in the middle of these minbars, one shall be erected for my successor, ʿAlī b. Abū Ṭālib, which will be higher than all their minbars.

God will then say:

"ʿAlī, deliver a speech.'

So he will deliver a speech that no successor has ever heard before. Then for the children of the prophets and messengers shall be erected minbars of light; among them shall be a minbar of light for my two sons, grandsons, and the two flowers of my life (al-Ḥasan and al-Ḥusayn). Then it shall be said to them:

"Deliver speeches."

So they will deliver two speeches like none of the children of the prophets and messengers have ever heard before!

A caller — Jibrā'īl — shall then call:

> `Where is Sayyidah Fāṭimah b. Muḥammad?' She ﷺ will rise..." (until he said):

'God ﷻ shall say:

> `O people of the gathering, to whom does honor belong today?'

So Muḥammad, 'Alī, Ḥasan, and al-Ḥusayn ﷺ will say:

> 'To God ﷻ, The one, The Mighty

'God ﷻ will say:

> "O people of the gathering: lower your heads and cast your eyes down, for this is Sayyidah Fāṭimah proceeding towards Paradise.' Jibrā'īl ﷺ shall then bring her a female camel from the female camels of Paradise; its sides shall be embellished, its muzzle with fresh pearls, and it shall have a saddle of coral. It shall kneel in her presence so she will ride it. God will then send 100,000 angels to accompany her on her right side, 100,000 angels to accompany her on her left side, and 100,000 angels to lift her onto their wings until they bring her to the gate of Paradise. Near the gate of Paradise, she will look to her side.

God ﷻ will then say:

"Daughter of My beloved, why did you look to your side after I command that you enter my Paradise?"

She will say:

"My Lord, I wished my position would be realized on such a Day!"

God will say:

"Daughter of My beloved! Go back and look for everyone whose heart was love for you or any of your progeny; take their hand and lead them into paradise!"

Abū Ja'far ؏ said:

"By God, Jābir, she will pick her Shī'ī (followers), and those who love her just like a bird picks good seeds from bad seeds. So that when her Shī'ī are near the gate of Paradise, God will inspire their hearts to look to their sides; when they do — God ﷻ, will say:

My beloved ones, why did you look around when Sayyidah Fāṭimah, the daughter of my beloved one, interceded for you?'

They will answer:

'Our Lord! We hoped that our position would be known on such a day!'

God will then say:

'My beloved ones, go back and look for everyone who loved you for your love for Sayyidah Fāṭimah; Look for everyone who fed you for the love of Sayyidah Fāṭimah; Look for everyone who clothed you for the love of Sayyidah Fāṭimah; Look for everyone who gave you a drink for the love of Sayyidah Fāṭimah; Look for everyone who prevented (ghībah) backbiting from being done against you for the love of Sayyidah Fāṭimah... Take their hands and lead them into Paradise...'"

5. Ibn 'Abbās said:

"I heard Amīr al-Mu'minīn, 'Alī say:

Once the Messenger of God entered the house of Sayyidah Fāṭimah and found her in a sad mood. So he said:

'What has made you sad, daughter?'

Sayyidah Fāṭimah replied:

'Father, I remembered the gathering (Day) and people standing naked on the Day of Resurrection!'

He said:

"Daughter, surely it will be a great Day. But Jibrāʾīl informed me that God ﷻ is He, said that the first one upon whom the ground shall be split opened is me, then your husband, ʿAlī b. Abū Ṭālib ؑ; then God shall send Jibrāʾīl accompanied by seventy thousand angels, and he will erect on your grave seven domes of light, after which Isrāfīl will bring you three garments of light and stand by your head and say to you:

"O Sayyidah Fāṭimah b. Muḥammad, rise towards your gathering place."

"You (Sayyidah Fāṭimah) shall then rise secure from fear and veiled (in privacy). Isrāfīl will hand you the garments, and you will wear them. Rafael will then bring you a female camel of light; its muzzle shall be made of fresh pearls, and on it shall be a howdah of gold. You will ride it, and Rafael shall lead it by its muzzle while seventy thousand angels holding the banners of glorification accompany you. When the caravan hurries with you, seventy thousand Huris shall receive you, rejoicing at seeing you, while every one of them will be holding a censer of light from which the fragrance of incense is spread without fire. They shall be wearing crowns of jewels embellished with green chrysolites."

6. Imām Bāqir ﷺ said[318]:

"I heard Jābir b. 'Abdullāh Ansārī says:

"God's Messenger said:

"On the Day of Rising, My daughter, Sayyidah Fāṭimah, shall arrive riding a female camel from among the camels of Paradise — to her right shall be seventy thousand angels and to her left shall also be seventy thousand angels; Jibrā'īl will be holding its muzzle and calling with the loudest of voices:

'Cast down your eyes so that Sayyidah Fāṭimah b. Muḥammad may pass!"

"Then shall no prophet, messenger, truthful one, or martyr remain without casting their eyes down until Sayyidah Fāṭimah passes... Then a call shall come from the side of God ﷻ:

My beloved one and the daughter of my beloved one; ask Us, and you shall be given (whatever you wish), and intercede, your intercedence shall be accepted. By my Honor and Exaltation, the oppression of no oppressor shall pass My (judgment) today.

---

318 Majlisī, 'Allamah Muḥammad Bāqir, *Biḥār al-Anwār*, Vol. 10, on the authority of Ṣadūq, Shaykh Muḥammad b. 'Alī, *al-Amālī*.

She (Sayyidah Fāṭimah) will then say:

> "O God, My Master; My progeny, My Shīʿī (followers), the Shīʿī of my progeny, those who love me, and those who love my progeny."

She will then hear a call from God's ﷻ side:

> "Where are Sayyidah Fāṭimah's progeny, her Shīʿī, those who love her, and those who love her progeny?" They will then come forward, surrounded by angels of mercy, and Sayyidah Fāṭimah will lead them into Paradise."

Interceding in the Noble Qur'ān

The narrations just mentioned prove beyond doubt that intercedence is a given fact and a right granted to some chosen worshippers of God.

Yet, some heedless Muslims argue that intercedence is a polytheism, as if they have not read the Noble Qur'ān. The following Qur'ānic verses explicitly speak of intercedence on the Day of Rising.

﴿مَن ذَا الَّذِي يَشفَعُ عِندَهُ إِلَّا بِإِذنِهِ﴾

﴾*man dhā lladhī yashfaʿu ʿindahū ʾillā bi-ʾidhnihī*﴿

﴾*Who is it that may intercede with Him except with His permission*﴿[319]

﴿وَلا يَشفَعونَ إِلَّا لِمَنِ ارتَضى﴾

﴾*wa-lā yashfaʿūna ʾillā li-mani rtaḍā*﴿

﴾*and they do not intercede except for someone He approves of*﴿[320]

﴿ما مِن شَفيعٍ إِلّا مِن بَعدِ إِذنِهِ﴾

﴾*mā min shafīʿin ʾillā min baʿdi ʾidhnihī*﴿

﴾*There is no intercessor, except by His leave*﴿[321]

---

319 Sūrat al-Baqarah, Verse 255.

320 Sūrat al-Anbiyā', Verse 28.

321 Sūrat Yūnus, Verse 3.

﴿لا يَملِكونَ الشَّفاعَةَ إِلّا مَنِ اتَّخَذَ عِندَ الرَّحمٰنِ عَهدًا﴾

﴿lā yamlikūna sh-shafāʿata ʾillā mani ttakhadha ʿinda r-raḥmāni ʿahda^{n}﴾

﴿No one will have the power to intercede [with God], except for him who has taken a covenant with the Beneficent﴾[322]

﴿يَومَئِذٍ لا تَنفَعُ الشَّفاعَةُ إِلّا مَن أَذِنَ لَهُ الرَّحمٰنُ وَرَضِيَ لَهُ قَولًا﴾

﴿yawmaʾidhin lā tanfaʿu sh-shafāʿatu ʾillā man ʾadhina lahu r-raḥmānu wa-raḍiya lahū qawla^{n}﴾

﴿Intercession will not avail that day except from him whom the Beneficent allows and approves of his word﴾[323]

﴿وَكَم مِن مَلَكٍ فِي السَّماواتِ لا تُغني شَفاعَتُهُم شَيئًا إِلّا مِن بَعدِ أَن يَأذَنَ اللَّهُ لِمَن يَشاءُ وَيَرضىٰ﴾

﴿wa-kam min malakin fī s-samāwāti lā tughnī shafāʿatuhum shayʾan ʾillā min baʿdi ʾan yaʾdhana llāhu li-man yashāʾu wa-yarḍā﴾

﴿How many an angel there is in the heavens whose intercession is of no avail in any way except after God grants permission to whomever He wishes and approves of!﴾[324]

---

[322] Sūrat Maryam, Verse 87.

[323] Sūrat Ṭā Ḥā, Verse 109.

[324] Sūrat al-Najm, Verse 56.

These verses speak of intercedence on the Day of Rising.

There are also Qur'ānic verses, which prove intercedence in this world; some of these verses are:

﴿وَلَو أَنَّهُم إِذ ظَلَموا أَنفُسَهُم جاءوكَ فَاستَغفَرُوا اللَّهَ وَاستَغفَرَ لَهُمُ الرَّسولُ لَوَجَدُوا اللَّهَ تَوّابًا رَحيمًا﴾

﴿*wa-law 'annahum 'idh ẓalamū 'anfusahum jā'ūka fa-staghfarū llāha wa-staghfara lahumu r-rasūlu la-wajadū llāha tawwāban raḥīma*[n]﴾

﴿*Had they, when they wronged themselves, come to* you *and pleaded to God for forgiveness, and the Apostle had pleaded for forgiveness for them, they would have surely found God Clement, Merciful*﴾[325]

﴿قالوا يا أَبانَا استَغفِر لَنا ذُنوبَنا إِنّا كُنّا خاطِئينَ﴾

﴿*qālū yā-'abānā staghfir lanā dhunūbanā 'innā kunnā khāṭi'īn*[a]﴾

﴿*They said, 'Father! Plead [with God] for forgiveness of our sins! We have indeed been erring.'*﴾[326]

﴿وَاستَغفِر لِذَنبِكَ وَلِلمُؤمِنينَ وَالمُؤمِناتِ﴾

﴿*wa-staghfir li-dhanbika wa-li-l-mu'minīna wa-l-mu'mināti*﴾

[325] Sūrat al-Nisā', Verse 64.

[326] Sūrat Yūsuf, Verse 97.

❨and plead *[to God] for forgiveness of* your *sin and for the faithful, men and women*❩327

﴿وَتُزَكِّيهِم بِهَا وَصَلِّ عَلَيْهِمْ ۖ إِنَّ صَلَاتَكَ سَكَنٌ لَّهُمْ﴾

❨*wa-tuzakkīhim bihā wa-ṣalli 'alayhim 'inna ṣalātaka sakanun lahum*❩

❨*and purify them thereby, and bless them. Indeed* your *blessing is a comfort to them*❩328

﴿مَن يَشْفَعْ شَفَاعَةً حَسَنَةً يَكُن لَّهُ نَصِيبٌ مِنْهَا﴾

❨*man yashfa' shafā'atan ḥasanatan yakun lahū naṣībun minhā*❩

❨*Whoever intercedes for a good cause shall receive a share of it*❩329

Moreover, 'Allamah Ṭabāṭabā'ī explained what intercession means, saying330:

> "When he (man) wants to get a reward without doing his task; or to save himself from punishment without performing his duty, then he looks for someone to intercede on his behalf. But intercession is effective only if the person for whom one intercedes is otherwise qualified to get the reward and has

---

327 Sūrat Muḥammad, Verse 19.

328 Sūrat al-Tawbah, Verse 103.

329 Sūrat al-Nisā', Verse 85.

330 Ṭabāṭabā'ī, 'Allamah Sayyid Muḥammad Ḥusayn, *al-Mīzān fī Tafsīr al-Qur'ān*, Vol. 1, p. 227-265.

already established a relationship with the authority. Suppose an ignorant person desires an appointment to a prestigious academic post. In that case, no intercession can do him any good, nor can it avail in case of a rebellious traitor who shows no remorse for his misdeeds and does not submit to the lawful authorities. It indicates that intercession works as a supplement to the cause; it is not an independent cause. The effect of an intercessor's words depends on one or the other factor, which may have some influence upon the concerned authority; in other words, intercession must have solid ground to stand upon.

The intercessor endeavors to find a way to the heart of the authority concerned so that the authority may reward or waive the punishment of the person who is the subject of intercession. An intercessor does not ask the master to nullify his mastership or to release the servant from his servitude, nor does he plead with him to refrain from laying down the rules and regulations for his servants or to abrogate his commandments (either generally or especially in that one case), to save the wrongdoer from the due consequences nor does he ask him to discard the canon of reward and punishment, (either generally or in that particular case).

In short, intercession can interfere with neither the institution of mastership and servitude nor the master's authority to lay down the rules, nor can it affect the system of reward and punishment. These three factors are beyond the jurisdiction of intercession. What an intercessor does is this: He accepts the inviolability of the three aspects mentioned above. Then, he looks at one or more of the following factors and builds his intercession on that basis:

a. He appeals to such attributes of the master as giving rise to forgiveness, e.g., nobility, magnanimity, and generosity.

b. He draws attention to such characteristics of the servant as justify mercy and pardon, e.g., his wretchedness, poverty, low status, and misery.

c. He puts at stake his prestige and honor in the eyes of the master.

Thus, the import of intercession is like this: I cannot and do not say that you should forget your mastership over your servant, abrogate your commandment, or nullify the system of reward and punishment. What I ask of you is to forgive this defaulting servant of yours because you are magnanimous and generous and because no harm would come to you if you forgive his sins; and because your servant is a wretched creature of low status and steeped in misery, and it is befitting of a master like you to forgive and pardon him in honor of my intercession. In this way, the intercessor bestows precedence on the factors of forgiveness and pardon over those of legislation and recompense. He removes the case from the latter's jurisdiction, putting it under the former's influence. As a result of this shift, the consequences of legislation (reward and punishment) do not remain applicable. The effect of intercession is, therefore, based on shifting the case from the jurisdiction of reward and punishment to that of pardon and forgiveness; it is not a confrontation between one cause (divine legislation) and the other (intercession). By now, it should have been clear that intercession is one of two causes; the intermediate cause connects a distant cause to its desired effect.

God is the ultimate Cause. This causality shows itself in two ways:

> First, in Creation, Every cause begins from Him and ends up with Him; He is the first and the final Cause. He is the actual Creator and Originator. All other causes are mere channels to carry His boundless mercy and limitless bounty to His creatures.
>
> Second, in Legislation: He, in His mercy, established contact with His creatures; He laid down the religion, sent down His commandments, and prescribed suitable rewards and appropriate punishment for His obedient and disobedient servants; He sent Prophets and apostles to bring us good tidings and to warn us of the consequences of transgression. The prophets and apostles conveyed His message in the best possible way. Thus, His proof over us was complete:

﴿وَتَمَّتْ كَلِمَتُ رَبِّكَ صِدْقًا وَعَدْلًا ۚ لَا مُبَدِّلَ لِكَلِمَاتِهِ﴾

﴿*wa-tammat kalimatu rabbika ṣidqan wa-ʿadlan lā mubaddila li-kalimātihī*﴾

﴿*The word of* your *Lord has been fulfilled in truth and justice. Nothing can change His words*﴾[331]

Both aspects of the causality of God may be, and in fact, related to intercession.

---

[331] Sūrat al-Anʿām, Verse 115.

1. Intercession in creation: Quite obviously, the intermediary causes of creation are the conduits that bring divine mercy, life, sustenance, and other bounties to the creatures, and as such, they are intercessors between the Creator and the created. Some Qur'ānic verses, too, are based on this very theme:

﴿لَهُ ما فِي السَّماواتِ وَما فِي الأَرضِ ۗ مَن ذَا الَّذي يَشفَعُ عِندَهُ إِلّا بِإِذنِهِ﴾

﴿lahū mā fī s-samāwāti wa-mā fī l-'arḍi man dhā lladhī yashfa'u 'indahū 'illā bi-'idhnihī﴾

﴿To Him belongs whatever is in the heavens and whatever is on the earth. Who is it that may intercede with Him except with His permission?﴾[332]

﴿إِنَّ رَبَّكُمُ اللَّهُ الَّذي خَلَقَ السَّماواتِ وَالأَرضَ في سِتَّةِ أَيّامٍ ثُمَّ استَوىٰ عَلَى العَرشِ ۖ يُدَبِّرُ الأَمرَ ۖ ما مِن شَفيعٍ إِلّا مِن بَعدِ إِذنِهِ﴾

﴿'inna rabbakumu llāhu lladhī khalaqa s-samāwāti wa-l-'arḍa fī sittati 'ayyāmin thumma stawā 'alā l-'arshi yudabbiru l-'amra mā min shafī'in 'illā min ba'di 'idhnihī﴾

﴿Indeed your Lord is God, who created the heavens and the world in six days, and then settled on the Throne, directing the command. There is no intercessor, except by His leave﴾*[333]

---

332 Sūrat al-Baqarah, Verse 255.

333 Sūrat Yūnus, Verse 3.

* Cf. 13:2; 32:5.

Intercession in the sphere of creation is only the intermediation of causes between the Creator and the created thing and effect, bringing it into being and regulating its affairs.

2. Intercession in legislation: Intercession, as analyzed earlier, is effective in this sphere too. It is in this context that God ﷻ says:

﴿يَوْمَئِذٍ لَا تَنفَعُ الشَّفَاعَةُ إِلَّا مَنْ أَذِنَ لَهُ الرَّحْمَٰنُ وَرَضِيَ لَهُ قَوْلًا﴾

﴾*yawma'idhin lā tanfa'u sh-shafā'atu 'illā man 'adhina lahu r-raḥmānu wa-raḍiya lahū qawla*^{n}﴿

﴾*Intercession will not avail that day except from him whom the Beneficent allows and approves of his word*﴿[334]

﴿وَلَا تَنفَعُ الشَّفَاعَةُ عِندَهُ إِلَّا لِمَنْ أَذِنَ لَهُ﴾

﴾*wa-lā tanfa'u sh-shafā'atu 'indahū 'illā li-man 'adhina lahū*﴿

﴾*Intercession is of no avail with Him except for those whom He permits**﴿[335]

﴿وَكَم مِّن مَّلَكٍ فِي السَّمَاوَاتِ لَا تُغْنِي شَفَاعَتُهُمْ شَيْئًا إِلَّا مِن بَعْدِ أَن يَأْذَنَ اللَّهُ لِمَن يَشَاءُ وَيَرْضَىٰ﴾

---

[334] Sūrat Ṭā Ḥā, Verse 109.

[335] Sūrat Saba, Verse 23.

* See Zamakhshari and Ṭabāṭabā'ī. Or 'except of those whom He permits.'

﴿*wa-kam min malakin fī s-samāwāti lā tughnī shafāʿatuhum shay'an 'illā min baʿdi 'an ya'dhana llāhu li-man yashā'u wa-yarḍā*﴾

﴿*How many an angel there is in the heavens whose intercession is of no avail in any way except after God grants permission to whomever He wishes and approves of!*﴾[336]

﴿وَلا يَشفَعونَ إِلّا لِمَنِ ارتَضىٰ﴾

﴿*wa-lā yashfaʿūna 'illā li-mani rtaḍā*﴾

﴿*and they do not intercede except for someone He approves of*﴾[337]

﴿وَلا يَملِكُ الَّذينَ يَدعونَ مِن دونِهِ الشَّفاعَةَ إِلّا مَن شَهِدَ بِالحَقِّ وَهُم يَعلَمونَ﴾

﴿*wa-lā yamliku lladhīna yadʿūna min dūnihi sh-shafāʿata 'illā man shahida bi-l-ḥaqqi wa-hum yaʿlamūna*﴾

﴿*Those whom they invoke besides Him have no power of intercession, except those who are witness to the truth and who know [for whom to intercede]*﴾[338]

These verses affirm the intercessory role of various servants of God ﷻ — both men and angels — with divine permission and pleasure. It means that God has given them some power and authority in this matter, and to Him belongs all the kingdom

---

336 Sūrat al-Najm, Verse 26.

337 Sūrat al-Anbiyā', Verse 28.

338 Sūrat al-Zukhruf, Verse 86.

and all the affairs. Those intercessors may appeal to God's mercy, forgiveness, and other relevant attributes to cover and protect a servant who otherwise would have deserved punishment because of his sins and transgressions. That intercession would transfer his case from the general law of recompense to the special domain of grace and mercy.[339]

God ﷻ clearly says;

﴿إِلَّا مَن تَابَ وَآمَنَ وَعَمِلَ عَمَلًا صَالِحًا فَأُولَٰئِكَ يُبَدِّلُ اللَّهُ سَيِّئَاتِهِمْ حَسَنَاتٍ﴾

﴿*'illā man tāba wa-'āmana wa-'amila 'amalan ṣāliḥan fa-'ulā'ika yubaddilu llāhu sayyi'ātihim ḥasanātin*﴾

﴿*excepting those who repent, attain faith, and act righteously. For such, God will replace their misdeeds with good deeds**﴾[340]

God ﷻ has the power to change one type of deed into another, in the same way He may render an act null and void.

---

[339] It has already been explained that the effect of intercession is based on shifting a case from the former's to the latter's jurisdiction; it is not a confrontation between one law and the other.

[340] Sūrat al-Furqān, Verse 70.

* Or 'their vices with virtues.'

He ﷻ says:

﴿وَقَدِمنا إِلىٰ ما عَمِلوا مِن عَمَلٍ فَجَعَلناهُ هَباءً مَنثورًا﴾

﴾*wa-qadimnā ʾilā mā ʿamilū min ʿamalin fa-jaʿalnāhu habāʾan manthūran*﴿

﴾*Then We shall attend to the works they have done and then turn them into scattered dust*﴿[341]

﴿فَأَحبَطَ أَعمالَهُم﴾

﴾*fa-ʾaḥbaṭa ʾaʿmālahum*﴿

﴾*so He made their works fail*﴿[342]

﴿إِن تَجتَنِبوا كَبائِرَ ما تُنهَونَ عَنهُ نُكَفِّر عَنكُم سَيِّئاتِكُم وَنُدخِلكُم مُدخَلًا كَريمًا﴾

﴾*ʾin tajtanibū kabāʾira mā tunhawna ʿanhu nukaffir ʿankum sayyiʾātikum wa-nudkhilkum mudkhalan karīman*﴿

﴾*If you avoid the major sins that you are forbidden, We will absolve you of your misdeeds, and admit you to a noble abode*﴿[343]

﴿إِنَّ اللَّهَ لا يَغفِرُ أَن يُشرَكَ بِهِ وَيَغفِرُ ما دونَ ذٰلِكَ لِمَن يَشاءُ ۚ وَمَن يُشرِك بِاللَّهِ فَقَدِ افتَرىٰ إِثمًا عَظيمًا﴾

341 Sūrat al-Furqān, Verse 23.

342 Sūrat Muḥammad, Verse 9.

343 Sūrat al-Nisāʾ, Verse 31.

﴾'inna llāha lā yaghfiru 'an yushraka bihī wa-yaghfiru mā dūna dhālika li-man yashā'u wa-man yushrik bi-llāhi fa-qadi ftarā 'ithman ʿaẓīman﴿

﴾Indeed God does not forgive that any partner should be ascribed to Him, but He forgives anything besides that to whomever He wishes. And whoever ascribes partners to God has indeed fabricated [a lie] in great sinfulness﴿[344]

The last quoted verse is certainly about cases other than true belief and repentance; with faith and repentance, even polytheism is forgiven, like any other sin. Also, God may nurture a small deed to make it greater than the original:

﴾أُولَئِكَ يُؤْتَوْنَ أَجْرَهُم مَّرَّتَيْنِ بِمَا صَبَرُوا﴿

﴾'ulā'ika yu'tawna 'ajrahum marratayni bi-mā ṣabarū﴿

﴾Those will be given their reward two times for their patience﴿[345]

﴾مَن جَاءَ بِالْحَسَنَةِ فَلَهُ عَشْرُ أَمْثَالِهَا﴿

﴾man jā'a bi-l-ḥasanati fa-lahū ʿashru 'amthālihā﴿

﴾Whoever brings virtue shall receive ten times its like﴿[346]

---

344 Sūrat al-Nisā', Verse 48.

345 Sūrat al-Qaṣaṣ, Verse 54.

346 Sūrat al-Anʿām, Verse 160.

Likewise, He may treat a nonexistent deed as existing:

﴿وَالَّذِينَ آمَنُوا وَاتَّبَعَتْهُمْ ذُرِّيَّتُهُم بِإِيمَانٍ أَلْحَقْنَا بِهِمْ ذُرِّيَّتَهُمْ وَمَا أَلَتْنَاهُم مِّنْ عَمَلِهِم مِّن شَيْءٍ ۚ كُلُّ امْرِئٍ بِمَا كَسَبَ رَهِينٌ﴾

﴿*wa-lladhīna 'āmanū wa-ttaba'athum dhurriyyatuhum bi-'īmānin 'alḥaqnā bihim dhurriyyatahum wa-mā 'alatnāhum min 'amalihim min shay'in kullu mri'in bi-mā kasaba rahīnun*﴾

﴿*The faithful and their descendants who followed them in faith — We will make their descendants join them, and We will not stint anything from [the reward of] their deeds. Every man is a hostage to what he has earned*﴾[347]

To make a long story short, God ﷻ does what He pleases and decrees as He wills. Of course, He does so according to His servants' interest, and per an intermediary cause and intercession of the intercessors (e.g., the prophets, the friends of God, and those who are nearer to Him) is one of those causes, and certainly, no rashness or injustice is entailed therein. It should have been clear by now that intercession, in its true sense, belongs to God only; all His attributes are intermediaries between Him and His creatures and are the channels through which His grace, mercy, and decrees pass to the creatures. He is the real and all-encompassing intercessor:

﴿قُل لِّلَّهِ الشَّفَاعَةُ جَمِيعًا﴾

﴿*qul li-llāhi sh-shafā'atu jamī'an*﴾

---

[347] Sūrat al-Ṭūr, Verse 21.

﴾Say, *'All intercession rests with God*﴿[348]

﴿ما لَكُم مِن دونِهِ مِن وَلِيٍّ وَلا شَفيعٍ﴾

﴾*mā lakum min dūnihī min waliyyin wa-lā shafīʿin*﴿

﴾*You do not have besides Him any guardian or intercessor*﴿[349]

﴿لَيسَ لَهُم مِن دونِهِ وَلِيٌّ وَلا شَفيعٌ لَعَلَّهُم يَتَّقونَ﴾

﴾*laysa lahum min dūnihī waliyyun wa-lā shafīʿun laʿallahum yattaqūna*[a]﴿

﴾*besides whom they shall have neither any guardian nor any intercessor, so that they may be Godwary*﴿[350]

The intercessors, other than God, get that right by His permission, by His authority.

In short, intercession with Him is a confirmed reality that does not go against the divine glory and honor."

Sayyid Ṭabāṭabāʾī also answers the following question:

Who are the Intercessors?

He writes:

[348] Sūrat al-Zumar, Verse 44.

[349] Sūrat al-Sajdah, Verse 4.

[350] Sūrat al-Anʿām, Verse 51.

"It has been described that intercession takes place in two spheres: creation and legislation. So far as the intercession in creation is concerned, all intermediary causes are intercessors because they are placed between the Creator and the created.

As for the intercessors in the sphere of legislation and judgment may be divided into two categories:

Intercessors in this life, and those in the hereafter.

1. Intercessors in this life: All the things that bring a man nearer to God and make him eligible for divine forgiveness. The following come into this category:

   a. Repentance: God ﷻ says:

﴿قُل يا عِبادِيَ الَّذينَ أَسرَفوا عَلىٰ أَنفُسِهِم لا تَقنَطوا مِن رَحمَةِ اللَّهِ ۚ إِنَّ اللَّهَ يَغفِرُ الذُّنوبَ جَميعًا ۚ إِنَّهُ هُوَ الغَفورُ الرَّحيمُ﴾

﴿qul yā-ʿibādiya lladhīna ʾasrafū ʿalā ʾanfusihim lā taqnaṭū min raḥmati llāhi ʾinna llāha yaghfiru dh-dhunūba jamīʿan ʾinnahū huwa l-ghafūru r-raḥīmᵘ﴾

﴿وَأَنيبوا إِلىٰ رَبِّكُم وَأَسلِموا لَهُ مِن قَبلِ أَن يَأتِيَكُمُ العَذابُ ثُمَّ لا تُنصَرونَ﴾

﴿wa-ʾanībū ʾilā rabbikum wa-ʾaslimū lahū min qabli ʾan yaʾtiyakumu l-ʿadhābu thumma lā tunṣarūnᵃ﴾

﴿Say [that God declares,] 'O My servants who have committed excesses against their own souls, do not despair of the mercy of God. Indeed God will forgive all sins. Indeed He is the Forgiving, the

Merciful. Turn penitently to Him and submit to Him before the punishment overtakes you, whereupon you will not be helped﴾[351]

It covers all the sins, even polytheism; if one repents from it and believes in One God, one's previous polytheism is wiped out and forgiven.

b. True faith; God ﷻ says:

﴿يا أَيُّهَا الَّذِينَ آمَنُوا اتَّقُوا اللَّهَ وَآمِنوا بِرَسولِهِ يُؤتِكُم كِفلَينِ مِن رَحمَتِهِ وَيَجعَل لَكُم نورًا تَمشونَ بِهِ وَيَغفِر لَكُم ۚ وَاللَّهُ غَفورٌ رَحيمٌ﴾

﴾*yā-'ayyuhā lladhīna 'āmanū ttaqū llāha wa-'āminū bi-rasūlihī yu'tikum kiflayni min raḥmatihī wa-yaj'al lakum nūran tamshūna bihī wa-yaghfir lakum wa-llāhu ghafūrun raḥīm*[un]﴿

﴾*O you who have faith! Be wary of God and have faith in His Apostle. He will grant you a double share of His mercy and give you a light to walk by, and forgive you, and God is Forgiving, Merciful*﴿[352]

c. Good deed:

﴿وَعَدَ اللَّهُ الَّذينَ آمَنوا وَعَمِلُوا الصّالِحاتِ ۙ لَهُم مَغفِرَةٌ وَأَجرٌ عَظيمٌ﴾

﴾*wa'ada llāhu lladhīna 'āmanū wa-'amilū ṣ-ṣāliḥāti lahum maghfiratun wa-'ajrun 'aẓīm*[un]﴿

351 Sūrat al-Zumar, Verses 54-54.

352 Sūrat al-Ḥadīd, Verse 28.

﴿*God has promised those who have faith and do righteous deeds forgiveness and a great reward*﴾[353]

﴿يا أَيُّهَا الَّذينَ آمَنُوا اتَّقُوا اللّهَ وَابتَغوا إِلَيهِ الوَسيلَةَ﴾

﴿*yā-'ayyuhā lladhīna 'āmanū ttaqū llāha wa-btaghū 'ilayhi l-wasīlata*﴾

﴿*O you who have faith! Be wary of God, and seek the means of recourse to Him*﴾[354]

There are many verses with this theme.

﴿يَهدي بِهِ اللَّهُ مَنِ اتَّبَعَ رِضوانَهُ سُبُلَ السَّلامِ وَيُخرِجُهُم مِنَ الظُّلُماتِ إِلَى النّورِ بِإِذنِهِ وَيَهديهِم إِلىٰ صِراطٍ مُستَقيمٍ﴾

﴿*yahdī bihi llāhu mani ttaba'a riḍwānahū subula s-salāmi wa-yukhrijuhum mina ẓ-ẓulumāti 'ilā n-nūri bi-'idhnihī wa-yahdīhim 'ilā ṣirāṭin mustaqīm*[in]﴾

﴿*With it God guides those who follow [the course of] His pleasure to the ways of peace, and brings them out from darkness into light by His will, and guides them to a straight path*﴾[355]

d. Anything related to a good deed, like mosques, holy places, and auspicious days.

---

[353] Sūrat al-Mā'idah, Verse 9.

[354] Sūrat al-Mā'idah, Verse 35.

[355] Sūrat al-Mā'idah, Verse 16.

e. The prophets and the apostles, as they seek forgiveness for their people.

God ﷻ says:

﴿وَلَو أَنَّهُم إِذ ظَلَموا أَنفُسَهُم جاءوكَ فَاستَغفَرُوا اللَّهَ وَاستَغفَرَ لَهُمُ الرَّسولُ لَوَجَدُوا اللَّهَ تَوّابًا رَحيمًا﴾

﴿*wa-law 'annahum 'idh ẓalamū 'anfusahum jā'ūka fa-staghfarū llāha wa-staghfara lahumu r-rasūlu la-wajadū llāha tawwāban raḥīman*﴾

﴿*Had they, when they wronged themselves, come to you and pleaded to God for forgiveness, and the Apostle had pleaded for forgiveness for them, they would have surely found God Clement, Merciful*﴾[356]

f. The angels, as they too ask forgiveness for the believers.

God ﷻ says:

﴿الَّذينَ يَحمِلونَ العَرشَ وَمَن حَولَهُ يُسَبِّحونَ بِحَمدِ رَبِّهِم وَيُؤمِنونَ بِهِ وَيَستَغفِرونَ لِلَّذينَ آمَنوا رَبَّنا وَسِعتَ كُلَّ شَيءٍ رَحمَةً وَعِلمًا فَاغفِر لِلَّذينَ تابوا وَاتَّبَعوا سَبيلَكَ وَقِهِم عَذابَ الجَحيمِ﴾

﴿*alladhīna yaḥmilūna l-'arsha wa-man ḥawlahū yusabbiḥūna bi-ḥamdi rabbihim wa-yu'minūna bihī wa-yastaghfirūna li-lladhīna 'āmanū rabbanā wasi'ta kulla shay'in raḥmatan wa-'ilman fa-ghfir li-lladhīna tābū wa-ttaba'ū sabīlaka wa-qihim 'adhāba l-jaḥīmi*﴾

356 Sūrat al-Nisā', Verse 64.

﴾*Those who bear the Throne, and those around it, celebrate the praise of their Lord and have faith in Him, and they plead for forgiveness for the faithful: 'Our Lord! You comprehend all things in mercy and knowledge. So forgive those who repent and follow Your way and save them from the punishment of hell*﴿[357]

﴿وَالْمَلَائِكَةُ يُسَبِّحُونَ بِحَمْدِ رَبِّهِمْ وَيَسْتَغْفِرُونَ لِمَنْ فِي الْأَرْضِ ۗ أَلَا إِنَّ اللَّهَ هُوَ الْغَفُورُ الرَّحِيمُ﴾

﴾*wa-l-malāʾikatu yusabbiḥūna bi-ḥamdi rabbihim wa-yastaghfirūna li-man fī l-ʾarḍi ʾa-lā ʾinna llāha huwa l-ghafūru r-raḥīmu*﴿

﴾*while the angels celebrate the praise of their Lord and plead for forgiveness for those on the earth. Look! God is indeed the Forgiving, the Merciful!*﴿[358]

g. The believers themselves, as they seek pardon for their believer brothers and themselves.

God ﷻ quotes them as saying:

﴿وَاعْفُ عَنَّا وَاغْفِرْ لَنَا وَارْحَمْنَا ۚ أَنْتَ مَوْلَانَا﴾

﴾*wa-ʿfu ʿannā wa-ghfir lanā wa-rḥamnā ʾanta mawlānā*﴿

---

[357] Sūrat Ghāfir, Verse 7.

[358] Sūrat al-Shūrā, Verse 5.

﴿Excuse us and forgive us, and be merciful to us! You are our Master﴾[359]

2. Intercessors in the hereafter: We use the term intercessor in the meaning explained in the beginning. The following come into this category:

    a. The prophets and the apostles ﷺ.

    God ﷻ says:

﴿وَقالُوا اتَّخَذَ الرَّحمٰنُ وَلَدًا ۗ سُبحانَهُ ۚ بَل عِبادٌ مُكرَمونَ﴾

﴿wa-qālū ttakhadha r-raḥmānu waladan subḥānahū bal ʿibādun mukramūna[a]*﴾*

﴿لا يَسبِقونَهُ بِالقَولِ وَهُم بِأَمرِهِ يَعمَلونَ﴾

﴿lā yasbiqūnahū bi-l-qawli wa-hum bi-ʾamrihī yaʿmalūna[a]

﴿يَعلَمُ ما بَينَ أَيديهِم وَما خَلفَهُم وَلا يَشفَعونَ إِلّا لِمَنِ ارتَضىٰ وَهُم مِن خَشيَتِهِ مُشفِقونَ﴾

yaʿlamu mā bayna ʾaydīhim wa-mā khalfahum wa-lā yashfaʿūna ʾillā li-mani rtaḍā wa-hum min khashyatihī mushfiqūna[a]*﴾*

﴿They say, 'The Beneficent has taken offsprings.' Immaculate is He! Rather they are [His] honoured servants. They do not venture to speak ahead of Him, and they act by His command. He knows that

[359] Sūrat al-Baqarah, Verse 286.

*which is before them and that which is behind them, and they do not intercede except for someone He approves of, and they are apprehensive for the fear of Him⟩*³⁶⁰

Those who were called sons of God are His honored servants and they do intercede for whom He approves. Among them is 'Īsā (Jesus), son of Maryam, and he was a prophet. It means that the Prophets do intercede for authorized persons.

Again God says:

﴿وَلَا يَمْلِكُ الَّذِينَ يَدْعُونَ مِن دُونِهِ الشَّفَاعَةَ إِلَّا مَن شَهِدَ بِالْحَقِّ وَهُمْ يَعْلَمُونَ﴾

⟨*wa-lā yamliku lladhīna yadʿūna min dūnihi sh-shafāʿata 'illā man shahida bi-l-ḥaqqi wa-hum yaʿlamūnᵃ*⟩

⟨*Those whom they invoke besides Him have no power of intercession, except those who are witness to the truth and who know [for whom to intercede]*⟩³⁶¹

b. The angels: The preceding two verses prove that the angels too may intercede because they too were called daughters of God.

---

³⁶⁰ Sūrat al-Anbiyā', Verses 26-26.

³⁶¹ Sūrat al-Zukhruf, Verse 86.

Moreover, God ﷻ says:

﴿وَكَم مِن مَلَكٍ فِي السَّماواتِ لا تُغني شَفاعَتُهُم شَيئًا إِلّا مِن بَعدِ أَن يَأذَنَ اللَّهُ لِمَن يَشاءُ وَيَرضىٰ﴾

﴿wa-kam min malakin fī s-samāwāti lā tughnī shafā'atuhum shay'an 'illā min ba'di 'an ya'dhana llāhu li-man yashā'u wa-yarḍā﴾

﴿How many an angel there is in the heavens whose intercession is of no avail in any way except after God grants permission to whomever He wishes and approves of!﴾[362]

﴿يَومَئِذٍ لا تَنفَعُ الشَّفاعَةُ إِلّا مَن أَذِنَ لَهُ الرَّحمٰنُ وَرَضِيَ لَهُ قَولًا﴾

﴿yawma'idhin lā tanfa'u sh-shafā'atu 'illā man 'adhina lahu r-raḥmānu wa-raḍiya lahū qawlaⁿ﴾

﴿يَعلَمُ ما بَينَ أَيديهِم وَما خَلفَهُم وَلا يُحيطونَ بِهِ عِلمًا﴾

﴿ya'lamu mā bayna 'aydīhim wa-mā khalfahum wa-lā yuḥīṭūna bihī 'ilmaⁿ﴾

﴿Intercession will not avail that day except from him whom the Beneficent allows and approves of his word. He knows that which is before them and that which is behind them, but they cannot comprehend Him in their knowledge﴾[363]

---

[362] Sūrat al-Najm, Verse 26.

[363] Sūrat Ṭā Ḥā, Verse 109-110.

c. The witnesses:

God ﷻ says:

﴿وَلا يَملِكُ الَّذينَ يَدعونَ مِن دونِهِ الشَّفاعَةَ إِلّا مَن شَهِدَ بِالحَقِّ وَهُم يَعلَمونَ﴾

﴿*wa-lā yamliku lladhīna yad'ūna min dūnihi sh-shafā'ata 'illā man shahida bi-l-ḥaqqi wa-hum ya'lamūna*﴾

﴿*Those whom they invoke besides Him have no power of intercession, except those who are witness to the truth and who know [for whom to intercede]*﴾[364]

This verse shows that those who witness the truth own (or have authority for) intercession. The witness mentioned here does not mean the one killed on the battlefield. It refers to the witness for the deeds, as was described in the Chapter of the Opening.

d. The believers shall be joined to the witnesses on the Day of Judgment; they may intercede like the Witnesses (*Shuhadā'*).

God ﷻ says:

﴿وَالَّذينَ آمَنوا بِاللَّهِ وَرُسُلِهِ أُولٰئِكَ هُمُ الصِّدّيقونَ ۖ وَالشُّهَداءُ عِندَ رَبِّهِم﴾

﴿*wa-lladhīna 'āmanū bi-llāhi wa-rusulihī 'ulā'ika humu ṣ-ṣiddīqūna wa-sh-shuhadā'u 'inda rabbihim*﴾

[364] Sūrat al-Zukhruf, Verse 86.

⟪*Those who have faith in God and His apostles —it is they who are the truthful and the witnesses* with their Lord; they shall have their reward and their light*⟫365

It is noticeable that Sayyid Ṭabāṭabā'ī did not mention the Imāms or Sayyidah Fāṭimah ﷺ in his categorization of the intercessors. This is because the Imāms are among the witnesses that he spoke of. In his explanation of the following verses, he implicitly stated that what is meant by the witness on the right path is the Imāms ﷺ. In addition, various narrations clearly state that the witnesses mean them ﷺ.

⟪اهدِنَا الصِّرَاطَ المُستَقِيمَ⟫

⟪*ihdinā ṣ-ṣirāṭa l-mustaqīmᵃ*⟫

⟪*Guide us on the straight path*⟫366

⟪وَكَذَٰلِكَ جَعَلْنَاكُمْ أُمَّةً وَسَطًا لِّتَكُونُوا شُهَدَاءَ عَلَى النَّاسِ وَيَكُونَ الرَّسُولُ عَلَيْكُمْ شَهِيدًا ۗ وَمَا جَعَلْنَا الْقِبْلَةَ الَّتِي كُنتَ عَلَيْهَا إِلَّا لِنَعْلَمَ مَن يَتَّبِعُ الرَّسُولَ مِمَّن يَنقَلِبُ عَلَىٰ عَقِبَيْهِ ۚ وَإِن كَانَتْ لَكَبِيرَةً إِلَّا عَلَى الَّذِينَ هَدَى اللَّهُ ۗ وَمَا كَانَ اللَّهُ لِيُضِيعَ إِيمَانَكُمْ ۚ إِنَّ اللَّهَ بِالنَّاسِ لَرَءُوفٌ رَحِيمٌ⟫

---

365 Sūrat al-Ḥadīd, Verse 19.

* Or 'martyrs.'

366 Sūrat al-Fātiḥah, Verse 6.

⟪wa-ka-dhālika jaʿalnākum 'ummatan wasaṭan li-takūnū shuhadāʾa ʿalā n-nāsi wa-yakūna r-rasūlu ʿalaykum shahīdan wa-mā jaʿalnā l-qiblata llatī kunta ʿalayhā 'illā li-naʿlama man yattabiʿu r-rasūla mimman yanqalibu ʿalā ʿaqibayhi wa-ʾin kānat la-kabīratan 'illā ʿalā lladhīna hadā llāhu wa-mā kāna llāhu li-yuḍīʿa 'īmānakum 'inna llāha bi-n-nāsi la-raʾūfun raḥīm^{un}⟫

⟪Thus We have made you a middle nation that you may be witnesses to the people, and that the Apostle may be a witness to you. And We did not appoint the qiblah you were following but that We may ascertain those who follow the Apostle from those who turn back on their heels. It was indeed a hard thing except for those whom God has guided. And God would not let your prayers go to waste*. Indeed God is most kind and merciful to mankind⟫[367]

Sayyidah Fāṭimah undoubtedly is included among the believers who are intercessors on the Day of Rising. If a particular class of believers has the right of intercession, then it is only reasonable that she is at the top of the category. Nevertheless, the previously mentioned narrations regarding her intercession deem it unnecessary for us to speak further about this matter.

Traditions Regarding Intercession

Sayyid Ṭabāṭabāʾī has also selected several traditions that speak of intercession on the Day of Rising by the Prophet and Ahl al-

---

[367] Sūrat al-Baqarah, Verse 143.

* '*Īmān*' here means prayers. God reassures the faithful that the prayers they have offered earlier facing towards Quds will not be wasted by the change of *qiblah*.

Bayt ﷺ. To become more familiar with the subject from this viewpoint, some of these narrations are mentioned here:

1. al-Ḥusayn b. Khālid narrates[368] from al-Riḍā ؑ, who conveyed through his forefathers from the Leader of the Faithful ؑ that he said:

   "Messenger of God ﷺ said:

   'Whoever does not believe in my reservoir, may God not bring him to my reservoir, and whoever does not believe in my intercession, may God not extend to him my intercession.'

   Then he said:

   'Verily, my intercession is for those of my Ummah who shall have committed great sins; as for the good-doers, there shall be no difficulty for them. "

   al-Ḥusayn b. Khālid said:

   "I asked al-Riḍā ؑ;

   'O son of the Messenger of God! What is then the meaning of the words of God, Mighty, and Great is He:

   ﴿وَلَا تَنفَعُ الشَّفَاعَةُ عِندَهُ إِلَّا لِمَنْ أَذِنَ لَهُ﴾

[368] Ṣadūq, Shaykh Muḥammad b. 'Alī, *al-Amālī*.

⟪wa-lā tanfaʿu sh-shafāʿatu ʿindahū ʾillā li-man ʾadhina lahū⟫

⟪Intercession is of no avail with Him except for those whom He permits*⟫369

al-Riḍā said:

"They only intercede on behalf of those whom God accepts their faith."

2. "Ṣumaʿah b. Mihrān370 narrates from Abū Ibrāhīm what he said about the words of God:

﴿عَسَىٰ أَن يَبْعَثَكَ رَبُّكَ مَقَامًا مَّحْمُودًا﴾

⟪ʿasā ʾan yabʿathaka rabbuka maqāman maḥmūdaⁿ⟫

⟪It may be that your Lord will raise you to a praiseworthy station⟫371

The people, on the Day of Resurrection, will remain standing for forty years; and the sun will be ordered so that it will ride over their heads and they will be bridled with sweat, and the earth will be told not to accept any of their sweat. So, they shall approach Ādam to intercede for them, and he will direct them to Nūḥ, and Nūḥ will direct them to Ibrāhīm, and Ibrāhīm

---

369 Sūrat Saba, Verse 23.

* See Zamakhshari and Ṭabāṭabāʾī. Or 'except of those whom He permits.'

370 al-ʿAyyāshī, Muḥammad b. Masʿūd, *Tafsīr al-ʿAyyāshī*.

371 Sūrat al-Isrāʾ, Verse 79.

will direct them to Mūsā, and Mūsā will direct them to 'Īsā, and 'Īsā will direct them saying:

> 'You should seek help from Muḥammad, the last Prophet.'

Thereupon, Muḥammad ﷺ will say:

> 'I'll do it'

and will proceed until arriving at the door of the Garden; he will knock on it. It will be asked,

> 'Who is it?' (While God knows better), and he will say:

> 'Muḥammad, '

Then it will be said:

> 'Open for him'.

When the door is opened, he will turn to his Lord, falling in sajdah. He will not raise his head until told:

> 'Speak up and ask, you shall be given; and intercede, your intercession shall be granted.'

He will raise his head and, turning to his Lord, fall (again) in sajdah. Then he will be promised as before; then he will raise his head. Thereupon, he shall intercede until he will intercede even for him who would have been burnt in the fire. Therefore, on the Day of Resurrection, no one among all the nations will be more eminent than Muḥammad ﷺ; this is (the meaning of) the words of God:

$$\text{﴿عَسَىٰ أَن يَبْعَثَكَ رَبُّكَ مَقَامًا مَّحْمُودًا﴾}$$

﴾*'asā 'an yab'athaka rabbuka maqāman maḥmūda^n*﴿

﴾*It may be that* your *Lord will raise* you *to a praiseworthy station*﴿372

3. 'Ubayd b. Zurārah said:

> 'Abū 'Abdillāh ☙ was asked whether a believer would have the right of intercession.
>
> He said:
>
>> 'Yes.'
>
> Then someone said:
>
>> 'Will even a believer need the intercession of Muḥammad ☙ on that day?'
>
> He said:
>
>> 'Yes, the believers too will come with wrongs and sins, and there will be none but shall need the intercession of Muḥammad on that day.'"

('Ubayd) said:

> 'And someone asked him about the words of the Messenger of God:

---

372 Sūrat al-Isrā', Verse 79.

'I am the Chief of the children of Ādam, and I say this without boasting.'

He said:

'Yes,'

then he said:

He will hold the chain-link of the door of the garden and open it; then he will fall in sajdah, and God will tell him:

'Raise your head, to intercede, your intercession shall be granted; ask, you shall be given.'

He will raise his head and intercede, and his intercession will be accepted; he will ask and be given. `

4. al-Qummī narrates a tradition in his tafsīr under the verse:

﴿وَلَا تَنفَعُ الشَّفَاعَةُ عِندَهُ إِلَّا لِمَنْ أَذِنَ لَهُ﴾

﴿*wa-lā tanfaʿu sh-shafāʿatu ʿindahū ʾillā li-man ʾadhina lahū*﴾

﴿*Intercession is of no avail with Him except for those whom He permits**﴾[373]

[373] Sūrat Saba, Verse 23.

* See Zamakhshari and Ṭabāṭabā'ī. Or 'except of those whom He permits.'

that Abū al-'Abbās al-Mukabbar said:

> 'A servant of a wife of 'Alī b. al-Ḥusayn ※, named Abū Ayman, came (to the fifth Imām ※) and said:
>
>> 'O Abū Ja'far! You mislead the people, saying intercession of Muḥammad, intercession Muḥammad.'
>
> (Hearing this) Abū Ja'far became so angry that his face took a glowering expression; then he said:
>
>> 'Woe unto you! O Abū Ayman! Are you deluded by the chastity of your stomach and genitals? Why, when you see the terror of resurrection, you shall certainly require the intercession of Muḥammad. Fie on you! Would he intercede except for him, who would have been sentenced to the fire?'
>
> (Then) he said:
>
>> 'There is not one from the early people to the later ones, but he will need the intercession of Muḥammad ※ on the Day of Resurrection.'
>
> Then again, Abū Ja'far said:
>
>> 'Certainly the Messenger of God has (authority of) intercession for his Ummah, and we have (authority of) intercession for our Shī'ī, and our Shī'ī have (authority of) intercession for their families.'

Then he said:

'And indeed a believer shall intercede for (vast numbers of) people like the tribes of Rabī'ah and Muḍar. And indeed, a believer shall intercede for his servant, saying:

"O my Lord! I owe this to him; he protected me from heat and cold."

5. The (fifth) Imām said about the verse,

﴿وَلَا تَنفَعُ الشَّفَاعَةُ عِندَهُ إِلَّا لِمَنْ أَذِنَ لَهُ﴾

⟨wa-lā tanfa'u sh-shafā'atu 'indahū 'illā li-man 'adhina lahū⟩

⟨*Intercession is of no avail with Him except for those whom He permits*⟩[374]

"No prophet or apostle may intercede until God permits him, except the Apostle of God; because God has already given him permission before the Day of Resurrection; and intercession is (allowed) to him and the Imāms from his progeny, and after that to the prophets."[375]

---

[374] Sūrat Saba, Verse 23.

* See Zamakhshari and Ṭabāṭabā'ī. Or 'except of those whom He permits.'

[375] al-Qummī, 'Alī b. Ibrāhīm, *Tafsīr al-Qummī*.

6. ʿAlī ﷺ said:

"The Apostle of God ﷺ said:

> `Three (groups) shall intercede with God, and their intercession will be accepted: the prophets, then the (religious) scholars, then the martyrs. "[376]

7. Abū ʿAbdullāh narrates through his father and grandfather, from ʿAlī ﷺ that he said:

"The garden has eight gates: one for the entry of prophets and the truthful ones, the other for the martyrs and the good ones; and five gates are for the entry of our Shīʿī, and lovers. I shall be standing on the as-Ṣirāṭ (the path, the bridge over hell) praying and saying:

> `My Lord! Save my Shīʿī and my lovers, my helpers, and those who followed me in the (life of the) world.'

Then suddenly, a voice from inside the throne will come:

> 'Your prayer is granted, and your intercession for your Shīʿī accepted.'

And every Shīʿī of mine and everyone who loves and helps me, and fights my enemies by (his) deed or word, shall intercede for seventy thousand of his neighbors and relatives; and (there is) a gate from which shall enter all the Muslims who witness that there is no god except God and in whose heart there is not an iota of enmity towards us, the people of the cause."

---

[376] Ṣadūq, Shaykh Muḥammad b. ʿAlī, *al-Khiṣāl*.

8. al-Kāẓim ﷺ narrated from his father ﷺ, through his forefathers ﷺ, from the Prophet ﷺ that he said:

> "My intercession is for those of my Ummah who would have committed big sins; as for the doers of good, there shall be no difficulty for them."

He was asked:

> "O son of the Messenger of God! How can the intercession be for those who have committed big sins while God ﷻ says,
>
> ﴿وَلَا يَشْفَعُونَ إِلَّا لِمَنِ ارْتَضَىٰ﴾
>
> ⟪wa-lā yashfaʿūna ʾillā li-mani rtaḍā⟫
>
> ⟪and they do not intercede except for someone He approves of⟫[377]
>
> and a committer of big sins cannot be approved?"

He ﷺ said:

> "No believer commits a sin, but he regrets it and feels ashamed. And the Prophet has said:
>
> 'Enough is regret as repentance,' and 'whoever is pleased by a good deed and displeased by a bad deed, he is a believer.'

---

[377] Sūrat al-Anbiyāʾ, Verse 28.

Therefore, if someone does not feel remorse for a sin he has committed, he is not a believer, and intercession will not avail him, and he will be unjust.

And God ﷻ says:

﴿ما لِلظّالِمينَ مِن حَميمٍ وَلا شَفيعٍ يُطاعُ﴾

﴿mā li-ẓ-ẓālimīna min ḥamīmin wa-lā shafīʿin yuṭāʿu﴾

﴿the wrongdoers will have no sympathizer, nor any intercessor who might be heard﴾[378]

It was said to him:

> "O son of the Messenger of God! How is it that he who is not sorry for a sin he has committed does not remain a believer?"

He said:

> 'Anyone who commits a big sin, knowing that he must be punished for it, will certainly feel remorse for his actions. And as soon as he is sorry, he is repentant, eligible for intercession. But if he is not sorry, he persists in it, and a persistent (sinner) is not forgiven because he does not believe in the punishment for what he has done. Had he believed in that punishment, he would have been sorry.

---

[378] Sūrat Ghāfir, Verse 18.

And the Prophet has said:

> 'No big sin abides with apologizing, and no small sin remains (small) with persistence.'

And as for the words of God,

﴿وَلَا تَنفَعُ الشَّفَاعَةُ عِندَهُ إِلَّا لِمَنْ أَذِنَ لَهُ﴾

﴾*wa-lā tanfa'u sh-shafā'atu 'indahū 'illā li-man 'adhina lahū*﴿

﴾*Intercession is of no avail with Him except for those whom He permits**﴿[379]

> it means that they do not intercede except for him whose religion He approves. Religion is an acknowledgment that good and bad deeds have to be recompensed. If one's religion were approved, one would feel remorse for the sins one committed because he would know their result on the (Day of) Resurrection."[380]

9. A similar theme is found in a tradition quoted from Abū Isḥāq al-Laythī, where he said[381]:

> 'O son of the Messenger of God! Tell me about a believer possessing religious understanding when he reaches (a high

---

[379] Sūrat Saba, Verse 23.

* See Zamakhshari and Ṭabāṭabā'ī. Or 'except of those whom He permits.'

[380] Ṣadūq, Shaykh Muḥammad b. 'Alī, *al-Tawḥīd*.

[381] Ṣadūq, Shaykh Muḥammad b. 'Alī, *'Ilal al-Sharāi'*.

point in) knowledge and becomes perfect. Does he commit fornication?'

He said,

`By God! No.'

I said:

`Then does he indulge in sodomy?

He said:

`By God! No.'

I said:

`Then does he steal?'

He said:

'No.'

I said:

`Then does he drink intoxicants?'

He said:

`No.'

I said:

> 'Then does he commit any big sins or indulge in these indecencies?'

He said:

> 'No.'

I said:

> 'Then does he sin?'

He said:

> 'Yes, and he is a believer, sinner, submissive.'

I said:

> 'What does submissive mean?'

He said:

> 'The submissive (servant) does not persist in it, does not keep doing it..."

10. al-Riḍā عليه السلام narrated through his forefathers عليهم السلام that the Messenger of God ﷺ said:

"When the resurrection comes, God, Great, and Mighty are He, will manifest himself to His believer servant, and will remind him of his sins one by one; then God will forgive him;

God will not let (even) a near angel or an apostle prophet know of his (sin), and will cover it least anyone becomes aware of it.

Then He will say to his bad deeds,

`Be good deeds."[382]

11. Abū Dharr said:

"The Messenger of God ﷺ said:

A man will be brought on the Day of Resurrection; and it will be said:

"Show him his small sins, and keep back from him his big sins."

Then it will be said to him:

"You did so and so on such a day."

And he will go on confessing while apprehensive of his big sins.

Then it will be said:

"Give him a good deed in place of every bad deed."

Then he will say:

"I had done some which I do not see (mentioned) here.

---

[382] Ṣadūq, Shaykh Muḥammad b. ʿAlī, *al-Khiṣāl*.

"Abū Dharr said:

'And I saw the Messenger of God laughing until his teeth were shown.'"[383]

12. As-Ṣādiq said:

"When the Day of Resurrection comes, God Glorified and Sublime is He, shall spread His mercy until even Iblīs will hope for His mercy."[384]

---

[383] Muslim b. al-Ḥajjāj, *Ṣaḥīḥ Muslim*.

[384] Ṣadūq, Shaykh Muḥammad b. ʿAlī, *al-Amālī*.

Visitation to Sayyidah Fāṭimah al-Zahrā᾿ عليها السلام

Sayyidah Fāṭimah عليها السلام said:

"My father said to me:

`He who prays on your behalf, God عزّ وجلّ shall forgive him and make him join me wherever I may be in Paradise."[385]

For this reason, and to benefit the dear readers of this book, we include her visitation here and accompany it with the English translation[386]:

In the name of God, the Beneficent, the Merciful

Peace be upon Muḥammad and his Progeny

O you who were tried;

God, Who Created you, tried

you before He Created your (flesh);

He found you patient with that which

He pushed you with. We claim that we are your followers,

believing in you, and (believing and) bearing with everything

that has been brought unto us by your father

---

385 al-Irdibillī, ʿAlī b. ʿIsā Hakkārī, *Kashf al-Ghumma fī Maʿrifat al-Aʾimma*.

386 This is the visitation mentioned in *Mafātīḥ al-Jinān* (Keys to Paradise).

and that which his successor brought unto us.

Therefore, we beg you (now that we believe) to make us

join both so we may rejoice at being purified for following you.

(It is recommended to add the following here.)

Peace be upon you, O daughter of the Messenger of God;

Peace be upon you, O daughter of the Prophet of God;

Peace be upon you, O daughter of the beloved of God;

Peace be upon you, O daughter of the friend of God;

Peace be upon you, O daughter of the sincere friend of God;

Peace be upon you, O daughter of the trusted (Messenger) of God;

Peace be upon you, O daughter of the best of God's creatures;

Peace be upon you, O daughter of the best of God's prophets, messengers, and angels;

Peace be upon you, O daughter of him who is the best of all creatures;

Peace be upon you, O wife of the friend of God and the best of creatures after the Messenger of God;

Peace be upon you, O mother of al-Ḥasan and al-Ḥusayn, who are the masters of the youth of Paradise;

Peace be upon you, the truth-teller (devoted one) and martyr;

Peace be upon you, O gratified and accepted one;

Peace be upon you, O well-mannered and chaste one;

Peace be upon you, O human ḥūrī;

Peace be upon you, O pious and pure one;

Peace be upon you who is spoken to by angels and who is knowledgeable;

Peace be upon you, O oppressed and usurped one;

Peace be upon you, O repressed and defeated one;

Peace be upon you, O Sayyidah Fāṭimah, daughter of God's Messenger;

and may the blessings and mercy of God be upon you and your soul and body;

I bear witness that you have perished while fully knowing your Lord.

(I also bear witness) that he who gladdens you gladdens the Messenger of God

he who deserts you deserts the Messenger of God

he who harms you harms the Messenger of God

he who bestows you (with a favor) bestows (a blessing) upon the Messenger of God and

he who deprives you of the Messenger of God (This is) because you are "part of him and his spirit which lies in his sides."

God, His Messengers, and His Apostles are my witnesses that I accept him whom you accept, resent him whom you resent;

I exonerate myself to God from whom you absolve yourself to God from, whom you befriend, hold as my enemy those whom you have (as your enemies), and dislike him whom you dislike.

God is the best Witness, the best-anticipated One, the best Rewarder, and the most Bountiful.

(It is recommended to pray on behalf of the Prophet and his progeny after this visitation).

All praise is due to God, the Lord of the Worlds.

www.ingramcontent.com/pod-product-compliance
Lightning Source LLC
Chambersburg PA
CBHW020246010526
44107CB00002B/119
* 9 7 8 1 9 5 6 2 7 6 4 4 2 *